About

Gib Bulloch is an award-winning social intrapreneur who consults, writes and speaks on topics relating to the role of business in society. Gib believes passionately in the power of business to change the world and in the power of the individual to change the world of business. After an early career spent at BP and Mars, Bulloch's epiphany came from a year as a business volunteer with Voluntary Service Overseas (VSO) in the Balkans in 2000. Over the following 15 years, Gib founded and scaled Accenture's global 'not-for-loss' consulting business, Accenture Development Partnerships. He left Accenture in 2016 to explore new ways of supporting purpose-driven insurgencies within the corporate world. Gib serves on the Board of the End Fund and the League of Intrapreneurs. He is an Intrapreneur in Residence at Business Fights Poverty and a Visiting Fellow at Cranfield School of Management.

www.gibbulloch.com

@gibbulloch

Praise for *The Intrapreneur*

'A story of courage, determination and persistence, told with a combination of wit, pathos and refreshing honesty'

Paul Polman, CEO Unilever

'An inspiring personal account of how purpose and well-being can transform the business world.'

Arianna Huffington

'It's refreshing to see business leaders like Gib Bulloch break the taboo surrounding mental health in the workplace by speaking up, openly and honestly, about their personal experiences.'

Alastair Campbell, writer and broadcaster

'This book by Gib Bulloch is a powerful reminder to all business leaders of the enormous potential of creating purpose driven innovative companies.'

Feike Sijbesma, CEO Royal DSM

'Accenture was a founding member of the Global Business Coalition for Education and under the leadership of Gib and his ADP team, provided new thinking about the role of the business community and use of innovative finance to bridge the funding gaps which keep so many kids out of school.'

Sarah Brown, Chair, Global Business Coalition for Education

'Few people combine the vision and passion needed to shape the organisation of the future with the professional skills and experience of having made it happen in a way that Gib does. His skill in helping companies and not-for-profits think and work differently is exceptional.'

Mark Goldring, CEO, Oxfam GB

'This is not another book on how to do intrapreneurship, but a deeply personal account of becoming a social intrapreneur and what that has meant in Gib's life and the many lives that his work touches.'

Professor Harry Scarbrough, Cass Business School

'An incredible account of changing the world from inside big business – and a wake up call that our corporate system needs to change to unleash the humanity within.'

Andy Wales, Formerly Senior Vice President,
Sustainable Development, SABMiller

'Gib may be the first to share his story so openly, but he is not alone. Employees everywhere are experiencing 'cognitive dissonance' as companies search for infinite growth on a finite planet. As our incumbent institutions prioritise short-term returns over compassion, community and human dignity. This story is a wake up call to find your purpose and align your values with your day job (stat!).'

Maggie De Pree, Co-Leader, League of Intrapreneurs

'A wake up call for all of us to reflect on the sanity of our current corporate system. With courage and vulnerability, Gib's story brings to light the power for innovative change that can be driven from the bottom up.'

Florencia Estrade, Co-Leader, League of Intrapreneurs

'Every story we tell of our own mental ill health is like a life boat being sent out into the ocean where those suffering in silence can cling onto and realise they are normal. Thank you Gib for your courage and the "life boat" you have sent to "the many" who may read this book. It too is a very inspiring account of how we as individuals who are "purpose led" can truly change the world and where network trumps hierarchy!, through the movements we can create.'

Geoff McDonald, Former Global VP HR Unilever; Global Campaigner, Advocate and Consultant for mental health at work

'Gib has walked the talk on the Intrapreneur's Journey, inspiring many others already and with this refreshing book, he will surely inspire many, many more would-be intrapreneurs!'

Prof David Grayson CBE, Emeritus Professor of Corporate Responsibility, Cranfield School of Management, co-author of *Social Intrapreneurism and All That Jazz*

'Gib's thoughtful and thought-provoking reflections on his personal and professional journey will offer inspiration to many. His story illustrates the enormous potential we all have as individuals to build a sense of shared purpose and make a positive difference in the communities and organizations where we live and work. At the same time, he offers an honest and courageous perspective on the limits and human frailties that each of us face individually, and the precious gift of nurturing family, friends, good colleagues, teachers and healthcare providers who support us along the way.'

Jane Nelson, Director, Corporate Responsibility Initiative, Harvard Kennedy School

'Since 2009, the Aspen Institute has supported nearly 200 corporate social intrapreneurs through its First Movers Fellowship. Gib's personal and engaging story will be an inspiration to them and to the many other intrapreneurs who will follow in their footsteps.'

Nancy McGaw, Founder, Aspen Institute First Movers Fellowship

THE INTRAPRENEUR

THE INTRAPRENEUR

CONFESSIONS OF A CORPORATE INSURGENT

GIB BULLOCH

This edition first published in 2018

Unbound

6th Floor Mutual House, 70 Conduit Street, London W1S 2GF

www.unbound.com

ISBN (eBook): 978-1-912618-41-5

ISBN (Paperback): 978-1-912618-40-8

Design by Mecob

Cover images:

© Shutterstock.com

Printed in Great Britain by Clays Ltd, St Ives plc

For Garmt van Soest (1977–2017)
Former Accenture colleague, friend and intrapreneur.
You certainly succeeded in 'Kicking ALS in the Balls'!

Dear Reader,

The book you are holding came about in a rather different way to most others. It was funded directly by readers through a new website: Unbound.

Unbound is the creation of three writers. We started the company because we believed there had to be a better deal for both writers and readers. On the Unbound website, authors share the ideas for the books they want to write directly with readers. If enough of you support the book by pledging for it in advance, we produce a beautifully bound special subscribers' edition and distribute a regular edition and e-book wherever books are sold, in shops and online.

This new way of publishing is actually a very old idea (Samuel Johnson funded his dictionary this way). We're just using the internet to build each writer a network of patrons. Here, at the back of this book, you'll find the names of all the people who made it happen.

Publishing in this way means readers are no longer just passive consumers of the books they buy, and authors are free to write the books they really want. They get a much fairer return too – half the profits their books generate, rather than a tiny percentage of the cover price.

If you're not yet a subscriber, we hope that you'll want to join our publishing revolution and have your name listed in one of our books in the future. To get you started, here is a £5 discount on your first pledge. Just visit unbound.com, make your pledge and type INTRA18 in the promo code box when you check out.

Thank you for your support,

Dan, Justin and John
Founders, Unbound

Super Patrons

Oddi Aasheim
Tom Abell
Ellen Agler
Joe Agoada
Gordon Alexander
Big Bert Alexander
Anne Alexander
Gordon Alexander
Mourad Ameziane
Rod Anson
James Arnott
Frederic Astier
Matt Axeen
Dan Baker
Hans Balmaekers
Rachael Barber
Jan Benedictus
Phoebe Bennett
Marilia Bezerra
Tim Bishop
Lionel Bodin
Sarah Brown
Michelle Brownlee
Jean-Marie Buchilly
Sarah Buckley
Franco Buehlmann
Brindusa Burrows
Robin Bush
Sarah Jane Bustin
Andrew Butler
William Campbell
Aileen Caskie

Kitrhona Cerri
Louisa Cervoni
Pascal Cervoni
Marit Chervier de Ruiter
Emeka Chukwureh
Sandrine Cina
Ciuki
Laura Clise
Steven Coates
Ivan Cowie
James & Deborah Crowley
Morven Davis
Caroline DSilva
john Duffy
Gene Early
Jacqueline Eatz
Kay Etherington
Roger Ford
DJ Forza
Kaori Fujii
Becky Galea
Amanda Gardiner
Mark Goldring
Shona Grant
Joanna Hafenmayer
Lincoln McNey & Cynthia Hansen
Edward Happ
Mike Hoffman
John Horspool
Derek Humphries
S. Raza Husain
Intrapreneurs Intrapreneurs
Louise James
Laura Johnson-Graham
Christopher Jurgens
Jacqueline Kay

Jon Khoo
Dan Kieran
Annalie Killian
Magdalena Kot
Chryssa Koulis
Raj Kumar
Steven Lang
Clary Leffel
Alasdair Lenman
Lesley
Ilana Lever
Tom Levitt
Jack Levy
Ian Lightfoot
Elizabeth Lillie
Mark Lillie
Gordon & Heather Lister
Sandy Lister
Jamie Lister
Dominic Llewellyn
Ian Lobo
Suzanne Locklin
Jessica Long
Lisl Macdonald
Kirsteen MacLeod
Neil MacLeod
Iain L. MacLeod
Helen MacLeod
Christopher Magennis
Mala Manku
Alex Manson
Wee Marj
Lucy Marti
Janet McAlister
Maureen McDonagh
William McFie

Gerry McGurk
Steve McKenna
Neil McLennan
Carsten Meier
Caroline Middlecote
Catherine & Ben Mile 91
Stuart Mills
John Mitchinson
Andy Moore
David Mowatt
Hilary Nathan
Jonas Nyberg
Connor OBeirne
Philip Otley
John Parker
David Pearl
Robert Phillips
Justin Pollard
Business Fights Poverty
Scott Powell
Tommy Robison
Mina Rodriguez
Martin Ryan
Dali Sanghera
Robin Schofield
Vishna Shah
Jon Shepard
Jason Simpson
Andrew Smith
Joanne Sonenshine
Eilidh Squire
Dominic Squire
Steffen Staeuber
Louise Storey
Losel Tethong
Mark Thain

Duncan THomson
VArcot VArcot
Andy Wales
Colin Wells
Angela Werrett
Ilana Wetzler
Michelle Staben Wobker
Nate Wong
Andrea Young
Stephen Zatland
Carlo Zavaroni

With grateful thanks to Business Fights Poverty for helping to make this book happen.

'We delight in the beauty of the butterfly, but rarely admit the changes it has gone through to achieve that beauty.'

Maya Angelou

Contents

Foreword

In many ways, our model of economic growth has served us well. Millions have been lifted out of poverty over recent decades. Livelihoods have been transformed and life opportunities expanded. The vast majority of us today are better educated and are living longer and healthier – if not always happier – lives.

Yet economic progress has come at a price. We face, among other things, the connected challenges of rising inequality, growing instability and runaway climate change. These in turn have contributed to a collapse of trust, causing many to openly question the validity of our political and economic systems. At a time when leadership is desperately needed, we are facing a crisis in global governance. In fact, we have entered the era of what one respected think-tank has described as 'the great power sclerosis'.

Business needs to step into this vacuum. It can – as this book so eloquently argues – be an enormous force for good in the world. Larger businesses have the opportunity to use their scale and resource to drive the kind of transformational change across industry sectors that is so badly needed, working closely alongside governments, agencies and civil society partners in the process.

And it is in businesses' interests to do so. A world where systemic social and environmental challenges persist is not a world in which business can thrive and prosper over the long-term.

Fortunately, the case for change is building. The evidence is amassing. This excellent contribution is but the latest in a growing body of books and studies that demonstrate beyond doubt that business as usual is no longer an option. And business itself is motivated to change, to be a part of the solution and not part of the problem. I have yet to meet a CEO, for example, who wants more air pollution, more refugees or more inequality in the world.

So, momentum is building. Two things I believe will help to accelerate further this turning of the tide.

First, we now have an agreed vision of the world we want. The UN Sustainable Development Goals (SDGs) – all 17 of them – and the related Paris Climate Change agreement, provide a shared roadmap for a more inclusive and sustainable future. Signed in 2015 by virtually all the nations of the world, these agreements provide a moral framework that leave no-behind , a blueprint for a better world.

But implementation cannot be left to governments alone. The total level of official development aid, for example, is put around $160 billion a year, yet the latest estimates from the United Nations Conference on Trade and Development (UNCTAD) put the investments needed to achieve the SDGs at a minimum of $5 trillion.

Only business can help get us there.

And there is a huge incentive to do so. The Business and Sustainable Development Commission, set up in 2016, has already identified in its flagship report, *Better Business Better World,* more than $12 trillion in commercial opportunities for businesses willing to contribute to a global economy that is fairer, more stable and inclusive, and more sustainable. Implementing the SDGs, the report argues, also has the potential to create up to 380 million jobs by 2030.

This makes the SDGs the world's business plan, and one of the most exciting business opportunities in a lifetime, as depicted – in typically original and creative ways – in one of the chapters in this book.

No wonder a growing number of businesses are embedding the SDGs in their strategies, whether they are larger businesses like Unilever – with our Unilever Sustainable Living Plan – or entrepreneurs and startups, where we see some of the boldest thinking and action being taken.

The second, and related, cause for optimism is that we are seeing powerful movements for change develop *inside* large organisations, with the rise – if you like – of the intrapreneur.

Most employees want to feel that their working lives are engaged in a purpose-led endeavour, that their personal values and instinct to do good in the world align with the long term aims of their organisation. More than ever, people want to know that their employers are net contributors in creating a better world and a healthier planet.

It starts with developing an overarching purpose – in Unilever's case, to 'make sustainable living commonplace' – and then giving individuals the space and freedom to express their desire to be part of a movement bigger than themselves.

For Unilever, this comes alive with our brands. Indeed, I have often likened managing our brand to running social enterprises. In many ways, these brand managers are the archetypal intrapreneurs of this story.

Take Lifebuoy, for example, one of our oldest brands. If you work on Lifebuoy, you are not selling soap; you are saving and improving lives by preventing the spread of infectious diseases through regular hand-washing, especially among the young and most vulnerable. In parts of Africa today, for example, nearly one-fifth of children under the age of five dies needlessly of diseases like diarrhoea or diphtheria.

If you work on Domestos, you are not selling toilet cleaner but are engaged in one of the most important and urgent social needs of our time: to reduce open defecation and improve sanitation. It surely cannot be right that nearly two and a half billion people around the world suffer from poor or non-existent access to sanitation.

If you work on Dove, you are engaged in a crusade to help improve self-esteem among young – mostly female – adolescents. In some parts of the world as many as nine in every ten girls suffer from low body esteem . Already, more than 20 million young people have been helped and supported through Dove's Self-Esteem Project.

I could go on. All of our brands are putting these kinds of social missions at the heart of their businesses. At the same time, they are using their scale and reach to help create wider movements for change. And in each case their work relates directly to supporting one or more of the Sustainable Development Goals.

The people behind these businesses will, I am sure, be encouraged and inspired by Gib Bulloch's story, as will many others. It is a story of courage, determination and persistence, told with wit, pathos and refreshing honesty. It is relevant not just for business, but for any organisation. The central message is clear: change can be inspired from the top, but it can only be sustained by movements of people driven by a sense of common purpose.

Paul Polman
CEO, Unilever

Prologue

The Business Case for Unleashing a Corporate Insurgency

Over the past three decades, my generation created the enormous machines we call multinational corporations. Today, over half of the largest economies in the world are global businesses – controlled by the few, impacting the many. Business has the power to change the world. But that will first require a profound change in the world of business.

The world we live in today faces challenges on an unprecedented scale – mass migration, religious extremism and gross inequality to name but a few – all exacerbated by the most pressing existential threat facing our planet: climate change. Efforts to address these issues by traditional state actors and multilateral institutions have thus far fallen short of what is required both in terms of ambition and impact. On a national level, democracy and the traditional role of the state is being challenged by left- and right-wing populism and by so-called 'fake news'. But such problems cannot be solved at the level of arbitrary geographic borders. Typically, we've turned to the likes of the United Nations and civil society for a solution, but challenges of funding, legitimacy and effectiveness have inhibited their response.

Multinational corporations have emerged as the new superstates. They recognise that today's world is highly interconnected and interdependent and pursue joined-up strategies that span arbitrary geographic borders or socio-political boundaries. Local business decisions are taken with this global context in mind.

As politics moves towards the poles of transient public opinion, might there be an opportunity for business to step into that central, expanding void and stand up for pragmatic, common sense solutions to problems that cannot be solved at a national level?

Cynics will argue that this is not the role of businesses and could undermine their fiduciary duty to shareholders and investors of maximising profit. They'll point to the underwhelming array of Corporate Social Responsibility(CSR) initiatives of the past, which focused far too much on reducing the negative effects of business and far too little on accentuating the positives.

But there doesn't need to be a trade-off between profit and purpose. I firmly believe that the significant socio-economic challenges facing our global community – the UN's Sustainable Development Goals[1] provide the best summary – represent a massive untapped commercial opportunity for business. In the latter sections of this book I will explain this belief in more detail but recognise it will require as much of a change in our mindset and priorities as consumer citizens, as it does in business leaders. Do we want the latest, smallest, snazziest gadget or might the same new technologies be applied to improving the educational outcomes of our kids, accelerating cures for disease or providing access to clean energy for those who lack it? There is a business case for both scenarios, but this will require a paradigm shift as to how these corporations are run and for whom.

I accept this vision is a far cry from where we are today, which begs the questions: who will drive the necessary change and how will this transformation be achieved?

I would have to accept, reluctantly, that top down isn't working. Certainly not fast enough. The CEOs of big businesses find themselves in fiscal straightjackets, risking the wrath of investors and, indeed, their own well-paid jobs if they are seen to have deviated too far from their primary goal of short-term profit maximisation. Paul Polman, Unilever's CEO, is one of the few exceptions that proves the rule (for the cynics out there, let me say that I believed this and said so long before he kindly agreed to write the Foreword, and this belief is, in fact, the main reason I asked him to do so). Despite there being significant business value in addressing social and environmental challenges in the long term, the current economic system rewards and incentivises short term behaviour. Despite their annual pilgrimage to The World Economic Forum in Davos, the global elite of today's multinational corporations are not, on their own at

---

1. http://www.un.org/sustainabledevelopment/sustainable-development-goals/

least, going to be the primary drivers of change. I challenge them to prove me wrong and will be the first to applaud those who do.

Instead, the answer must come from the bottom up, by unleashing the power of purpose–driven *corporate insurgencies* amongst employees – individually as so-called 'Social Intrapreneurs', and collectively through sheer force of numbers. By *intrapreneurs*, I'm talking about the misfits, the rebels and the oddballs who are hanging on to some crazy idea for a new product or service that has potential commercial *and* social value, but feel disempowered, disengaged or downright ignored by their business leadership. These aspiring intrapreneurs are dormant changemakers, lurking deep within all roles and functions of large corporations – they're exactly the people I'm targeting with this book, together with the more savvy senior executives who hold the keys to unleashing their potential.

I'm also using the book as a medium to share thoughts on how to give greater voice to those outside the Wall Street bubble or the corporate boardroom, on how global businesses are run, what they do and for whom. Yes, given we as citizens are all impacted by their decisions, I believe we urgently need to find ways of *democratising* the multinational corporation.

I'd be the first to admit that trying to drive change is hard and have some of the scars to prove it. But as I write, nearing the end of the second decade of our new millennium, we have the perfect storm that could just make this feasible. Firstly, the significant business opportunities of solving social issues that I've eluded to; secondly, disengagement and longing for career purpose amongst today's employees; thirdly, the sheer power of new media to connect and inspire around ideas.

Globally, levels of employee engagement stand at about 13 per cent. To put that in simple terms, just over a tenth of the working population don't want to turn up for work. At the same time according to Deloitte's survey of Millennials[2] the majority of these employees believe that business is not doing enough to tackle social and environmental challenges and are keen to find roles that give them

2. https://www2.deloitte.com/global/en/pages/about-deloitte/articles/millennialsurvey.html

the opportunity to contribute. Most importantly, they are willing to shift employer to do so. Millennials are also 'super-connected' through social media and well placed to mobilise collective action around a more purpose-oriented business agenda.

That explains the context in which I've written this book. But I do not intend it to be a traditional 'business book' full of graphs, charts and jargon-filled bullet points of advice and learnings. I want it to be accessible to people on the outside of business too. Instead, I believe in the power of story to capture hearts and minds and have written *The Intrapreneur* as a memoir – it's the personal story of a career and life journey with a difference that I believe may have relevance to others, and I hope will convince employees of the potential for driving change bottom-up and inspire them to act on their ideas.

As in most good stories, there are plot twists, heroes, villains and hopefully a degree of candidness and personal reflection on my own career successes and failures along the way. I'd like to think that these topics provide the opportunity for some humour as I poke fun at the 'craziness' of today's business environment,

Throughout the book, I've sought to share sometimes complex business ideas in laymen's terms as part of the narrative on what business could and should be. Not on what it is today. I have plenty more ideas where these came from, but am more interested in hearing the brilliant and innovative ideas that are inside the heads of the multitude of intrapreneurs out there, and to think about how we bring them to life. If just one single person who reads this takes action, which catalyses an initiative that has meaningful impact in their organisation or beyond, then I'd consider this book a success. Well worth the time and effort in writing it.

It should have become clear that if you were hoping for an anti-business book, look elsewhere. There are plenty of these around. Neither is this book anti-Accenture – I worked there for 20 years and am hugely grateful for the opportunities and support I was given. I firmly believe Accenture and its consulting competitors such as PwC, Deloitte, EY and IBM have a massive potential role to play in harnessing the latent power of business for good. No, this is not an anti-business book, but it is, quite unapologetically, anti–business-as-usual. Now is the time for change.

Finally, what makes *The Intrapreneur* a bit different from more traditional business books is that it is set in the context of a psychiatric ward. Statistically, one in four of us will experience some kind of mental health issue in our lifetime. I always assumed that I was comfortably in the three out of four majority. I had a good upbringing on a beautiful Scottish island, was happy, relatively healthy and felt fulfilled in my job. Mental health issues were something other people had to deal with – people who hadn't perhaps been dealt quite as good a hand in life as I had. But five days and five nights spent in a psychiatric hospital in Glasgow provided pretty convincing proof I was wrong. I feel strongly that if people like me, who've always considered themselves 'normal', do not speak out openly about the real and growing issue of mental health in the workplace, then it will always remain the taboo that it is today.

At its heart however, the book is less about the mental health of the individual and more about the *mental health of the organisations* and the economic system in which they work. It's about creating a business environment which is more aware of and receptive to the latent potential of social intrapreneurs in their midst.

Let me leave you with a question to keep in the back of your mind as you read this book. Did I really go nuts, or was it the system that's insane? Or, to put it another way, might *madness* in fact be the sanest response to a system that has indeed gone crazy?

Read on and I'll let you be the judge.

Introduction

More than forty years had passed but it felt just like yesterday. In some strange way it was a bit like a homecoming. A return to my roots. Here I was, now a grown man, standing at the top of the grey steps that led from the front door of my old primary school out into the large square playground which was encircled by high stone walls. They'd seemed enormous back then, but I suppose I was barely 3ft tall at the time. Yes, my unexpected return to Rothesay Primary School could have been a pleasant, nostalgic experience. Had it not been for the fact that it was to visit the local shrink.

It was a damp drizzly day, like so many growing up on the west coast of Scotland. When the sun shines I'd argue there's nowhere more beautiful in the world. But that was unfortunately all too rare an occurrence and, from what I hear, even climate change hasn't helped. The brick-walled outside toilets are no longer standing and with them, thankfully the attendant aroma had gone too. The whole playground is now a car park, both the boys' area to the right of the school building and the girls' one to the left.

I reckon the school was well over one hundred years old but I'm sure it still has at least another hundred years of life left in it. It was in the mid '70s that this fabulous old building got repurposed for other local government use. That was when the new Rothesay Primary was built on an idyllic plot of land overlooking a loch on the outskirts of the town. It was a very modern open-plan building which, I recall from the local gossip, had cost a vast fortune at the time. You know, about the same amount you'd now need to scrape together for the deposit on an apartment in London or New York. Of course this grand edifice lasted less than 30 years before being demolished and rebuilt on the same site under the UK government's 'Private Finance Initiative' – no doubt earning some clever banker-types a decent commission.

Meanwhile, my good old original school building remains standing in Union Street almost as if in contempt. It's been repurposed from a school to now fulfil many different functions within the community – tax office, Citizens Advice Bureau, Job Centre. It's also home to the community psychiatric nurse or CPN, Mary, whom I'd just been to visit for the sixth time in the past month, while staying with my parents on the Isle of Bute. There's a beautiful irony in the fact that these one-to-one CPN meetings took place in the very 'classroom' that I'd sat in 42 years previously while attending Primary 2. Back then, I recall, it was a place with lots of screaming, playing with bricks and scribbling with wax crayons. On that basis it's hardly changed at all.

As I gazed out of the high arched windows of the room I remember being gripped by nostalgia (which, according to my dad, is not what it used to be). I still had vivid memories of my first happy few years at school in this building. Kissing Lindsay Cox under the desk in Primary 2. Starring in *The Sound of Music* school concert in Primary 3. Learning to play the Viola in Primary 7 – that lasted all of about 6 months, and my thespian aspirations never got off the ground either. Kissing girls lasted quite a bit longer I have to admit, but we'll come back to that, and the fact that I never married, a little later on.

My daydreaming was brought to a fairly abrupt halt by Mary's dulcet Scottish tones.

'Well, Gib, ye seem pretty much back tae yer normal sel now,' she said reassuringly, her thick Glasgow accent betraying the fact that she was not born and bred on the island. 'I'll be happy tae let you go back hame tae Geneva next week, but ye'll need tae check in wi' a local psychiatrist there every few weeks, just to make sure there's no recurrence of yer little wobble.'

My little wobble. Well, that was quite a nice gentle way of referring to what happened during the last week of November. She made it sound like I'd had a bout of flu or an ear infection that had affected my balance. Looking back, the whole situation I found myself in was a bit surreal to say the least. I'd been living a very happy and fulfilled life by anyone's standards. I was passionate about my job working in Accenture, one of the largest multinational consulting firms in the world. I had a fancy job title – 'Executive Director, Accenture Development Partnerships' read the business cards. Sounds impressive, right? Accenture Development Partnerships, or ADP as it was more often known (not to be confused with the US provider of 'cloud-based Human Capital Management (HCM) solutions', that goes by the same name), is an organisation I'd founded back in 2002 together with a small group of kindred spirits. Over the years I'd led the team that grew it into a well-established and highly respected part of the company. That's right, they'd given me my own little bit of the corporate train set to play with.

Turn to Camera

I'm going to pop up from time to time throughout the story where I think something needs a bit of explaining or additional context outside the main narrative. Think Frank Underwood in *House of Cards*, addressing the viewer directly.

I describe ADP as a "corporate social enterprise" – an internal business unit that was tasked with bringing Accenture's business and technology expertise to parts of the world with the greatest need but the least access. We'd do this on a not-for-profit basis although I prefer to use the tongue in cheek term "not-for-loss" instead. My job for all these years had been to try to make the organisation break even, or "cost-neutral for shareholders", to use the jargon. To do that we'd effectively had to turn the traditional consulting business model upside down, i.e. we'd challenged the standard equation of high salaries + high margins = high fee rates. Instead, ADP requires Accenture's employees to work on a voluntary pay cut of up to 50%, the company waives the profit margin and the client pays what's left – typically about 20% of the normal market rates. Sim-

ple but effective – and that was the secret of our success.

So I was one of the lucky few who found that the difference between
their day job and their hobby is pretty blurred. I got to travel around
the world to exotic countries, meeting interesting people who were
doing fascinating things. I was in charge of a growing team of really
smart, highly motivated consultants. I got lots of kudos and recognition (perhaps more than my fair share given we were a team effort)
for the fact that we were not just raising the bar, but actually redefin-
ing the notion of Corporate Social Responsibility or CSR. ADP was
finding new ways to bring *private* innovation, entrepreneurship and
investment into the traditionally *public* sector domain of international development – the sector that cares about health, education,
water and sanitation, humanitarian relief – in the poorest parts of the
world. What's more, I'd been pretty well paid for the privilege. Yes,
life was indeed sweet.

I don't want to give you the impression it was all plain sailing.
Far from it. Accenture, like its peer group of household names –
EY, Deloitte, PwC and others – is all about working for some of
the biggest, most profitable multinational companies in the world,
mostly in the richest countries in the world and for a very healthy
profit. I found myself in a role that was almost diametrically opposed
to these norms. My clients were mostly charities, working in many
of the poorest parts of the world and I was trying to grow an
organisation that was explicitly *not* trying to make a profit. Most
days I'd find myself having to challenge, navigate around or even
break (shhh!) some company policy or other. Sure, I had lots of support from many of the senior leaders in the firm. But swimming
against a strong tide for over a decade had started to take its toll.
Somewhat paradoxically, the more I saw a great opportunity to take
ADP to a whole new level of impact, the less I seemed able to get

support from a new leadership team. It felt like I'd lost my mojo – my knack for winning over the bosses, for getting my own way. My fabulous, dedicated team were increasingly frustrated.

Looking back, the retreat in India couldn't have come at a better time for me. I'd signed up for an event organised by a group called Leaders' Quest that would see me spend four days in the Rajasthan desert. The retreat offered a mix of activities – discussions in small focus groups about the state of the world, visits to impoverished villages, talks by inspiring NGO leaders – even yoga and meditation classes. I'd gone to get myself out of the rut, out of the comfort zone – to find new inspiration to break the internal impasse I'd been facing. I got more than I bargained for.

I'll probably never know for sure what caused The Incident – or my wobble, if you prefer. Perhaps I'd been working far too hard and was under more stress than I realised. It might have been the fever I contracted during the trip that acted as a catalyst. Some have even suggested there was a more spiritual explanation – an epiphany or enlightenment experience. Take your pick. But what I do know is that I would find myself spending the better part of a week locked up in a psychiatric hospital in Glasgow. The fall was pretty spectacular – only a few weeks earlier I'd been shaking hands with President Clinton in some glitzy New York hotel. Then bang. I found myself playing a cameo role in *One Flew Over the Cuckoo's Nest.* I'd describe the experience as fascinating, frightening and funny, in about equal measure.

Now here I was standing on the steps of my old Primary School. I couldn't resist a smile when I thought of how my young six-year-old self in short trousers, standing on the same step in 1973, could never have imagined the journey he'd experience over the next 40 or so years. A journey that would take him from the excesses of a career in the business fast lane to not-for-profit work within some of the poorest countries in the world. This six-year-old would grow up to be a man who ate food in the fanciest Michelin-starred restaurants but also tripe cooked in a Soweto Township. Whose hand, which had been shaken by several Presidents, also shook the stump of a leper in Ethiopia.

It's a journey I want to now share. We'll get to the more glamorous and exciting stuff in due course. But let's start with a visit to a place that few of us ever expect to be in, let alone be locked up in: the Thomson Psychiatric Ward of Glendevon Hospital, Glasgow.

NIGHT I – GROWING UP

'*Experience is not what happens to us – but what we do with what happens to us.*'

Otto Scharmer, MIT

Chapter 1 - Island Life

Thomson Psychiatric Ward, Glendevon Hospital, Glasgow. November 2014

As a management consultant, I'd got used to sleeping in strange beds. No, I don't mean that in any risqué sense. I'm talking more about working remotely at a client site, eating a late dinner in a restaurant and staying in a bland room in one of the big-name hotel chains. It didn't matter which particular hotel – the only thing that differed was the brand of free toiletries. But my 'check-in' at Glendevon Hospital in Glasgow was a little different, despite the fact I was wearing my usual grey business suit. No spa or fitness room on the second floor. No credit card imprint required for incidentals. No payment required at all, for that matter. I'd be the guest of the UK's beloved National Health Service. Yes, that first evening spent in Room 17 of the Thomson Ward, was an altogether new experience.

I lay half-dressed on top of a little single bed in the corner of the room – a bed just like the one I'd slept in for all of my childhood and for most of my time at university too, for that matter. But the surroundings were far from familiar to someone who'd grown used to the luxuries of business travel. No nice goose-feather pillows, big fluffy white Egyptian cotton duvet or massive plasma screen to channel-surf on. Instead, just bare white walls. A basic wardrobe of cheap wood laminate stood in the corner and, to its left, the door to a small toilet and shower room stood ajar. There was a chair in the corner with a grey suit jacket hung over it and a black tie draped on top. Strange, no? Let me explain. I'd been in Glasgow intending to go to my old schoolmate Mowatti's dad's funeral, together with two other friends, Johnny and Carlo. All three of us had grown up on the Isle of Bute. But my 'uncharacteristic behaviour' in the morning had given cause for concern and they'd taken me to the hospital down the road for a check-up. That's when all the fun started.

I checked my watch – 4.20pm. Lying on my back staring at the ceiling, I tried to piece together the events of the day. I remembered being taken in the back of an ambulance to the sprawling outbuildings of what looked like a hospital, then being led up a long curved ramp, with a selection of amateur-looking paintings hanging on the walls – no doubt the handiwork of whoever resided in this strange place. Then I remember walking through two sets of double doors into a corridor. On the left were large windows looking into some kind of canteen full of round tables. Oddly, no one sat together, each apparently preferring empty chairs to company. At one table, an old man slept, head drooping, wearing the strangest-looking straw hat. At another, a woman sat sobbing. A young girl, alone in the corner, stared blankly into space. There were only seven or eight people in the room. A mixture of young and old. Male and female. Wherever this place was, it would get a high ranking on one of our corporate diversity indices. On the opposite side of the corridor was what appeared to be an office with large glass windows offering a view of two wooden desks with some scattered papers and desktop computers that might have been original Charles Babbage prototypes. Clearly, this was where the staff hung out – some wore turquoise-green uniforms, while others were more plain-clothed. I'd later discover that this could make it quite tricky to distinguish between staff and patients – I mean, just who's 'normal' anyway, right?

I hadn't felt scared in the least when I arrived. In fact, I was on a high. It was all so different. I was curious at being given a glimpse into a different world. My first encounter with the ward staff was when a smiling nurse in a green uniform stepped out from the office and greeted me with a cheery, 'Welcome tae the Thomson Ward, Gilbert.'

With a quick scribble of the pen on a clipboard, she effectively took 'custody' of me from the two ambulance drivers who'd escorted me up the ramp to the door and who gave me a parting wave as they left.

'Eh, thanks guys. Enjoyed the drive. First time in an ambulance, you know,' I shouted after them. I then turned to the nurse.

'Good afternoon. Nice to meet you. Call me Gib, by the way. Everyone else does.'

'OK, Gib, nae problem,' she said. 'Ma' name's Gillian and I'm the supervisor on the day shift today. You seem a little bitty excited, are you no'? Speakin' dead fast. I need ye tae be very calm.'

'Sorry, Gillian.'

She had a point. I was a little bit hyper.

'Now, let me check – yes, you're going to be staying in Room 17 which is jist at the end of the corridor, four doors doon on the left-hand side.'

'Oh, thanks, I should be able to find that.'

'Nice suit, by the way. We don't often get people arriving quite as well dressed as you. Are ye straight frae the office today?'

'Oh no. I don't work in Scotland any more. I was actually here for a friend's dad's funeral in the borders, but I think I'll have missed that now. If you were to sign me off, then maybe I could head down there a bit late and arrive in time for the wake.'

'Oh, ah'm sorry tae hear aboot yer pal's dad. But you'll be staying here for a wee while tae get some rest. Don't worry aboot anythin', son. We'll take guid care o' ye here. Now, ah shid tell yae that dinner is served from 5 to 6.30pm every night, lunch 12 to 1pm and yer brekkie is from 7.30 and the kitchen closes at half past eight sharp. So ye can ask one o' the nurses tae give ye a wee knock in the mornin' tae make sure ye don't sleep in or ye might huv tae go hungry.'

I smiled and thanked Gillian before wandering off in search of my room at the end of the corridor. Odd numbers were on the left-hand side, even on the right – I started counting under my breath as I passed each door – '11, 13, 15' – and then… I came to two quite burly-looking blokes sitting outside the door of Bedroom 17, both in light-green staff uniforms. One had his sleeves rolled up revealing tattoos on both forearms.

'How are you doin', lads?' I asked. 'Are you here to guard my door so that I don't escape? I've no plans to, you know. In fact, I've been made to feel quite welcome so far.'

'We're fine, Gulbert. But could you just stand a little to the side please so that we can see the door opposite. It's that room across frae ye that we're watchin'.'

'Oh, really?'

'Yeah, there's some poor bloke in there that's been praying for the last two days solid. We have tae keep an eye on him as he's been known tae have the odd bad turn – even a wee bit violent, you know.'

'I see,' I said, glancing at the whiteboard beside my door, which read *'Gilbert Bulloch'* in blue marker pen with *'Date of admission: 26th November, Consultant: Dr Ratner'* written below. 'Gilbert' is what I'd term as my 'Sunday name'. Not one I'd inflict on any child of mine, but it did have some historical significance on my mother's side of the family – my great->grandfather and his son had both been Gilberts. It had always seemed very old-fashioned and stuffy to me. Any protests or queries during childhood would be greeted by, 'It's a very fine name and yer gran and I both like it,' from my mum. Then sometime around the age of 13 or 14, my friends in school started to call me *Gib*, perhaps because they found it less of a mouthful. I've no idea where it came from but it's stuck with me ever since.

'Oh, and it's Gib, by the way, lads, not Gilbert, whatever the sign may read. You might want to change that. And who are you both?' I said, reaching out to shake their hands.

'I'm Mick,' said one, nodding and smiling.

'Johnny, pleased to meet you, Gib,' said the other, shaking my hand firmly.

'Pleased to meet both of you,' I said as I entered the room, closed the door and locked it behind me. I had the feeling that staff could get in from the outside if they needed to. But perhaps the lock would be another line of defence against a visit from my pyscho neighbour across the corridor.

I'd been lying on my back on the bed for what must have been several hours, hands behind my head, staring at the ceiling thinking, 'Is this some weird dream or am I actually lying here on a bed in some loonie bin? WTF is going on?!' Ordinarily, I'd have had a quick Facebook fix or checked my WhatsApp messages, but I was under an enforced digital detox. They'd taken my briefcase, computer, iPhone – the lot. But I was OK with that. I wanted to be alone with my thoughts. The whole situation felt quite surreal, almost dreamlike. But the events of that day and the previous week had been all too real.

Then a thought crossed my mind – *I wonder if someone has told my parents where I am?* I'm sure they're worried sick. I knew that at the weekend I'd just spent on the island I'd been giving a bit of cause for concern. I'd been a little over-excited. Talking a lot. Yes, even more than normal. Not sleeping. The flow of energy and ideas had just kept on coming. But we'll come to that crazy stuff, all in good time. First, I owe you a bit more background on who I am and where I'm from, in case you're curious.

Isle of Bute, Scotland. 1970s–80s

I come from quite a small, close family of four – Mum, Dad and sister. My father and mother – happily together for well over 50 years, having gone on their first date when they were just 19 – were both teachers. Lyn, my father, taught Art all his life and played the organ in the local church on Sundays as his 'weekend job'. He used that additional salary to fund his wine habit.

'Teachers can't afford to drink wine every night,' he'd quip, 'but organists can.'

To be honest, it was a paltry salary he earned. Weddings would provide an extra tenner and funerals the same, although he'd always give back that fee when there were dependants left behind.

'How come you get ten quid for just half an hour's work playing at that wedding, Dad?' I once asked obnoxiously, aged about eight or nine.

'They're not paying me for the half->hour's organ playing, son, it's the 25 years of practice before it.'

This was one of these life lessons that would come in useful in my later consulting career when justifying eye-watering fee rates to clients.

My mother, Majorie, or 'wee Marj' as she is affectionately known given her 5ft frame, taught English and History. Despite her size, she developed a fairly fearsome reputation as a disciplinarian, but her

25

bark was definitely worse than her bite. At home she had a completely different, warm and gentle persona – thank goodness. My sister Louisa, or Looby as most friends call her (due to her having the same pigtails as Looby Loo in the kids' cartoon *Andy Pandy*), is two years older than me. We're really close now but as kids we fought like cat and dog. I jokingly refer to her as the 'white sheep' of the family – she got married in her twenties to a nice Frenchman called Pascal, while both were living in Paris, and had two great kids, my niece Fiona and my nephew Gordy, students of engineering and music, respectively.

It seems pretty unusual these days, but we'd eat all our meals as a family seated round a little wooden kitchen table; breakfasts, dinners and sometimes even lunches, when my sister and I didn't have a school meal. Dinner was at 6pm prompt every night with a strict ban on TV during meals – the Facebook of its day, I suppose. Given we only had one old black-and-white TV that sat in the living room, it was a moot point. We each had our own favourite seats around the table, mine on the bench beside my mum, opposite my sister and diagonally across from my father.

'I'm starving. What's for dinner, Mum?' I'd often ask, partly just to solicit Mum's standard response.

'Baked white rat with mouse trimmings,' she'd reply, poker-faced, in a slow deliberate voice.

'Yum, my favourite.'

It was a set-piece move – a bit like the classic one-two in football.

At the end of the table, next to the wall, my father placed a large 'Sasco Year Planner' that he dutifully filled with colour-coded appointments or coloured stars and red shading for any of the family who had a birthday on that day. A bright flower might mark a wedding he'd been booked to play at, black shading for a funeral, and so on. The wall behind the kitchen table held several maps that got progressively larger in sequence. There was a map of our home Island of Bute near the door, followed by one of the UK, then Europe and eventually a huge world map at the far end. Of course, this made for a variety of different quizzes, one of the drawbacks of having teachers for parents, I suppose. That said, it was handy knowledge for someone who went on to spend most of his career working in the international development sector.

'Name the capital city of... <pause>... Libya?' was a typical question.

'Without looking, Gib, you cheat!' my sister would interject.

The kitchen was certainly the nerve centre of the family, where all the action took place: the cooking, the washing up (done in teams on a strict rota) and the place where visitors might drop in for a quick coffee and chat. The more formal dining room was saved for when guests came for dinner or for Sunday lunch; typically, this would include my gran (my mum's mother, widowed since her late forties), a close family friend called Moira, who was the local radiographer, and my grandad (Dad's father), who'd been on his own since my granny died when I was about 11. In contrast to the kitchen, the formal dining room was a dank, dark room, cluttered with lots of old furniture. Not a place to linger, and my sister and I would be creative in coming up with reasons for being excused from the table.

'I'll just go through and put a bit more coal on the fire to be ready for when you all come through,' was one of my sister's favourites.

'OK, thanks love. Gib, you stay there and tell your gran about that nice new teacher you've got at school.'

The real skill was getting the excuse in first.

I reckon I could count on the fingers of one hand – OK, maybe two hands max, the number of nights during my childhood that we didn't all sit together at breakfast or for evening meals. It's not that my parents weren't active – far from it. They were immersed in the local community and would take turns attending some event or other most evenings while the other would be back in the house looking after my sister and me. OK, at least until our teens. My dad would be chairing meetings of the local Community Council, playing the organ at an evening church service, or the piano at a rural concert. My mum would be out at her Keep Fit Club, playing badminton in the winter or regularly walking from door to door in the neighbourhood, collecting for some charity or other – Christian Aid, Cancer Research and Save the Children were her perennials.

Given that my working life for the past 20 years has required me to spend half my time on the road, this upbringing feels like a throwback to a bygone age. I remember it being a very happy family environment, and I never wanted to settle for anything less for my own family – were I ever to conquer my commitment phobia of course. OK, I suppose while I'm on the subject, I did promise to address the whole *still single in late forties* issue and won't procrastinate any longer. Yes, I've never been married. Never divorced. Never even engaged although I toyed with the notion once. OK, maybe twice. For many of you that'll no doubt make me a bit weird. I mean most other 'normal' people (there's that word again) get married and settled down in their twenties and thirties. If they're single in their forties, then they'll probably have at least a kid or two and maybe one divorce under their belt. I remember having to make a speech at the wedding of a friend who was getting married for the second time. I said I felt like I'd been lapped.

No, conforming is not something I've ever been that good at. But the chorus of, 'Look, everyone else is settling down/getting married/having kids,' has never held much sway as an argument. It's not that I haven't met some amazing women or that I'm against marriage. It's just never happened for me and I wasn't prepared to live someone else's conventional narrative as my life. I'm not sure who it was that once said, 'I spent over 20 years looking for the perfect woman only to find that she was looking for the perfect man.'

I do remind myself of that quote from time to time. Especially given my parents seemed to have found 'the one' in a school year of fewer than 50 kids. A shrink would probably lay the blame at their door – for setting the bar too high. Of course, I'd never met a shrink. Shrinks were for crazy people. As I glanced around the bare, white walls of my bedroom, something told me that might all be about to change.

Given it was a small island with only one secondary school, quite a few kids in my class had parents who were teachers. It wasn't such a big deal, although it was like having a parents' night every single day. Feedback on laziness or misbehaviour could be shared in the staffroom real time and then brought up over dinner that same evening. There were some perks too of having parents as teachers:

my sister and I would get a lift to school each morning, although only during secondary school where they both taught. For primary school it was 'Shanksie's Pony' (my mother's favourite term for having to walk somewhere – I've no idea where it comes from) which, from Primary 4 onwards, was across the park to the 'new' primary school – yes, the one built at vast expense, and that has long since been replaced. It was a modern, open-plan building, in a beautiful setting overlooking a loch and with views to the mountains of the neighbouring Isle of Arran in the distance.

On nice sunny days, the 15-minute walk was no real hardship. On colder winter days, more typical of the west coast of Scotland, it was a bit less fun. Especially considering my mum insisted I wear short trousers to school for much of my childhood. Why, I don't know, but it made me the only boy in the school in short trousers, which, of course, meant a teasing from time to time – especially if there was snow on the ground and my legs turned pink with cold! Over time I had to become comfortable with being a bit different, but I did yearn for my first pair of long trousers – a pair of Wrangler jeans like every other boy on the island seemed to have at the time. My mum dangled this incentive like some kind of rite of passage for when I would get into secondary school aged 12. At last, my chance to conform – to look just like the other kids – not to stand out in the crowd.

Well, I had no idea at the time, but the feeling of conformity and normality would be short lived.

Chapter 2 – The Bald Facts

Losing all my hair at the age of 12 was not the most fun part of my childhood. But then again there are worse things that can happen to you. Well, that's what I always told myself and it seemed to help. The cause was alopecia – a disease I couldn't even spell for many years, let alone understand. It's one of those autoimmune diseases that are all the rage these days. It normally causes small, random bald patches that in most cases will grow back, albeit often a different colour. That's where you see people – men or women – with a strange grey or fair wisp. You know the sort, a bit like the evil Cruella de Vil in *101 Dalmatians*. But it was no little bald patches or stylish wisps for me. I had to go one better – I had *alopecia universalis* (AU). Now, you don't need be a Latin scholar to guess it's the aggressive form of the disease when all the little bald patches join up, making the victim entirely bald. Indeed, your entire body rejects hair – no eyebrows, eyelashes, body hair – zilch, nada. My understanding was and is that nobody really knows what causes it – some say stress or a shock, diet, air pollution and the like. I have no idea and don't really care either – well, not now at least. Back then it was different.

Those were interesting days. The entire period from the first sighting of a tiny small bald patch on the back of my head to total hair loss took just six months. I'd wake up in my bed each morning to find clumps of fluffy fair hair on the pillow. Each night my poor mum would ritually wash and blow-dry my hair in an attempt to cover over the growing number of bald patches before the next day at school. But we both knew we were fighting a losing battle – alopecia was winning hands down.

The irony was that I had just started secondary school and had at last graduated into long trousers – the first time in years I was able to blend in with the other kids, to look like a 'normal' school pupil. What's more, I was the proud owner of a brand new pair of dark blue Wrangler jeans. Scant reward for seven years of bare legs through primary school. They got their first outing at one of the school discos that took place about once a month in the main assembly hall. We're talking way back in 1979 when disco was in its prime. It was all about these fabulously theatrical bands like Earth, Wind & Fire, the Bee Gees, Kool & The Gang – complete with high-heeled shoes, spangly trousers, suits with big flared collars – the lot.

I have vivid memories of that first-ever school disco – opening the doors at the back of the hall to be hit by a thumping wall of sound. 'Street Life' by the Crusaders, featuring Randy Crawford on vocals and with a really catchy baseline – you know the one. I found the atmosphere electric as I walked forward through a dark sea of bodies, barely able to see who was who. The DJ was up on the stage with all sorts of flashing and spinning lights – I'd never experienced anything like it and was completely mesmerised. This was around the time that *Grease* had gone huge, featuring a young (and much slimmer) John Travolta and the gorgeous Olivia Newton-John. As a result, the fashion was for guys to have a metal comb sticking out of the back pocket of their jeans – it was the height of 'cool'. In an effort to blend in I'd turn up in my Wrangler jeans, black shirt and the ubiquitous metal comb in my back pocket. It became a habit – my disco uniform. But by January 1980 I had but a few strands of hair left. During the evening disco that month I went to the boys' toilet and looked in the mirror with my comb at the ready. Then the realisation hit me like a baseball bat to the head: it wasn't particularly cool to have a shiny metal comb sticking out your back pocket when you've barely got a strand of hair on your head. While no one was looking, I quickly jettisoned the comb into the rubbish bin. I'm sure that was the last comb I ever owned or am ever likely to own. Who cares?

Thomson Ward. Thursday evening

I checked the time on my watch: 6.15pm. *Shit* – I realised I'd better hotfoot it down to the canteen if I was to get any dinner. This early eating would take a bit of getting used to. Over the past 20 years of 50–60-hour working weeks, I would typically have dinner anywhere between 8pm and 10.30pm, which, on reflection, was not particularly healthy. But it fitted in with busy work and social schedules. Now I had a new, very different schedule to get used to. How would I adjust to being very un-busy?

I threw on my suit jacket and headed off briskly towards the canteen, nodding and smiling at anyone I passed by in the corridor – still not quite sure who was staff and who was a patient. I got there in the nick of time.

'Yoor just in time, son,' said the large bare-armed woman behind the counter. 'Ah wiz just aboot tae clear awe this nice food away.'

'Oh, I'm sorry – lost track of time. My name's Gib, by the way. I've just arrived today and have still to get used to the timings.'

'Nae problem, Gib, ah'm Mary. Whit can a get ye from this delightful selection, son? Ah made it awe w' ma own fare hawns.'

'Really? It's all homemade, Mary?'

My sarcasm was clearly lost on her. She gave me the kind of withering look that implied she felt I must have been born yesterday. Oh, or perhaps the resident of a psychiatric hospital. Take your pick.

'Nawe, son, o' the NHS food is made doon in Wales then frozen an sent oot aroon the country.'

I'd discover that a little insight would go a long way to explaining the taste and quality of my diet for the next few days. Mary was quite clearly Glasgow born and bred and seemed to have the characteristic warmth, friendliness and sense of humour that Glaswegians are famous for. The delightful selection of 'Welsh' cuisine included a choice of reconstituted mince or slices of what might (once upon a time) have been pork, in a thick gravy sauce, accompanied by soggy-looking vegetables, served on one of these big metal trays. But my eyes lit up at the sponge cake with custard – a throwback to my old school dinners diet. Every cloud…

I thanked Mary, took my tray of food and scanned the room for where to sit. There were a few empty round tables I could have gone to. That was the easy option. I chose to head for a table that had a solitary, dark-haired, older woman sitting at it.

'Mind if I join you?' I asked as I approached.

She frowned and sprang up quickly from her seat, gathered the plates onto her tray and headed towards the large trolley where the used trays were stacked after use.

'Mmm. It appears you do, then,' I muttered under my breath.

'You can sit here if you want,' came a voice from behind me. It came from the one other table that had someone sitting at it. A young-looking guy, I'd guess early thirties. Slight build.

'Oh, thanks, that would be great,' I said. 'I'm Gib, by the way, just arrived today.'

'I'm Danny. Been here about a week. So I was wondering how come you don't have any hair?'

It's funny. For the past couple of decades, it no longer crosses my mind that I'm bald. Then every now and then I get asked a question like that from out of the blue and I'm instantly reminded that I look a bit different. I think most people assume that I shave my head – it's so normal these days and I've been lucky that it's become a fashion for men who start to lose it up top. Thank god the total shave has replaced the comb-over favoured by the middle-aged men of my youth. I actually found Danny's honest direct curiosity quite refreshing. I gave him my quick, well-rehearsed spiel about alopecia. He nodded while chewing away at his plate of pork.

'You know you look just like that swimmer Duncan Goodhew?'

'You're not the first person to say that, Danny. If I had a penny for every time…'

Duncan Goodhew had become a bit of a celebrity figure in the UK during the 1980s when he'd won a gold medal in the breast-stroke at the Moscow Olympics. He'd gone on to a career in TV and became quite a well-known face – well, head actually, as of course Duncan had also lost all his hair as a boy. Apparently, he'd fallen out of a tree as a kid and, as a result of the shock, woke up the next day completely bald. When I was in my early twenties and he was at the height of his fame, I used to often get mistaken for him when visiting a big city like Glasgow or London. It wasn't just the fact we were both bald – there was also quite a facial similarity. Try Google Images and make up your own mind.

This fact actually allowed a bit of fun and mischief, if I'm honest – role-playing a celebrity based on mistaken identity, signing the odd fake autograph, you name it.

'Do you want to hear a good Duncan Goodhew story, Danny?' I asked.

'Absolutely.'

My favourite Goodhew story took place at Gleneagles Hotel, a very posh country hotel in Scotland where my then Danish girl-friend, Winnie, had decided to take me as a graduation present (yes, I'll explain who Winnie was a bit later).

'I'd been playing a round of golf and got paired up with a nice old bloke called Billy, who turned out to be hotel magnate from Ireland. He'd turned up in a Rolls Royce together with some old aunts for some kind of family celebration. I'd explained to Billy that Gleneagles is such a posh hotel that people almost expect to see celebrities there, so I would get the odd knowing smile from staff and guests alike. I went for a swim at the plush spa, which even had a little bridge over the swimming pool. When I noticed a small crowd gathering on the bridge, nudging each other and pointing, I realised they were now totally convinced that they were in the company of the great British Olympic Gold Medallist Duncan Goodhew. I tried to swim the breaststroke as fast as I could, ducking my head under the water like the pros do, but I'm sure they must have been very disappointed at how far downhill Goodhew had gone since his 1980 Olympic triumph.'

'That's brilliant,' said Danny. 'Were they all not asking for autographs?'

'Well, when I told this to Billy on the golf course, he made me promise to come to his table that night at dinner and be introduced to his entourage as his golf partner, "the famous Duncan Goodhew". Rather naughtily I went along with it and they told me how excited Billy had been to play golf with an Olympic legend. One even turned round to Winnie and said, "You must be so proud of your husband, Mrs Goodhew," which left her speechless. I even agreed to sign a couple of autographs at the poolside the next day – but thankfully Billy had let them in on the secret by that time.'

'Seems like you're a bit of a storyteller, Mr Bulloch,' came a voice from behind me. 'We've got quite a few of them in here. I'm Tony, the Duty Nurse this evening. I see you've just arrived at Thomson today.'

'Oh, hello, Tony. I was just chatting with Danny here and sharing some childhood memories.'

'No problem – always good to socialise. But you might want to get a bit of an early night as you've had a big day. Why not come with me and we'll pass by the little medicine kiosk on the way to your room and get you something to calm you down and help you sleep.'

As if I needed it. I'd barely slept in the past seven nights and was desperate for some rest.

I said a quick goodbye to Danny and followed Tony out of the canteen and down to a space which, in daylight, I could imagine would be bright and airy, with a few sofas placed against the walls. It was pitch black outside but I could see that the big, full-length windows led out onto a small garden with some kind of glass conservatory-style roof. Against one wall there was a little kiosk, almost like a tuck shop.

'Marion's just got a wee something for you that you can swallow with this glass of water,' he said.

Inside the kiosk another smiling face looked out at me and handed me two white plastic cups, one with water, the other with two small pink pills.

'I feel like I'm in a scene straight out of *The Matrix*. Are these pills going to do me any good?' I asked glibly.

'Yes, of course,' replied Marion in a friendly, reassuring voice. 'They're just going to help you get some sleep. I hear you've barely slept at all in the last week.'

She had a point. My body felt completely exhausted. I was both mentally and physically drained of all energy.

'OK, Marion. I don't know you and we've just met. I've no idea what you're giving me but I have to trust you completely. That goes for all of you,' I said, glancing at Tony as I popped the two pills into my mouth and gulped down the water. Marion nodded and smiled.

I said goodnight to Tony and walked back down the corridor towards Room 17, sneaking a quick glance in through the windows in the doors to the other bedrooms as I passed. Silhouetted figures sat, lay or stood in the small confines of most rooms. Mick and Johnny were still sitting slumped down, arms crossed, continuing their vigil outside my door.

'Evening, Mick. Evening, Johnny,' I said as I glanced through the window on the door opposite and could just about make out a shadowed figure kneeling by the bed.

'Hi Gib,' they both chimed. I smiled when I saw the whiteboard beside my door – the *Gilbert* had been crossed out and replaced by *Gib* in blue marker pen.

'Did ye huv a good dinner, Gib?' asked Johnny.

'Absolutely delightful, Johnny,' I said somewhat sarcastically. 'Will you be staying there all night lads?'

'Yep, we'll both be sittin' here quietly until the morning,' Mick, the bigger of the two men answered.

'OK, great. Well, I'm going in here to get some rest. I'm completely knackered. But if you two fine men can just stop whatever is in there from getting in here,' I said gesturing inside my room, 'then I'd be extremely grateful and will sleep a little easier.'

'Nae problem, Gib' said Mick with a smile. 'Sleep well, son'.

I started to undress, putting my things onto the back of the little chair, and checked the time as I took off my watch. 7.12pm. Well, this would be my earliest bedtime in over 40 years but, God, did I need it. I climbed into bed and pulled up the thin duvet. My eyelids felt like they'd had weights attached to them. My mind slowly drifted back to childhood and happy memories of trying to fall asleep in my little single bed, while, very faintly, the gentle piano music of my father drifted up the stairs. It wasn't until I was much older that I learnt that the piece I remembered hearing, my favourite, was 'Sonatina No. II' by Kenneth Leighton[1]. A beautiful, haunting melody that had seemed to penetrate my very soul – one of these

1. Sonatina II, Kenneth Leighton. Played by Lyn Bulloch in Gib's flat in Geneva, Summer 2015. https://www.youtube.com/watch?v=oaetQ8r6wn0&t=0s&index=1&list=PLWCXUu-Vav7JQJjqznQb99u3Lr8IEDB0Lk

melodies that plays in the back of your mind like the soundtrack to a film. I love all kinds of music. I have many favourite songs that remind me of different places – of happy or sad moments in my life. You know the feeling. But there was something very different about this gentle piano melody that gave me a comfort – a special warmth inside. I've often wondered if there's such a thing as a natural frequency of the body or spirit, something each person responds to in the same way that dogs can hear high-pitched sounds that are inaudible to the human ear. If so, Leighton's 'Sonatina No. II' was certainly my natural frequency.

I wondered if I might wake up the next day back in my flat in Geneva and discover this had been some kind of weird and vivid dream. As my eyes closed over, my mind drifted back to the curious events of the past few days and my childhood growing up on the island.

Chapter 3 – Daring Greatly

They say it takes a village to raise a child. I wouldn't disagree. I've always felt very fortunate to have grown up within a close-knit island community. Throughout my childhood I was exposed to a whole array of larger-than-life characters – each of them adding something colourful, something special, to daily life. I've never had that feeling in adulthood, no matter where I've lived. London always felt transient, although I ended up spending more than 15 years there. The Isle of Bute remained my spiritual home and I always have an inner buzz of excitement when I go back – the lure of a whisky with my dad by the warm coal fire, my mum's delicious home cooking on the kitchen table. 'Baked White Rat' remained a fixture on the menu well into adulthood, or 'The Fatted Calf', if my mum felt it had been too long since my last visit. These culinary delights would often manifest themselves as haggis, neeps and tatties, *boeuf bourguignon*, or one of Wee Marj's other home-cooked classics that she'd have 'slaved over a hot stove all day' to provide for her Prodigal Son as a home-coming treat.

I'd headed back to Bute from Geneva (where I'd lived since 2011) the previous Friday to combine a parental visit with poor Mowatti's dad's funeral, which I should have attended earlier in the day. Such trips would often provide an opportunity to catch up with some of the other heroes and heroines of my childhood – those who are still alive, of course. Too many phone calls home would have my mum remember someone's passing halfway through the call – 'Oh, you'll be sad to hear this, Gib, but that's poor old Tam Ferguson gone' – or some well-known elder statesman or stateswoman of the island. That's life, I suppose. But Mowatti's dad's death meant that the steady march of *Anno Domini* was very much on my mind. So on Saturday afternoon I'd paid a visit to the local ironmonger's shop, Bute Tools, to see one of these remaining 'elder statesmen' of the island. Indeed, one of the main role models of my life – the first and still the best boss I've ever had in the past 30 years.

Isle of Bute, Scotland. Summer 1984

I'd landed a weekend job in the local ironmonger's when I was 15, but during the school holidays I worked there six days a week. The shop was owned by a unique and charismatic individual, Willie McFie. Willie was a big man but softly spoken and very quick witted – he was rarely seen without a lit cigarette in his mouth, or one stuck behind his ear ready to be lit. He was something of a legend, locally: having trained as a blacksmith, he progressed to owning a small ironmonger's-come-general store, which got progressively larger over the years. Bute Tools was an institution within the community and seemed to sell just about everything from hardware and crockery to tools, lawnmowers and bottled gas cylinders. My job had originally been to repair the lawnmowers in the little back workshop, but after passing my driving test three months after my 17th birthday (I was obsessed by cars), I had progressed to doing home deliveries in the cool white Ford pick-up truck.

I loved the job and the banter was second to none. The little workshop round the back would be the focal point for jokes, teasings and socio-economic debates on island life. For example, how many pubs had been visited and how much alcohol consumed the previous night, who'd run off with whose wife, how much Auchincheerie farm had paid for a new tractor and so on. You know – the important stuff in life. But to me it was fascinating and the workshop acted like a lightning rod for all sorts of local worthies who, having gradually worked out the schedule of coffee breaks, would time visits accordingly.

My colleague in the workshop and on the delivery runs was another local legend, Scooby MacMillan. Scooby had been on Willie's payroll for many years. He left school without a paper qualification to his name but was and still is one of the most sharp-witted people I've ever met. Scooby and I worked in the shop for many years, including the first two summers during university, which helped me earn a little bit extra to augment my student grant. Each day had its own funny encounters, stories, jokes to be told. I'll share here what has to be my favourite tale from the Bute Tools part of my career – the plotting of a veritable coup at the Highland Games.

It was a bright summer's morning in July 1984 and, after the usual 8am start, I'd made good progress on the lawnmowers Willie had given me to repair. I got all three Flymos back up and running before coffee break and then headed out on the mid-morning pilgrimage to pick up the rolls with egg and sausage from More's the Bakers shop along the street. By the time I got back, Scooby had made the coffees and one of our most regular visitors, old Mr Henry, had stopped by the workshop for a cuppa.

'Morning, Mr Henry,' I said politely. I'd never heard anyone call him by his first name and have no idea what it was to this day. 'Morning, Master Bulloch. No roll for me, thanks son. I'm watching my weight,' Mr Henry replied in a slightly sarcastic tone, given he was a rather frail-looking octogenarian. Mr Henry was a lovely old man who reminded me of my grandad; always had a story to tell and was quite a raconteur. According to Willie, he'd been the CEO of one of the largest companies in Scotland, Coates Paton, having risen from tea-boy to the boardroom in a 50-year career. He retired to the island a few years previously and lived in one of the very large detached houses far out on the south shore.

He sat crossed-legged in his tweed cap, perched on one of the larger lawnmowers smoking a cigarette, and was clearly halfway through one of his legendary tales. I was transfixed by the accounts of his rich life. He appeared to pick straight back up where he'd left off.

'So I sold that Korean company in the morning and, believe it or not, had signed a contract to buy the bloody things from the Japanese instead by that very same afternoon!' he exclaimed, which was clearly the punchline as Willie and Scooby were both bent over double with laughter.

Then glancing over his shoulder towards me he said, 'So I hear from Willie that you're going to the University of Strathclyde in the autumn to study Engineering. Congratulations, young man.'

Willie took this as his cue.

'Well, he might have got all these fancy qualifications at school and be going to that big university, but ma' shop is the University of Life,' he interjected. 'Oh, and don't forget, son, ah'm the fuckin' Dean!'

Then it was Scooby's turn to have a dig. 'Ye know, a went thru' University of Strathclyde ma self,' which took as all a bit by surprise and caused Mr Henry to raise an eyebrow.

'Aye, a got lost on the way tae Queen Street Station!'

A loud roar of laughter went out of the open door of the workshop and onto the street. I'm not sure if it was the laughter he'd heard or the smell of the sausage rolls, but it marked the arrival of another regular guest, Big Craigie. As his name would suggest, Big Craigie was a giant of a man – he filled the whole doorway of the workshop like a mini eclipse. He was close to 20 stone, had an enormous chest and hands the size of shovels. He drove an HGV for a living but was also a leading light in the local Highland Games, where a few years previously he'd won the World Cumberland Wrestling Championship in the heavyweight division.

'How's it goin' Big Man?' Scooby enquired.

'No tae bad, mate,' said Craigie. 'You boys got the kettle boiled? Do me a favour, Gib, and make yer old mate, Craigie, a cup o' tea.'

'Milk and two sugars?' I asked.

'That's the one. Willie's had you well trained these past few years. You'll go far, son,' said Craigie.

Suddenly, Willie stood up and put his mug down on the workbench – 'Gentlemen, I've just had a brainwave. We'll enter Bute Tools for the team event at the Highland Games!' he exclaimed to looks of astonishment from Craigie and Scoobie. They did their best to explain that this event was aimed at local sports teams like the Rugby or Shinty Clubs, but Willie was undeterred. With a couple of phone calls, he built a rag bag team of farm labourers, nightclub bouncers and even Jim Hines who represented the British Army in the 100m, who happened to be on leave over the summer.

After weeks of clandestine training at Knockanreoch Farm, it came to Highland Games Day, which is held on the third Saturday of August each year. The sounds of the bagpipes floated across the meadows as the dozens of pipe bands warmed up under their chosen trees. I'd always loved the Highland Games; it reminded me of why I was so proud to be Scottish. We'd been blessed with the weather, too, and the sun was splitting the sky. I made it down to the shop for the team gathering at 11.30am sharp. Entries had to be received by 12.30pm and we'd chosen a surprise tactic. I looked at my watch: 12.25pm. Just in time!

'Good afternoon, sir. I'd like to enter Bute Tools, the local hardware store, into the team event, please,' said Scooby, confidently.

'You want to enter a shop? But the team event is intended for the sporting clubs of the island to compete against each other,' replied the rather plucky-voiced old official.

Scooby pulled another piece of paper from inside his lab-coat pocket.

'Well, I've studied the rules carefully an' a canny see any mention of the event bein' limited tae sports teams. Can you mister?' he said, sticking the sheet of paper in front of the nose of the official who perused it briefly with a frown across his face.

'Very well. I'll accept your entry,' he said reaching for the tannoy. 'A last-minute entry by Bute Tools for the team event this afternoon!' boomed across the park.

Scooby turned, grinning at the six of us standing behind him with Big Craigie standing at the back alongside his equally big brother, who'd also been cajoled into the unlikely team of misfits.

'Right, men. Boiler suits off and warm up,' shouted Scooby loudly. Then, with a glance at the bemused-looking Bute Rugby Club team standing next to us, he exclaimed, 'Let the competition begin!'

To say it was a walkover would be an understatement. Our sprinters won by a mile. Big Craigie and Johnny were unstoppable in the heavy events. Johnny threw the hammer outside the limits of distance marker lines, requiring an extra-long measuring tape; Craigie tossed the caber over on its end like he was flicking a cigarette butt. He scored a perfect '12 o'clock' throw five times in a row. But the tug-o-war was probably the biggest thrill. I'd been allowed to join to make up the numbers to the official team of six. It was no contest with the shinty and football clubs, but the rugby club had some bigger lads in it. Big Craigie dug himself in as the anchor at the back, wrapping the rope over his shoulder and under one arm. The rest of us fell in line, grabbing the rope with both hands and digging our heels in as we'd done in practice up on the farm.

'OK, boys. Straight backs, bent legs, get low!' shouted Scooby from the side lines.

'Ready. Hold. And… Pull!' the official called out.

'Heave, boys!' Scooby shouted, but it was hardly necessary. The rope started coming back towards us and I felt myself back-stepping quickly as six of the biggest players in the rugby team fell over themselves before being dragged along the grass on their stomachs.

It was the first time anyone had beaten Bute Rugby Club in the past 12 years. And they clearly were not amused at being beaten by the local hardware shop. I'm good mates with many of these ex-Rugby Club lads to this day, but it still hits a bit of a raw nerve if it comes up over a pint in a local pub. We, on the other hand, were ecstatic, and Willie took great pride in going up to the podium to collect the Waddell Shield. When it came to the traditional 'march past', where about 50 pipe bands would march one after the other down the High Street, our team fell in behind the local Isle of Bute Pipe Band and Willie stood at the front holding the shield above his head, victoriously. The crowds lining the streets clapped and cheered wildly as we strode past. We celebrated late into the night and I've rarely had as bad a hangover to this day.

Turn to Camera

I had a bit of a debate with my Editor about whether to keep this rambling Highland Games anecdote or ditch it. She made the very fair point that it might lose the reader through an unnecessary departure from the central themes of the story.

I argued that 'chutzpah' was fairly central to the story. That Highland Games as was one of the happiest days of my childhood and no doubt left an indelible mark into adulthood. It was a triumph of idealism over adversity and winning against the odds. Willie had inspired us all to take on the might of the 'unbeatable' Rugby Club and through a fairly creative interpretation of the rules, he'd challenged the accepted system and won. It's that David v Goliath theme that I hope comes across loud and clear throughout the book. So if you've read the passage about the 1984 Bute Highland Games and this justification for keeping it, it means she was convinced. Hope you are too.

Willie was certainly a mentor to me in his self-appointed role as the Dean of the University of Life. That remains my real Alma Mater – more than the Engineering and Business degrees I went on to get at the University of Strathclyde. Having had a teacher-centric upbringing, I'd also been given my first exposure to the world of big business. I always loved hearing Mr Henry's tales of how he'd travelled to high-powered meetings in a chauffeur-driven Rolls Royce or flown in aeroplanes to exotic countries around the world, always First Class. It sounded like a James Bond kind of lifestyle and just the sort of career in the fast lane that I could aspire to. Yes, I think I'll become a businessman one day, I had thought to myself. Little did I know what that would actually entail.

Chapter 4 – Finding My Feet

'So, what do you want to do when you grow up?' must rank as the most irritating, yet favourite question of every grandparent, aunt or family friend. Personally, I used to dread it. It's always puzzled me that society expects kids in their mid- to late-teens to know what they want to do for the rest of their lives. At the age of 17 I hadn't the faintest idea what I wanted to do. But I had, admittedly, been quite enamoured with old Mr Henry's tales of the business high life. The glitz of a yuppie lifestyle had been immortalised for my generation by Gordon Gekko in the film *Wall Street*. His catch phrase, 'Greed is good', seemed to sum up the eighties zeitgeist. Well, look on the bright side – at least business leaders have learnt the error of their ways since then, right? If only.

I'd always assumed I would go to university – partly because that had been an implicit parental expectation from early childhood and partly for lack of any better ideas. But what should I study? The careers advice wasn't particularly sophisticated or imaginative at Rothesay Academy on the Isle of Bute.

'Your grades in Maths and Physics aren't bad – you'd probably be most suited to a career in Engineering,' proclaimed the careers advisor. His prediction, I was soon to discover, was dead wrong. I blindly took his advice, however, and by a process of elimination opted for a course in Naval Architecture & Offshore Engineering at the University of Strathclyde in Glasgow. 'Naval what?' is the typical response I get. Well, it's basically ship design and I was attracted by the small intake of about 20 students each year. They seemed to spend their time drawing boats and towing little models up and down a wave tank. *Looks quite fun*, I thought to myself. So that was that. And I managed to defer any further life decisions for the next four years.

I remember enjoying university life although for the first two years I felt quite disorientated by the 'big city' and discovered just how cocooned my upbringing had been on the island. My confidence and ego were to get a huge boost as I entered my third year and met my first proper girlfriend – remember Winnie who I promised to give you the lowdown on, the Danish girl who'd taken me to Gleneagles Hotel? Well, she was tall, blonde and had a gorgeous smile; she was simply stunning. She had come to the island for a year to work as an au pair for a local family. I'd known her by reputation – everyone did. People would literally stop in their tracks and turn to ogle her as she walked down the street, sometimes sporting her signature white leather miniskirt. I'd been introduced to her on a weekend trip to the island and was immediately smitten. She could have had the pick of any boy on the island – or frankly, just about anywhere for that matter. However, to my amazement and delight, Winnie chose me, a slightly shy (at the time) 20-year-old Scottish island boy with no hair. Why? I often asked myself that question. I think it was because she liked to be different, to fly in the face of norms or expectations, and I offered just that. In return, she gave my ego the most almighty kick up the backside and, looking back, it was quite a big turning point in my life. Winnie decided to stay in Scotland to study and we were together for about two and a half years before the relationship went tits up – although a different metaphor might be more appropriate. She'd gone back to Denmark for a holiday at Easter and never came back. Hardly surprising given a distinct lack of commitment on my side – a recurring theme throughout my adult life – but it still hurt a lot at the time and probably left me with more lingering trust issues than I'd care to admit. I'll leave the armchair shrinks amongst you to speculate on that one. Suffice it to say that looking back I feel ashamed to have dismissed Winnie as something of a trophy girlfriend. It's taken me almost 30 years to fully appreciate the pivotal role that she played in my life and the debt of gratitude I owe her.

Glasgow and Aberdeen, Scotland. Late 1980s

In my final year of Naval Architecture, I'd courted the romantic notion of becoming a yacht designer in the South of France. In reality, such jobs were about as common as tap-dancing unicorns –

landing a low-paid job in a small shipyard in Northwest England, designing the back end of a tug, was far more likely. However, upon graduating in 1989 I chose to join BP for a career in the oil industry, having been won over by their corporate presentations on glamorous international careers and the spoils that go with it: company cars, corporate credit cards and the like. Yes, this was back when there was no talk of climate change and low carbon economies – the days when coal was cool (groan).

Reality bites, as they say. On joining BP, I soon found myself in not-quite-so glamorous Aberdeen and spending half my time on a floating oilrig in the middle of the stormy North Sea, sometimes in waves over 18m high. But the money was good and I had only half the time to spend it, given life was fully funded when offshore. I discovered that my graduate starting salary of £18,000 was more than my poor father was on after 30 years as a secondary school teacher and as Head of the Art Department – it just didn't seem right to me. The view that we undervalue public sector skills, particularly teachers and nurses, and, in many cases, overvalue some private sector skills, has stuck with me ever since.

Life on the oilrigs was quite fun to be honest and a bit like a residential version of my weekend job in the ironmongers with Willie and Scoobie: the stories, the banter, the jokes and the windups made it a fascinating and exciting place to be, but it wasn't for the faint hearted. They were wary of young, 'wet-behind-the ears' graduates who would turn up armed with a degree and a know-it-all attitude, then start preaching engineering theory and equations to old hands who were 30 years their senior. These types would soon be brought down to earth with a bump and learn the hard way. My experience over many years in Willie's 'University of Life' had taught me a degree of humility and lots of respect. It turned out to be fabulous preparation for how to handle the large-than-life characters I encountered offshore and to understand that graduating from university with a bit of paper is only the start of the learning process. The real education begins when you start learning how to deal with *real* people in *real* life.

I only lasted a couple of years in BP, having quickly come to the conclusion that a long-term career in Engineering was not for me, and I was probably not for it. My honest assessment is that I was a fairly crap engineer. That said, there was one thing I did which I was proud of. It was a short project where I proposed a 'patently absurd' solution to an engineering problem – directly challenging the views of experts and conventional wisdom – but stood my ground. Without going into lots of techie details (partly because I doubt I can remember them now) there had been quite a major incident on the Buchan Alpha oilrig the previous year. The so-called 'separators', or large tanks that receive the crude oil and separate out the oil, sand and water, had all blown their high-pressure relief valves and forced an emergency shutdown. You can imagine how much one of these shutdowns costs an oil company – literally millions of dollars every hour. Safety was also a massive issue, so the company was keen to find out what had happened and ensure it wouldn't happen again. The mystery was that the pressure readings in the control room had been showing normal before these high-pressure relief valves had lifted. This dichotomy had confounded many senior engineers for several months and when I was in between projects, my boss tasked me this puzzle. I doubt he expected a new graduate to solve it but it would keep me occupied for a few weeks and out of his hair. I had nothing more than a bunch of squiggly lines of pressure recordings on graph paper and some technical drawings of the inlet and outlet pipes and the high-pressure relief valves themselves. 'Think out of the box, son,' was the only instruction I was given.

I discovered there had been a pressure build-up on the downstream side of the valves that was caused by a technician closing off the gas flaring. But intuitively that would only serve to hold the valves closed – a bit like putting downward pressure on a plug in a sink. I know this is sounding a bit involved, but bear with me. You see, having pored over the technical drawings, my hypothesis was that there was a design flaw in the valve that would cause it to trigger on backpressure. If I was proved to be right, it would explain the mysterious shutdown, but it was something that the manufacturer dismissed as physically impossible. Indeed, there was no shortage of sceptics regarding my idea amongst colleagues in BP.

I arranged a laboratory simulation at the manufacturer's factory – it was the only way I could prove my theory. They were clearly humouring me. In an effort to re-create the conditions of the shutdown, the backpressure on the top of the valve was slowly increased to see what would happen. The pressure was increased to quite a significant level and the damned valve remained doggedly closed. The technical experts from the manufacturer stood, arms folded and with a smug, 'We told you so, you young graduate upstart,' look on their faces. I stood, watching the pressure needle rise and feeling my own pressure, probably blood, start to build up inside me. The situation was shaping up to be the greatest embarrassment of my life. My palms were sweaty and I could feel my face getting redder and redder – deep, burning, cringing, mortification was imminent. All of a sudden, to everyone's astonishment, the valve did the supposedly impossible: it defied gravity and lifted, triggering an alarm bell, which was the equivalent of an emergency shutdown. My crazy hypothesis had been proved right and I tried to conceal a smug grin that was more out of sheer relief than conceit. At the risk of sounding a bit sanctimonious, it was my first taste of standing my ground in a business setting and fighting for what I believed to be right, even while knowing I was right out on a limb.

The victory was short lived, however, and I knew in my heart that I just didn't want to be an engineer for the rest of my life. I had to think about an escape plan, and business school was the best idea I could come up with at the time.

University of Strathclyde Business School, Glasgow. 1991–92

It was the early 1990s – the time when the Master of Business Administration degree, or MBA, really started to come into fashion. As it turned out, business was far more my forte than engineering ever was. It may partly have had to do with the fact that I was paying for the MBA myself out of a loan from the bank. That certainly focuses the mind! Or it may be that I was just more interested in business in general and had a greater aptitude as a result. Either way, for the first time in my career I was properly motivated, I was eager to learn; I wanted to be the best I could be. That said, even back then I remember feeling a little bit uncomfortable with the standard doctrine about business and its role in society being solely about making money.

I vividly recall a lecture in Corporate Finance where we'd been learning about bonds, yields, equities, debt, gearing ratios and other jargon terms and the lecturer was talking about the purpose of business. He was almost preaching to us: 'There is only one sole purpose of business that transcends all other goals,' he declared with total conviction, 'and that is for business management to fulfil their fiduciary duty to shareholders by maximising their return on investment.'

This jarred with me at the time and still does.

'You mean that's it?' I recall asking quite indignantly. 'What about their employees, their customers or the rest of society? Surely they matter just as much?'

'Well, if it wasn't for investors there would be no equity and there would be no company,' he replied confidently. 'In fact, this is a legally binding duty of all CEOs, as you'd know if you'd done the pre-reading for this module.'

The memory of this exchange with my Finance lecturer has stuck with me throughout my career. And, to be fair, the guy was only representing the conventional wisdom of the time and a viewpoint that pervades business to this day. The required pre-reading was a book by a certain Professor Michael Porter, a Harvard Professor and business guru, entitled *Competitive Advantage*. No self-respecting MBA student would be seen dead without a copy. It proclaimed the creed that shareholder value trumps every other possible consideration and is the Holy Grail of business success. But that was then. I'd like to think that things are changing, and relatively quickly, too. Even Professor Porter is preaching a different gospel these days. Instead of 'Shareholder Value', he's now promoting a focus on what he terms 'Shared Value' – the idea that businesses should balance profit with a shared benefit to broader society. Well, as they say, leopards sometimes can change their spots!

The highlight of the MBA was the final team project. Each year the Business School would lay down the gauntlet with a challenge country – in our year it was Russia. Remember that this was 1992, less than a year after President Yeltsin had dramatically seized power after Gorbachev stepped down. Russia back then was a bit like the Wild West, which made it all the more exciting. We'd conceived a project that would build partnerships or joint ventures between Scottish textile companies and manufacturers in Russia. We'd sent out lots of begging letters in search of funding, and about two weeks before we left, we hit the jackpot – a £7,000 grant from Scottish Enterprise. Our budget had assumed a nominal £50 per night per person for accommodation alone. But the student complex south of Moscow where we ended up cost us all of one pound a night. This meant we had several thousand pounds to blow in just a few weeks. That might not sound like a lot of money for a team of seven, but with everything dirt cheap, it actually was quite difficult to get through it all. Looking back now, I'm ashamed to think that a chunk of hardworking Scottish taxpayers' money got spent on vodka, *champanski*, gambling, helicopter trips over St Petersburg and on breaking the record for the highest bill in Russia's first McDonald's restaurant near Red Square. About 20 quid.

It was a month-long adventure that I'll never forget. One of our team had gone out to Moscow on a recce some days earlier in order to try to find us accommodation and generally case the joint. Television footage from Western media had stoked our fears that we'd be on a diet of cabbage and water for our entire stay. We couldn't have been more wrong. On our first night we went to eat in the old Hotel Russia just off Red Square. We'd learn that the standard menu option was 'meat or fish'. In rare cases, if we were lucky, that might extend to include a chicken Kiev. However, the fact it wasn't cabbage meant we were over the moon. More to the point, a bottle of vodka was all of 70 pence and champagne even cheaper at just 50 pence a bottle. We sat with our interpreter; the restaurant was empty except for a traditional Russian wedding party. Feeling flush, we sent several bottles of champagne over to the boisterous gathering in the corner. Their gesture in return was to send us a large plate of caviar and a bottle of vodka. Before too long we found ourselves totally integrated with the wedding party. After a few dances with the bride and bridesmaids, a number of toasts followed and it was then down to a vodka drinking competition. We were quickly drunk under the table by our Russian hosts. This very first night set the scene for what was to follow – a month of fun, heavy drinking and general debauchery with a few visits to local Russian businesses sprinkled in. Yet we managed to complete the project report and even sell a few copies to some retailers like Littlewoods and M&S.

London. Mid-1990s

The Russian adventure meant that I'd completely neglected looking for a job during what was one of the worst recession periods in years – late 1992. I got to the final interview stage with a couple of consultancies but fell at the last hurdle. In the end, I got a job with Mars, the confectionery company, where I spent almost four years of my career. I was in my late twenties, living in London and meeting lots of young like-minded colleagues, many of whom are my friends to this day. I didn't work particularly hard. Mars gave the job a fancy title such as 'Sales Research Associate', I think, but it basically amounted to designing confectionery displays and convincing retailers to place two to three Mars bars in a row. We'd conduct research to show that this would increase their sales by 29 per cent or something like that. No, I'm afraid that negotiating the number of Mars bars on a confectionery display was not my vocation.

Then, in 1996, a tip-off from a friend quite unexpectedly landed me a job with what was then Andersen Consulting (Accenture as of 2001). At last I'd found a role in a prestigious company that would allow me to utilise my MBA skills. What's more, they'd pay me shed loads more money. I was gradually elbowing my way towards the front in the London rat race. I'd soon discover that career success would simply make me a winning rat.

NIGHT II – THE EPIPHANY

'The two most important days in your life are the day you are born and the day you find out why.'

Mark Twain

Chapter 5 – A Winning Rat

Turn to Camera

So just before we dive into Night II and share the experiences that led to a fairly significant career shift in the late nineties, I want to clarify one thing, thinking of the cynics amongst you in particular.

Throughout the book, I'll be sharing my recollection of conversations I had with staff and patients in the hospital, as well as former colleagues I encountered during my career at Accenture. Are the characters real? Yes – but many names (all in the hospital) have been changed for obvious reasons. Do I recall these conversations verbatim? No, of course not. I was on a heavy dose of Diazepam at the time for goodness sake. But I do remember the encounters fairly well and have tried to represent the gist of what was said. With that small clarification and a degree of poetic licence, I'll continue with the story.

Thomson Ward. Friday morning

I was awoken by a loud knock on the door.

'Wakey wakey, Gib!' came the brash Glaswegian accent in the corridor. 'If ye don't get up noo, then y'll miss yer breakfast, son.'

'Ah, er OK, thanks,' I stammered as I checked my watch.

Ten past eight – just 20 minutes left before breakfast would be cleared away. Without my iPhone, I'd been unable to set my alarm as I normally would. I must have had over 12 hours' sleep – *God, when was the last time that happened?* I thought to myself. With a low-

57

pitched grunt, I swung my legs over the bed, got up and jumped into the little shower cubicle, using the blast of hot water on my face in an effort to kick-start my heavy, lethargic body. I reckoned the pills I'd been given the night before might have something to do with how tired I still felt.

Oh fuck! There was a leak in the bottom of the shower tray causing a large pool of water to seep under the door and create a large dark wet patch on the cheap blue carpet. No time to sort that now.

I threw down a towel to absorb some of the water and quickly pulled on my grey suit that was draped on the back of the chair. I had no choice but to wear the same white – now white-ish – shirt I'd had on the day before in preparation for Mowatti's dad's funeral. Well, needs must, as they say, and I doubted there was a strict dress code within your average psychiatric ward – apart from the clichéd straight jacket, of course, but I'd not seen any of those, thankfully. Well, not yet.

I checked the time again as I put on my watch, the only bit of 'technology' I'd been allowed to keep. It was 8.24am. If I rushed, I knew I'd just make it to breakfast in time. I opened my bedroom door and ventured out into the corridor. Mick and Johnny's night-time vigil outside my door seemed to have been suspended and, with a quick glance, I couldn't see anyone in the room opposite. I wondered where my troubled neighbour had gone. Released? Doubt it. Escaped? Hopefully not.

I walked briskly down the corridor, turning right to make a bee-line for the canteen. There were a few other patients sitting in the bright day room area where the various corridors converged – one elderly man gave a puzzled glance as this apparent business-man passed by in a hurry. Perhaps he thought I was one of these managerial types that the UK Health Service seems to be constantly criticised for having too many of. I yanked open the door of the canteen and marched up to the counter.

'Ah, here's last minit' Larry yet agin,' came the friendly voice from behind the counter.

'Morning, Mary,' I panted. 'Sorry, but I only just woke up and lost track of time'

'Nae problem, son, there's plentae a scran left,' she said, reassuringly. 'You've got Corn Flakes over there an' ye can hae toast, beans
an' scrambled egg afterwards, if ye wante.'

'Perfect, thanks Mary'.

'Did you sleep well, Gib?' came a voice from the corner. It was
Danny.

'Oh, hi, Danny. Sorry, I didn't even notice you there I was in such
a rush to make breakfast.'

'I'm not sure you'll find it was worth it,' he said with a smile, 'but
that's your call.'

'You're probably right but make sure you don't let Mary overhear
you say that. Mind if I join you for 10 minutes?'

'Feel free, mate.'

I loaded my tray with Mary's culinary breakfast delights and
walked across to Danny's table. There were only two other patients
left in the room – an old man wearing a straw hat, sleeping in the
corner, and a middle-aged woman, gently rocking back and forth as
she stared into space.

'Do you always dress up for breakfast, Gib?' said Danny, with a
sarcastic nod of his head in the direction of my suit.

'No, but I thought I might be joining someone important for
breakfast and here it turned out to be you,' I countered with a smile.

'Touché, mate. Well you've certainly won the prize for best-
dressed man on the ward.'

'Thanks.'

'So, you must be in business then, are you?'

'Good guess. I do work in business, but I was actually on my way
to a friend's dad's funeral when I got taken in here. I thought the
black tie might be overkill this morning.'

'Ah, right. Sorry to hear that. I work as an accountant in the city
centre. Dull job but pays the bills, I suppose. What do you do?'

Looking back, I shouldn't have been that surprised, but at the time
I remember being a bit taken aback to find another business professional in the same psychiatric ward as me.

'Well, I suppose you could say I'm a management consultant,

although what I do nowadays is actually quite different,' I said, somewhat apologetically.

Many people have asked what I do for a living over the years and the question tends to make me cringe. Management consultancy is a very broad and, in my opinion, pretentious term, which spans a variety of sins. There are management consultants who are more IT focused, some who look at operations, supply chain or the so-called re-engineering of business processes. Others focus on change management or business strategy. I landed in this last area, strategy, largely due to the fact that I had an MBA. Of course, my ability to bullshit was also quite useful. At the time of joining what was then called Andersen Consulting in 1996, about 70 per cent of my colleagues also had MBAs and mostly from the top schools around the world. University of Strathclyde Business School wasn't one of the 'Ivy League' or other prestigious universities and business schools they targeted, but I must have managed to slip through the net. The intellectual calibre of my peers was actually quite intimidating and I often wondered if I'd find myself out of my depth. At times I did, quite frankly, but it was a very supportive environment and the people in the firm were surprisingly nice and incredibly helpful – not always the reputation on the outside, I'd freely admit.

Actually, there are a lot of other misperceptions about consultancy and it tends to get looked at with a degree of cynicism by others in business. Here are these young, jumped-up professionals who are paid lots of money and charged out to clients at even higher day rates. How can they possibly be worth it? One of the most popular and more pejorative descriptions for consultancy is 'it's just like stealing someone's watch and then telling them the time'. Yeah, I must have heard that hundreds of times. My personal favourite definition for a management consultant is 'someone who can turn bullshit into air miles'. I'd often use that as a self-deprecating introduction when I couldn't be bothered to explain the details. These criticisms were, and still are, like water off a duck's back to me. I'd arrived. As someone who likes change and variety, I was as happy as the proverbial pig in shit.

I'd joined with visions of a glamorous corporate lifestyle – of business-class commuting to New York, or at least working on a project in some exotic European capital – Paris, Brussels or maybe Milan. The reality couldn't have been more different – for the first couple of years at least. A week after joining in June 1996, I was dispatched to work in the least sexy sector of all: UK Utilities. You know, electricity metering, gas storage, water and sanitation – and staying in a basic hotel in a rundown suburb of Manchester. The next project was in Solihull, near Birmingham. Livin' the dream, eh? Not exactly in line with my vision of where the likes of Gordon Gekko and his Wall Street mates would hang out. However, things started to change as I edged my way up the corporate hierarchy. Three years into my consulting career, I was enjoying the job, getting paid a fair chunk of money and at last getting to travel business class to the US and around Europe. This was more the role I'd envisioned. Someone described the lifestyle as 'a high standard of living but a low quality of life'. I think that's quite an apt description: we'd often eat in good restaurants and stay in very nice hotels – all on expenses, of course. But it came at a price. Long, unpredictable hours and having to work many weekends. If we were working towards a deadline for a client, our team might find itself getting back to the hotel really late at night, having eaten takeaway pizza in the client's offices. No, it wasn't the healthiest lifestyle and many of my senior colleagues who'd been there a decade or more, began to develop physiques worthy of the average taxi driver. No, it wasn't easy to motivate yourself to go to the hotel gym after what could sometimes be a 12- to 14-hour day. The most frustrating aspect of the consulting lifestyle of the late '90s was never really knowing if you might need to cancel the holiday you'd booked, due to all-important client deadlines. The client *always* came first.

Yet the spoils of success and a life in the fast lane were so seductive. My briefcase and luggage handles became adorned with a selection of high-status, loyalty programme plastic tags – pretentious git that I was. I was a Gold Card member of the British Airways Executive Club and a Starwood's 'Preferred Guest' no less. It always made me wonder how Starwood's marketing department referred to their other customers – 'Tolerated Guest', perhaps?

Looking back, life was pretty good. By 1999, I was still enjoying the job a lot and feeling I was learning. But I was questioning myself more – questioning what I wanted out of my career and out of life in general. Asking myself, 'Is this really all there is to life?' I was also getting increasingly uncomfortable accepting the received wisdom on the role of the multinational corporation in society – simply to maximise value for shareholders. Was I going to be content continuing to help already large and successful multinational companies become even more successful and more efficient, help them to employ even fewer people to do more work through so-called 'productivity improvements'? That was beginning to lose its appeal despite the considerable financial rewards and all the other fringe benefits of the job. Each year, the small bonus or promotion to a new management grade were beginning to mean less and less to me. There was something missing that I couldn't quite put my finger on at the time. An itch I couldn't scratch. I suppose I'd now put it down to a lack of purpose in my career. Isn't that what everyone's striving for, ultimately? Sure, the money was still good and you get used to a certain lifestyle and I'd achieved many of these boyhood material goals – you know, living a James Bond jet-set lifestyle or owning a Porsche. Boxes ticked. But was I really going to be highly motivated to buy a second Porsche, the very latest model? No, not me. I wanted something more, but at the time I didn't know what.

Then it came to me in an instant. When I'd least expected it. It had been just another ordinary day, like any other, but it was a day that would have an extraordinary impact on the direction of my life over the next two decades.

Chapter 6 – The District Line to Damascus

Most people believe that their lives are defined by big set-piece events, like marriage, the birth of a child or the death of a parent. Not me. On the contrary, I've found that it's the somewhat insignificant, unpredictable experiences and, more importantly, how we respond to them, that profoundly shape our destiny. Of course, hindsight makes it easier to identify such epiphanies. For me, it was reading a short article in the *Financial Times* (*FT*) one dreary day in March 1999. I was on my daily district line commute to central London on the underground – hardly the Road to Damascus, I'll admit – yet it was to catapult me on a journey that would transform my career, my life and, indeed, I'd like to think, the lives of many others, too. You know how they say that a butterfly can flap its wings and a monsoon takes place on the other side of the world? Well, that's a bit the way that I felt about the experience on that cold, drizzly day in London.

So, how did it all happen? Well, as a consultant I tended to read the *FT* often, but certainly not every day – had I not read the paper on this particular day or had that short article not caught my eye, then god only knows which direction my life would have taken and what I'd be doing now. You'd probably not be reading this book for a start (no, that's not a cue to cheer). But I did happen to buy the *FT* that day and the impact was, well, profound. The article was about a volunteering charity called Voluntary Service Overseas or VSO – a household name in the UK, a bit like the Peace Corps is in the US – and was actually penned by none other than Peter Mandelson, one of the controversial architects of Tony Blair's New Labour. I'm sure many people might claim that Peter Mandelson changed their lives, but I actually mean it in a *positive* sense. Mandelson's short article talked of a new programme VSO were launching that was seeking business professionals to work as volunteers in developing countries. They wanted motivated employees to be given on loan by participating companies and have their jobs held open for them to come back to at the end of their 6–12-month stint.

This article more or less leapt out of the page at me. Boom! From a career perspective, I felt like an anthropologist who'd just stumbled across *the missing link*. You see, I'd always associated international development work with doctors, nurses or teachers – you know, nice people, do-gooders, with beards, sandals, etc. – certainly not people like me who'd gone over to the dark side, to the murky world of big business. Instead, of striving to make a fortune, here was a chance to *make a difference* – here was an organisation that was crying out for accountants, project managers, business professionals or even strategy consultants like me. I reckon this was the trigger point – the moment when I awoke to that elusive sense of purpose that so many of us yearn for in our careers.

I ripped the article out, folded it up and stuck it deep into my briefcase where it would sit for several months. I was on a particularly intensive project and completely swamped with crunch deadlines for clients – running to standstill, to use the cliché. There certainly wasn't any time to pause and call some random charity guy. However, one day in the summer of 1999 I did find the time to pull the crumpled article out of the bottom of my briefcase and re-read it. Even several months on, it still had the same impact on me. Had I any hairs on the back of my smooth bald neck then I'm pretty sure they would have been standing up. I called the VSO contact name at the end of the article – a certain Michael Shann – and arranged a meeting at Andersen Consulting's offices in central London.

Back in those days we had 'dress-down Fridays', which were the opportunity to escape the grey suit consultant uniform and wear casual clothes. I decided that one such casual Friday would be the perfect day for my meeting with Michael. Jeans were discouraged but I breached that rule on this particular day given I was expecting some hair-shirted hippie charity worker to turn up. Of course, when VSO's Michael did arrive, he was wearing his best two-piece suit and a nice bright tie. I'm not sure who looked the more surprised – but the juxtaposed stereotypes made us both laugh and it was something we would joke about in the years ahead.

The VSO Business Partnership programme sounded just like everything I hoped it would be. Instead of VSO's normal two-year placements, they would create six-month roles for busy business professionals. Long enough to do some worthwhile work but not so long as to deter companies from releasing their employees. Partner companies would agree to grant employees a Leave of Absence and pay a small contribution to fixed costs such as mortgage repayments. Crucially, they'd also agree to keep the job open for the employee on their return. VSO's role was to create the placements with a local non-profit partner or government entity in a developing country, who would in turn pay a monthly stipend and provide basic accommodation. It seemed pretty straightforward. All I'd need to do now was get Andersen Consulting to sign up to the programme.

As a relatively junior manager at the time, my first port of call was my direct boss, who pointed me in the direction of the Head of Strategy in London. From there I was bumped upwards until I was told the decision would have to be made by none other than the UK Managing Partner for Operations himself, Willie Jamieson. I only knew of Willie, a fellow Scot, by reputation. And his reputation was that of a fairly fierce, straight-talking leader who didn't suffer fools gladly. Willie's PA grudgingly granted me an audience with the great man – a phone call of no more than 15 minutes as he was travelling in the US at the time. Beggars can't be choosers, so I took what I was given and sent him a few briefing slides in advance.

My mouth was bone dry. No one wants to fuck up, least of all in front of a big cheese, and for me at the time, Willie represented a very mature Scottish cheddar. I'd rehearsed my lines and gave what I thought was a fairly passionate and well-argued case. The VSO partnership would be good for employee morale. Good for Andersen Consulting's reputation. Good for attracting employees into the firm. I made sure I was factual, concise, to the point and kept my pitch to no more than six or seven minutes. Willie asked a few tough questions on costs, duration of placements and the like, which I'd anticipated and was able to handle reasonably well. Then came something of a curveball.

'In my experience, people who go on these types of extended

Leaves of Absence are on their way out of the firm anyway. They tend to leave for good soon afterwards. That's a major risk for our firm.'

'Well, Willie, er, I mean Mr Jamieson, I can only speak for myself,' I countered, hesitantly, 'but if I were granted one of these overseas placements, it would only serve to motivate me and enhance my sense of loyalty to the firm.'

I remember there being a long, nail-biting silence that followed this short conversation. My nerves convinced me it lasted about half an hour, but it may only have been five or six seconds in reality. Then Willie spoke in a curt, decisive voice.

'OK, we'll do it.'

I felt like I'd just won *The Apprentice* and fist-pumped the air mouthing a silent 'Yes!', while jumping up from my desk in the London office. Then I quickly tried to regain my composure.

'Thanks, Willie,' I said, in the calmest voice I could muster. 'You won't regret this decision.'

He rhymed off a string of names of people he'd bring on board – HR, finance, legal – and over the next few days, the corporate machine swung into action.

I often reflect on how that short, 15 minute call, five PowerPoint slides and four simple words, 'OK, we'll do it,' would define the next 15 years of my career and undoubtedly re-shaped the direction of my life. A few months later I would find myself on a flight to Macedonia, to take on a role as a business advisor as the country sought to recover from a refugee crisis caused by the war in neighbouring Kosovo.

However, that short call had far wider repercussions and would prove to be a significant milestone in Willie's career, too. I attended his retirement dinner a few years later and was touched by his speech outlining four big highlights of his three decades with Accenture. Championing the VSO Business Partnerships programme was one of them – a programme that saw dozens of the firm's staff volunteer all over the world, something he was justly proud of. Willie's leadership spawned a relationship between the two organisations that is still going strong today, some 20 years later. I can't think of many

other partnerships between a business and a charity that have survived as long. Accenture's charitable foundation donated millions to
VSO and, once the partnership went viral, thanks to an Intrapreneur
called Paul Gurney, hundreds of Accenture employees raised millions more by climbing Mount Kilimanjaro in multiple teams over
many years. I still get a Christmas card from Willie and allow myself
a little chuckle as I open it each year, thinking just how unlikely
that scenario would have seemed to the nervous, young consultant
in 1999.

My daydreaming ended abruptly with the sound of a plate smashing
on the floor and a piercing scream from the young girl who'd been
sitting in the corner.

'Wow, that sounds amazing! I wish my company would allow me
to do something like that,' said Danny, apparently oblivious to the
commotion on the other side of the canteen.

I hadn't meant to give him my life story, but with time on our
hands and no interruptions, that's more or less what I'd done. Before
I could reply to Danny, the door of the canteen suddenly opened
and Tony, the Duty Nurse, shouted across the room.

'Sorry to interrupt, Gib, but you've got a couple of people here
to see you. Think it's yer old man and old dear. Ah think Meeting
Room 2 is free just now.'

Tony had filled me in on the rules around visitors when I'd first
arrived. There were fairly strict times: 2 to 3pm each afternoon and
7 to 8pm each evening. Visitors could not go any further than the
canteen and the three or four small meeting rooms that lined either
side of the corridor near the ward entrance. To protect the privacy
of patients, visitors were prevented from going any further into the
ward. The fact that it was just after 10 o'clock in the morning meant
they must be making an exception for my folks, who'd travelled all
the way up to Glasgow from the island. Lucky me.

I said a quick goodbye to Danny, put my empty tray on the rack
and walked briskly out of the canteen. I turned the corner and there,
at the other end of the corridor, were the familiar silhouettes of my
parents: the slight, 5ft frame of my mother and my somewhat taller

5ft 8in father, standing side by side with beaming smiles. As I drew closer I could make out their faces and felt that familiar warmth and love that tended to greet me every time I paid a visit to the island. But these were unfamiliar surroundings and, though their faces smiled, I could read the worry in their eyes. Their erstwhile happy-go-lucky, contented, low-maintenance son was now residing in the psychiatric ward in one of the largest hospitals in Glasgow.

'Hello there, Wrinklies,' I said with a smile.

'Enough of your cheek, my boy,' said my mother. 'We've brought a couple of other visitors you might be pleased to see.'

Standing further down the corridor, hidden just out of sight, were my sister, Looby, and my niece, Fiona, who stepped out into view with a, 'Te-Da!'

'Ah, what a lovely surprise!' I gasped, giving them all a great big hug. 'You don't know how great it feels to see some familiar faces in here.'

'Hiya, Gibster,' my sister said. 'It's good to see you, too.'

I led them towards Meeting Room 2, a small room with six padded chairs and a window out onto the gardens.

'Let's go in here. I've been told it's free and will give us a bit of privacy from the canteen.'

We all sat down and I remember my mum leaning forward, wringing her hands slightly, eagerly awaiting an update.

'So, tell us how you're doing? We've been so worried, you know,' she asked.

'I'm doing fine, don't worry,' I said. 'I feel great. The only exception is that the food in here is really crap. I know about the NHS budget cuts, but how do they expect anyone to get well on reconstituted meat pie and frozen mashed potatoes?'

'You've just been spoilt by your mother's home cooking and all these fancy business-class restaurants all your life,' Dad said, smiling over at my mum.

'Well, maybe, but I'm pretty sure Jamie Oliver would agree with me.'

'So, take your time and tell us a bit about how you're doing and what you remember,' Dad continued. 'You've no doubt had a bit of a fright.'

I started to think back to what I could remember of the past couple of days, as I had been for the past 24 hours. But it was all a bit vague in my mind – a bit hazy, no doubt due to whatever tranquilisers I'd been taking. I could remember feeling really great. Some kind of happiness, even euphoria that I hadn't felt in a very long time. But I struggled to recall exactly why. I did remember flying to Scotland from Geneva a few days earlier.

'It's all a little bit confused in my head, to be honest,' I said. 'The nurses have told me that it's pretty normal and a side effect of some of the drugs they're giving me. Chill pills, I think.'

'Well,' said Dad, 'You spent several nights with us where you'd sit up really late after we'd gone to bed. I came downstairs during the night a couple of times expecting to find you lying sleeping by the fire in your usual pose. But instead you were sitting up typing away on your computer. It was a bit worrying latterly, to be honest.'

'Clearly you were overdoing things and no doubt stressed out. That company works its people too hard – that's what's landed you in here, I'm sure of it,' Mum interrupted, having found a familiar theme.

'You know, it's the only exercise she gets these days,' said Dad, glancing at Looby and me with a mischievous smile. I knew what was coming next – we all knew. It was one of Dad's favourite and admittedly fairly witty one-liners. I dutifully provided the set-up.

'So, what kind of exercise would that be, Dad?' I asked, innocently.

'Jumping to conclusions!'

Dad and I chuckled to ourselves while Mum, Looby and Fiona all rolled their eyes. My dad never had an issue with reusing old comic material and felt his jokes actually improved with age – a bit like a fine claret. They were 'set pieces' that would lie dormant in his head, eagerly awaiting the right trigger. But then, I have no issue with that and find myself doing exactly the same. We're both each other's best audience and, to a certain extent, best source of new material.

We spent the next hour discussing my erratic behaviour in the build-up to The Incident, each of us trying to piece together the facts; what I'd said to whom and when. Had I really, as my parents told me I'd claimed, had a phone call with Accenture's CEO? I wonder what I might have told him? Or might that conversation be part of the reason for my being in a psychiatric hospital?

These were all questions for another time. For now, it was big hugs all round and they were off. As they left I wondered what they'd be talking about on the way out of the hospital. How did they think I was doing? Were they now even more worried about their son/brother/uncle who'd lost the plot and gone a bit loopy? Or were they reassured that I was more myself? Indeed, am I more myself, more… normal? Besides, who decides what constitutes 'normal' anyway, and would I even want to be it? These were questions that I'd ask myself repeatedly over the days, weeks and, indeed, the months that followed.

As for what had actually been going on in my head during these euphoric few days, who knows? Was it a mental breakdown or more of a mental breakthrough? Either way, I'd experienced an intensive high worthy of a cocktail of illegal drugs. But I knew that I'd get some clarity in due course. I'd captured each thought, each idea, in hours of voice recordings I'd dictated into my iPhone day and night for an entire week. I'd digitally documented the entire episode, ready to be interrogated as soon as I was released from hospital and reunited with my precious mobile. It was the mental health equivalent of a black box flight recorder and, by God, had I been flying.

Chapter 7 - Bringing Business to the Balkans

Thanks to Willie Jamieson, in November 1999, Andersen Consulting became one of the first corporates to sign up to VSO's Business Partnership programme, together with Shell. I'd put myself forward to be the first employee to go on a volunteering assignment – a guinea pig for both sides, given that VSO had no real experience with short-term volunteering. Their normal volunteers would sign up for two years; the Business Partnership programme only required companies to release their staff for 6-12 months: 'VSO Lite', you could say.

There was a pretty rigorous selection process and pre-departure training to undergo. The former involved a day of team exercises and fairly challenging interviews. The interviews were there to check on people's motivations and make sure they'd thought through the implications of spending a prolonged period of time away from loved ones and the impact that might have on relationships. According to VSO, these were the most common reasons for assignments failing. My interviewer was a very sweet old lady, probably in her mid-eighties, a former volunteer, who was tasked with my personal interrogation process. She probed delicately into my personal life and I explained that I was in a relationship that had lasted almost four years – incidentally, that's still my record to this day.

'… and, may I ask, is this a physical relationship?' she enquired innocently.

Picture yourself sitting in front of your own grandmother being asked the same question and you'll have some sense of the degree of the embarrassment I felt. The slow, shameful nod of a bowed head confirmed that my longest ever relationship was indeed more than platonic. To be fair to my interviewer, she evidently wanted to make sure I was aware of risks such as HIV/AIDS and the importance of practising safe sex, and it was an important point to raise.

The pre-departure training courses were mostly held at Harborne Hall, a large old house on the outskirts of Birmingham that had been gifted to VSO. I remember rocking up for the two-day retreat in my Porsche 911 Cabriolet and parking beside an array of camper vans, Beetles emblazoned with CND logos and clapped out 15-year-old Ford Fiestas. As I reflect on my decision to drive there, I'm having the exact same reaction, no doubt, as most staff and fellow colleagues on the training course that weekend. Namely, 'What a wanker!'

I didn't pick to go to Macedonia – it kind of picked me. In fact, to be honest, I'd have struggled to pinpoint the country on a world map. Indeed, how many of you could now? Precious few, I bet. But I was more interested in the skills fit and finding a placement where I could have a chance to contribute something. The role VSO proposed seemed perfect. I'd be working as a business advisor for a small enterprise support agency in Gostivar, an ethnic Albanian town in the west of Macedonia. *Great, bring it on!* I thought to myself.

Macedonia, The Balkans. September 2000

Culture shock would be an understatement for what I experienced on arrival in the Macedonian capital, Skopje, on 18 September 2000. My first two weeks were spent on an immersion language course in Macedonian (fairly similar to Serbo-Croatian), and I was allocated a host family to live with. The contrast in my daily routines could not have been more different. For most of the previous year I'd been leading a team of consultants on an e-Business strategy project for a major multinational oil company, which required me to split my time between London and Houston. My fast-lane life of C-suite workshops, Club Class flights and flash restaurants ended abruptly one Friday. On the following Monday, I found myself sleeping on a lumpy sofa bed and learning the names of fruit and veg written in Cyrillic. I loved it. I'd stepped into the unknown and had no idea where it would lead.

The host family was really friendly, but the parents didn't speak any English and were clearly very poor. Blaje, the father, had been out of work for over a decade after the local glass factory closed – a victim of Eastern Europe's transition to the market economy in the early '90s. Anica, or Annie, the mother, had a part-time job in a local kindergarten, which brought in less than 100 Euro a month to support the entire family. They had two kids, Borce and Cece, who thankfully both spoke basic English and were willing to help me learn the local language.

After breakfast each morning, I'd walk 20 minutes to where the language classes were held and join a mixed bunch of fellow VSO volunteers who'd become my new friends. Social workers, teachers, nurses – yes, I was the token business guy. We learnt the Cyrillic alphabet, Macedonian grammar and, of course, some useful vocabulary for everyday items. Towards the end of the first week, our teacher gave us each a shopping list and accompanied us to the market to try out our new skills on the locals. In the end, it was really quite fun and I managed pretty well with my list, although my mispronunciation of the word for white cheese, 'sirenje', caused a great deal of mirth among the stall owners.

'Adno pole kilo serenje, ve molem,' I'd said confidently, thinking I was ordering half a kilo of feta cheese. The local stall owners seemed to find this hilarious and kept asking me to repeat myself. Their laughter attracted the attention of my teacher, who explained that I'd been asking repeatedly for half a kilo of 'shit'!

I'd usually arrive back at the family home by 3.30pm, as dinner was served at 4pm sharp – much earlier than I'd ever been used to eating. We'd always eat in the small dining-cum-living room off the kitchen, where Annie would have been slaving away after work. This room was the fulcrum of action within the house and, it seemed to me, the whole neighbourhood. During mealtimes – and when visitors were around – the TV would always remain on in the corner. If Milosevic appeared on the News, he'd be greeted by loud cheers in Serbian. *Wasn't he meant to be the bad guy?* I thought to myself. The room was always thick with cigarette smoke. Indeed, smoking appeared to be the national sport across the entire Balkans – right up there on a par with handball.

Annie was a great cook and seemed determined that I should sample as many of the local delicacies as possible. Every night was something of a banquet with different guests, who seemed to come and go quite freely. It appeared to be an open house for neighbours, uncles, aunts, cousins, you name it. The local homemade brandy, known as 'rakija', was always flowing copiously, and at about 8 or 9pm most evenings, the singing would start. Cece, in-between helping me with my homework, explained that these were old folksongs and that they were a very proud and nostalgic people.

The contrast with my life in London could not have been any starker. A good night out back home would involve a long commute in both directions, dinner at an expensive restaurant or drinking with semi-strangers and no change from £100 or sometimes £200. In Macedonia, nobody had much money. Entertainment, like the food, was homemade and inexpensive. Yet there was a happiness that was deeper, warmer and somehow more genuine. My first two weeks of the Macedonian adventure reminded me of the community spirit of my childhood in Scotland. It had confirmed my strong belief that the people who have the least in this world seem to be willing to give the most.

At the end of my fortnight of language immersion, I was taken to Gostivar, a rather rundown town on the western border with Kosovo, about an hour's drive from the capital. I discovered that Macedonia was a very divided country with deep tensions between the Muslim, ethnic Albanian population, who lived in the West, and the two-thirds majority Slavic population, who mostly lived in the East. Both were poor, often unemployed and saw the future as bleak. Throw into the mix the fact they dressed differently, were of different religions and spoke different languages, and you have a fairly explosive combination. I would go on to discover, quite literally, just how explosive these underlying tensions were.

However, I was there for adventure and really enjoyed my first six months working in the Enterprise Support Agency in Gostivar. They were a small team of six – four men and two women, all in their mid- to late-twenties apart from the boss, Musafer, who, I guessed, was more like my age at the time: early thirties. Some months later I discovered they'd been speculating why I'd been sacked from my job – they didn't buy the fact I was there on a voluntary sabbatical. I mean, who in their right mind would give up a career in the London fast lane to come to a small town in one of the poorest countries in Europe? I'm sure the eminent psychologist Abraham Maslow would have had something to say about that.

The job itself wasn't all that different from my normal management consulting role, but on a much smaller scale, providing business advice and consultancy to small and medium-sized enterprises – the SME sector. We also ran training programmes designed to encourage more women to get into business, particularly from the ethnic Albanian minority. There was great need for access to credit from banks and I'd coach my young colleagues on how to develop half-decent business plans. It's strange – I must have been on a salary reduction of over 90 per cent but had never felt more motivated in my life. I could at last see very tangibly where my skills and knowledge could be utilised for a purpose beyond just making money. Whether I had a good, productive day or a bad day could actually affect someone's life and livelihood – as opposed to being a rounding error on the profit of a multinational business. Yes, that focused the mind just a little.

The working culture was also very different – in some ways better, and in other ways, less so. The custom was to shake everyone's hand when you arrived at the office before sitting down at your desk; I liked that. Lunches and the regular coffee breaks would all be taken collectively around the meeting table – quite a contrast to my regular takeaway sandwich stuffed into my mouth while I sat working in front of my computer in London. Working hours were far shorter than I was used to. Again, perhaps no bad thing with hindsight, given the epidemic of burnout we're facing in the West.

Other practices were, well, less orthodox or, indeed, Orthodox in some cases. I accompanied one of my young colleagues, Maja, on a business trip to see the Mayor of Mavrovo, a nearby town and, instead of coffee, I was served about half a pint of rakija. It was barely 10am, but I took it as part of my cultural immersion and graciously accepted the offer. Maja looked quite shocked initially but then accepted a glass too. Then there was the day I asked an innocent question in the workshop I ran for managers of local businesses in the region.

'What do you see as the role of the manager within a business?'

I nodded to one stern-looking businessman who had put his hand up.

'To punish!' came the reply, without a hint of irony.

In my future consulting career, I'd go on to discover that apparently he wasn't alone in this view.

I was loving my time in Macedonia. Each day was like a new adventure, where I never quite knew what to expect. I jumped in with both feet, learning the language as well as I possibly could in two-hour, one-on-one lessons twice a week. I was invited to friends' houses for dinner with their parents or grandparents, or to parties with traditional dancing, even a wedding. However, the ethnic tensions lingered in the background. There was news that the remnants of the notorious Kosovo Liberation Army – the KLA – had formed a rebel group that planned to mount an offensive to 'free' the ethnic Albanian population in the west of Macedonia. It resulted in one of the most surreal experiences of my life, and put my presence in Macedonia in severe jeopardy.

'So, what car do you drive in London, Gib?' asked Borce, standing beside the old Suzuki Vitara Jeep that I'd bought as a local runaround.

'Er... a... BMW. An old one.' I replied, hesitantly. It was a lie. The truth – a Porsche 911, yes, the one I'd arrogantly driven to the VSO training – would have given me too much of a guilt trip. My dad had gladly offered to look after my 'Porker' for me while I was away and took great delight in giving white-knuckle tours of the island to his mates.

I'd just had one of Annie's massive banquet lunches and was ready to set off for home. It was early afternoon as I drove down the twisting route between Skopje and Gostivar. As I approached Tetovo, some 45 minutes to the south, I saw some flashes on the hillside in the distance and heard loud bangs. I pulled over to the side of the road and jumped out of the Jeep.

A few kilometres away on the hillside, I could see the red flashes of tracer bullets and, after a fraction of a second delay, the crackling of gunfire followed. A small, white house exploded on the hillside. A couple of tanks jostled for position. A piercing screech forced me to put my fingers in my ears as two jets flew past overhead. Yet, to my amazement, in the field in front of me a shepherd wandered along with his flock of sheep. In the neighbouring field, an old woman was bent double, planting what looked like potatoes. And in front of me, folk music was blasting from a loudspeaker in a roadside café, with an old man sitting solemnly, nursing a cup of coffee. I'd seen war films before – *Full Metal Jacket, Platoon, Good Morning Vietnam*, etc. – but none of them had anything on this.

I got back into the Jeep and drove the 15 minutes towards the little Enterprise Support Agency in Gostivar. As I approached the tollbooth at the end of the strip of motorway, a soldier stepped out from behind a wall of sandbags and asked for my passport. A second soldier stood in front of the car pointing a machine gun directly at me as I very gingerly handed it over

It would be putting it mildly to say that I was a little shaken by the time I got to the office. Normally I'd expect the team to be at their desks behind their computers, but today they were all gathered around the coffee table, deep in conversation and looking concerned. *Time for an upbeat greeting*, I thought to myself.

'Dobro Utro Seta, Kako ste? Sto pravic?' ('Hi, guys, how are you? What's up?')

They looked around at one another as if trying to decide who was going to be the bearer of bad news. As usual, Maja took on the role of spokesperson for the team. She was an extremely capable and highly motivated young woman who was always eager to learn. She broke the traditional mould in many ways – not only was she a working mother with a young son and a businesswoman in a very male-centric business environment, she was also Slavic, a minority in Gostivar and a big disadvantage compared with being an Albanian man. The word 'diversity' hadn't made it into the Macedonian business vocabulary back then.

'Dobro Utro, Gib,' replied Maja. 'Will you come and join us for coffee? I don't know if you've seen the latest news, but we're all really worried. The rebels are only 10km away and they've vowed to take over this town next.'

'Yes, I saw what must've been clashes with the national army as I drove down from Skopje. It does seem pretty serious,' I answered.

'I'm not sure whether I should close the office or not and allow the team to go back to their houses and families,' Musafer whispered to me, clearly not wanting the others to hear.

'We were also talking about you just before you came in to office, Gib,' added Maja. 'We expect that you'll be leaving soon. Most foreign embassies have been recommending that their nationals go back to Skopje and there's talk of potential evacuations.'

'Well, I hate to disappoint you, guys, but I'm going nowhere,' I said, faking the most confident voice I could muster, despite being more than a little scared. The team looked at each other a bit surprised.

'Really?' said Visar, the most senior consultant on the ESA team. 'But what's the point in staying around the office? No clients have come in all day and none of us can really concentrate with all this bad news in the background on the radio.'

'Well, maybe we should switch the radio off then and get back to work. It seems to me like you're all working each other up into a frenzy of worry,' I replied. 'Don't we have two business plans that were meant to be submitted to the bank yesterday and another four due by the end of the week?'

'And, don't forget we've got the monthly Cetvrti Cetvrtok on Thursday evening,' said Vlora, the office assistant and the youngest on the team.

'But surely that will be cancelled given all the troubles; I doubt anyone will turn up,' said Visar.

Cetvrti Cetvrtok was a new idea we'd been trying out quite successfully for a couple of months and is perhaps the one thing I was most proud of from my time in Macedonia. Literally translated, it means 'Fourth Thursday' and was a blatant rip-off of the first Tuesday concept, which used to bring investors together with eBusiness entrepreneurs on the first Tuesday of every month. Our version was a little lower key but had proved to be really popular and the first time anything like that had been seen in Skopje. What's more, it had been a great way of bringing the two different religious factions together. Cetvrti Cetvrtok seemed to give them the common language of business, which, I'd like to think, started to build bridges of cross-cultural understanding.

'Of course we shouldn't cancel it, Vlora. In fact, it is more important now than ever before that we go ahead,' I said, once again feigning self-confidence. 'It seems to be one of the few things that's uniting people these days and might just boost morale.'

They looked around at each other and shrugged their shoulders.

'What's more, we can either sit around all day and worry about something we can't control, or we can distract ourselves by writing these business plans. Who wants help with theirs?'

At that very moment, there was an incredibly loud bang – an explosion that shook the glass of the office window.

Chapter 8 – Faking it

The explosion had been a grenade going off a few blocks away from the office. After the initial shock, the team regained their composure and, to their credit, got back to work. Cetvrti Cetvrtok had gone ahead as planned, against the odds and during one of the periods of heightened tensions between the two ethnic factions.

Over the weeks and months that followed, I gradually became accustomed to seeing men in military fatigues or being stopped at gunpoint. Oh, let's not forget the odd curfew in the evening. I remember going out running after dark one evening from my apartment – a fairly regular routine, during which I'd often find myself getting barked at or even chased by stray dogs along my route. This particular evening the town was deathly silent – neither a car nor another soul on the streets. *How weird is that?* I thought to myself. As I passed the petrol station near my apartment, I saw a large 4×4 Lada jammed full of men in camouflage uniforms, all holding guns. I won't lie – I was scared shitless. To my mind, the rebel incursion that the BBC News website had been warning of must have taken place and here I was, out on the street in my bloody jogging gear. I ran home as fast as I could, bounded up the three flights of stairs and hastily locked the door behind me. My mind raced with wild notions. They must have seen me. Wouldn't the fact that I was the only ex-pat left in the town make me prime kidnapping material? A bargaining chip? I barely slept that night. However, the next day I discovered that Gostivar had not in fact fallen to the former KLA rebels. I had witnessed a training exercise for the town's Home Guard who had put in place the curfew. I'd seen no warning of this. Suffice to say, my visit to the local laundry took a little longer that particular week.

In the end, the troubles died down and the European Union, having learnt the sorry lessons of too little action, too late, in Bosnia, forced a peace settlement on the warring factions. It was called The Ohrid Agreement, named after the beautiful lakeside Macedonian town where the agreement was reached in 2001. Thankfully, I was able to stay on in my role and even extend it by a few extra months.

I've kept in touch with many friends and colleagues from my days in Macedonia and visited periodically during the 15 years that have elapsed since the initial adventure ended. ESA Gostivar still exists with Musafer at the helm, but many of the old team have gone on to bigger and better things – Maja is now a Principal Manager with the European Bank for Reconstruction and Development (the EBRD), Vlora, the young office assistant, is now heading up Microsoft's Education programmes in the region, and Visar worked for USAID in Skopje for many years and now runs an NGO. Their career success is a huge source of vicarious pleasure and pride for me, not that I'd claim to have had much of a hand in it. In fact, I'm convinced that I got far more out of the volunteering experience than I was ever able to give. Who knows? As for the country at large, I visited in the summer of 2016 after several years of absence and found Macedonia to be unrecognisable from how it was in those days. As the economy has risen, unemployment and, to a certain extent, ethnic tensions, appear to have fallen. The whole experience has left me with a firm belief that many of the conflicts we see in the world today – East versus West, Islam versus Christianity, the rise of Boko Haram, ISIS, al-Qaeda, Al Shabaab – are largely symptoms of much deeper issues: the extreme and growing inequality and injustice that exists across and within nations. If we don't tackle that issue head on and offer a future to youth with no education, no job, no money and no hope, then the ideology of grievance and the gun peddled by extremists will sadly prevail.

OK, sermon over. Looking back, I probably didn't realise at the time just what a profound impact the Macedonian experience would have on me. I'd broken out of the London bubble and seen a whole other side of life. In these long, winter evenings, I'd often reflected on why companies like my own were conspicuous by their absence in the Balkans. The obvious answer was that our fee rates were an order of magnitude too high. But I couldn't stop wondering how much more could I have achieved if I'd been surrounded by my usual team of consultants. How might our company go beyond sending a handful of volunteers to 'do some good' for VSO and instead bring our capabilities on an industrial scale to parts of the world with greatest need but least access to these skills? Was there a way of turning the traditional, high-cost, high-profit management consulting business model on its head? Create a market that didn't exist, but where there was a clear need for our expertise? My big idea wasn't rocket science; it was based on the premise that not every management consultant, or business professional for that matter, is hell-bent on just making money. Instead, I was convinced they craved *meaning*. No, I'm not talking about some spare time bullshit of digging wells or painting schools, rather using their core skills and business expertise. Moreover, I firmly believed they'd even accept a significantly lower salary to do it, just as I had done. So my thinking was that if the firm were willing to reduce overhead charges and waive the profit on this kind of work, and if employees would voluntarily give up half their salary, then my rough calculations indicated that we could make the business self-sustaining and therefore scalable.

These thoughts percolated through my head as I sat in a café in Thessaloniki on my way back to my 'normal' life in London. It was an article in the *FT* that had brought me to Macedonia. How might the *FT* describe the launch of a new consulting business with a difference – a non-profit business unit? As my daydreaming continued, I began to type into my laptop. I chose the dramatic headline – '*Accenture Hails CaeSaR*' – a play on the acronym for Corporate Social Responsibility or CSR, which was all the rage at the time. I copied-and-pasted an *FT* logo into it and set the date as one year into the future. I described what the business would do, the non-profit clients it would work for and the fact that it had a mission driven by purpose instead of profit. Without doubt, that little fake *FT* article I spent an hour creating was the most impactful thing I've ever written.

London. July 2001

By the time I returned from Macedonia, almost two years had elapsed since that first hesitant call with the formidable Willie Jamieson. He'd become fairly engaged with VSO as the champion of the Accenture relationship and we'd actually become quite pally as a result. That's right – Accenture. Did I not mention that the company had changed names while I was on my VSO sabbatical? I left when the firm was called Andersen Consulting and returned to a firm called Accenture – the result of a flotation or 'IPO' following the divorce from Arthur Andersen, who would go under just nine months later as a result of the Enron scandal, exposed in October 2001.

Willie and I agreed to 'do lunch' shortly after I returned from Macedonia in the summer of 2001. I decided to send him my fake *FT* article prior to meeting, just to see what he thought of the not-for-profit business idea. We talked at length about my time away and Willie seemed genuinely fascinated by the experience I'd had. Then the discussion moved on to my little article. He really loved the idea and, with my permission, wanted to forward it on to Vernon Ellis, then Head of Accenture in Europe, Middle East and Africa, or EMEA, to use the common business jargon. Indeed, Vernon was soon to be the International Chairman. Bingo! I was moving from mature Scottish cheddar to an ageing Roquefort in the 'Big Cheese' league table.

I'd never met Vernon Ellis but knew him by reputation both inside and outside the company – everyone did. He was heading a new UN digital business task force and was also Chairman of the English National Opera. I'd featured Vernon in the fake article as 'Sir Vernon Ellis' who'd announced the launch of the new venture at the World Economic Forum at Davos one year into the future. Giving Vernon a fictitious knighthood turned out to be prophetic, as he did end up becoming *Sir* Vernon several years later. I'm not sure whether it was the 'Sir' that grabbed Big Vern's attention or the idea itself – but either way, I was granted an audience with the demigod over breakfast. Willie would join us, as would Liz Padmore, The Global Head of Corporate Affairs. Breakfast was set for 8am one Friday in the client dining rooms at Accenture's central London offices and would probably rank right up there as one of the most important meetings of my career. It's funny to think that it so nearly didn't take place, thanks to my alarm clock not going off.

Ealing, London. July 2001

Fuck! Fuck! Fuck! Fuck!…

You remember the beginning of *Four Weddings and a Funeral* where Hugh Grant sleeps in on the day of his friend's wedding and comes out with that string of profanities? Well, that will give you a reasonably good picture of my bedroom as I woke at 7.32am at my flat in Ealing, West London, on the morning of the all-important breakfast with Vernon and Co. I leapt from my bed, pulled on a suit and was in a mini-cab within about five minutes. Forget the shower, forget the teeth brushing; it normally took me an hour door to door and I had just 25 minutes to avoid being late. *What a dickhead*, I thought to myself – you're given an amazing break and you screw it all up by over-sleeping.

Remarkably, I was probably no more than a few minutes late in the end – embarrassing, but not a showstopper – and blamed it on a signal failure on the London Underground – an all-too-believable excuse that was greeted with silent, almost sympathetic nods.

Despite the rather frenetic arrival, the meeting seemed to go very well. I'd never eaten in the posh client dining rooms before, let alone with three of the most senior folks in the firm. I was in awe on both fronts, but kept my composure and put forward my case for the non-profit with passion and confidence. Vernon later told me that for most of his 30-year career, he'd been used to having consultants show up at his office trying to negotiate a pay rise. Evidently this had been the first time anyone had voluntarily requested a *pay cut*. That got his attention.

The good old fake press release had done the trick again – the vision it set out had captured their imagination. However, they'd need more flesh put on the bones. They'd need to see a business case. Fair enough.

I'd gone back into my old role in the strategy consulting business and was assigned to a new project. However, I couldn't get the idea out of my system and pulled together a small group of colleagues as a volunteer team to develop the business case for 'Big Vern' et al. Our merry band would meet each week, either in person or on the phone, and would divvy up the various tasks. The fact that the 9/11 attacks on the World Trade Centre in New York took place during this period only served to strengthen our resolve and, for me at least, highlighted the need for a shake-up in the socio-economic system. By the end of the year we'd pulled together quite a comprehensive case, all working in our spare time. Vernon, Liz and Willie were suitably impressed. The next hurdle would be to develop a full-blown feasibility study and get the buy-in of the UK business leadership to fund it.

It was at about this time that the guerrilla tactics began. I knew two of the five UK Industry Leads quite well from my days in the Strategy Practice – Mark Spelman, who headed Resources back then – that's Accenture code for energy and utilities – and Adrian Lajtha, who was head of Financial Services in the UK. Both Mark and Adrian, I reckoned, would be supportive as they'd backed me with the VSO relationship. The other three 'big cheeses' I didn't know at all and they had a reputation for being hardliners. I approached Mark and Adrian first, both of whom agreed to fund one consultant each for the feasibility study team. I plucked up the courage to approach the others and remember giving them the distinct impression they'd be the odd ones out amongst their peers if they didn't provide support. Yes, I know, it was slightly massaging the truth but it had the desired effect and I was able to pull together a small team of some of the smartest consultants in the firm. This is when 'Gib's dream' became 'our shared dream' + vision + strategy to achieve it. Yep, I'll always be grateful to the fellow pioneers who joined me on the journey.

There were three basic questions we needed to answer in the Feasibility Study:

One: was there a market for our services at reduced rates in the non-profit world?

Two: could the business be economically viable?

Three: would enough Accenture employees be interested in working on the other side of the world on half their salary?

To answer the first question, our team went out and spoke to quite a few charities and foundations to gauge their interest. It was clear there would be a market for our services, but only if the fee rates were reduced dramatically, which, of course, was our intent. Tick. For the second question, the financial model seemed to suggest the business could indeed break even at 20–25 per cent of our normal rates, but only if employees took a voluntary salary reduction of 50 per cent. Sort of tick. Which leads to the third and arguably most critical question, which required a survey of the entire UK workforce. It evidently provoked one of the highest response rates of any survey of its kind.

What were we asking them? Well, not only did we want to know about levels of interest, we were also curious as to how they'd done in their last appraisals. Accenture, like most corporates, is obsessed with measuring performance and putting people into categories. You know, the top performers, the above average, average or below and then, well, the 'pull your socks up, or else' bucket.

The results were powerful: they'd shown a disproportionate number of the better performers were particularly interested in the 'CaeSaR' proposition. We were appealing to the very people Accenture wanted to attract as employees, retain and develop into future leaders. From a business case perspective, we'd just won the lottery.

Chapter 9 – Corporate Guerrilla Movement

ADP Pilot, London. Summer 2002

If you'd asked me to describe my dream job, then this was it. I was now working full time on turning that dream into reality. It was as if I'd been given my hobby to do as a job. Yep, I felt like the luckiest guy in the world, and by May 2002 we transitioned from feasibility study to a full-blown pilot. Well, I say 'transitioned' – what I mean is that no one told us to stop and so we just kept going. I was given the budget to build a small team and actually go out and find willing clients and deliver projects. That's when my salary cut started; it was to last 12 years. But I was happier than ever. That said, we were off-piste – no methodologies, no guide books – it was something of a business first in the consulting industry which had, up to then, only ever done bits and pieces of 'pro bono' work, often for their clients' favourite charity to curry favour for when the next mega-buck deal would be tendered. No, the industry needed to go far beyond that. We needed to create nothing less than a blueprint for a different kind of business model, one where *purpose* was on a par with *profit*.

Despite improbable odds, our small, dedicated team was finally up and running. But where to start? Well, we knew that we'd have to give our consultants a couple of days of training before dispatching them onto projects. We weren't trying to create experts in International Development – we'd rely on the clients for that knowledge. Instead, the training gave them the basic principles as well as how to keep themselves safe, both physically and emotionally. Cultural empathy was also important – they should not go with the impression that they were going out to share their great business wisdom with less educated or less fortunate people. Far from it. It would be a two-way process and they would be learning as much as they would be teaching.

We went to our friends in VSO to see if they could help identify a suitable trainer and were very lucky to find Andrew Butler and his colleague Evelyn Harold. Most Accenture Training Programmes were carried out by well-dressed professional-looking men or women standing at the front of the room in slick business attire. That's what our employees had got used to throughout their careers. Andrew could not have been more different. He'd arrive at Accenture's offices in London in a T-shirt and jeans. I'd love watching the looks this bald-headed, tattooed 'misfit' would get as he strode confidently down the corridor flashing his visitor badge with a wink as he passed the rather bemused security guards. He was supported by the more orthodox, but equally experienced, Evelyn, to jointly develop ADP's training curriculum. The consistent feedback from employees was that this training ranked as some of the most enjoyable of their careers. Evelyn and Andrew are still loyally running ADP's training programmes to this day and the feedback remains every bit as positive.

We started with three initial projects in the pilot, all of which had come through warm leads gained during the feasibility study interviews. We worked with CARE, one of the largest international development charities, to create a new strategy for their Country Office in Vietnam. Another team worked for the British government's aid arm, DFID, to design Humanitarian Information Centres – basically, a technology-enabled approach to improve aid coordination in the aftermath of a humanitarian emergency. Thirdly, we worked with the World Bank to provide consultancy and training services to small businesses in Serbia. That was ADP's first project and would have its share of excitement with a major security alert shortly after the team arrived in Belgrade.

Natalie, one of the three consultants on the team, had been at home asleep in her rented apartment in Belgrade when she was awoken by gunshots in the early hours of the morning. Bear in mind that this was only a couple of years after Belgrade had been pounded by US Scud missiles targeting the regime of then President Slobodan Milosevic. Understandably shaken, Natalie nonetheless remembered the emergency drill from her training – namely, that she should keep calm and call the 24hr emergency helpline for advice. She was quickly put through to one of Accenture's global security experts and described the situation.

'There's intermittent loud gunfire coming from the street just below me. It's like really loud cracking sounds... ehmm... sounds like some kind of gun fight, perhaps.'

'OK, Natalie. I want you to stay very calm. Keep yourself down low on the floor. Whatever you do, don't put your head up near the window. I'm going to get in touch with the local security services and find out what's going on,' the security expert said, reassuringly. 'You'll be fine. Don't worry. I'll call back shortly.'

Security called back five minutes later and were able to put poor Natalie's mind at rest. Evidently, the local basketball team in Belgrade had just won a major league match that night and the Serbs traditionally celebrate such victories by driving around the capital firing gunshots into the air out of car windows. In most places they might honk your horn, but hey, that's the Balkans for you.

In spite of this little mishap, the CaeSaR pilot was deemed to be successful and transitioned into the launch of Accenture Development Partnerships in 2003. We weren't a separate company but were set up to have our own budgets, staff and, indeed, premises, when we were given a floor of a small building in central London that Accenture had recently vacated. It was exciting and we felt like we were pioneering something very different.

As I think back to those early days, I was really very naïve. I'd thought that if we were offering high-quality business and technology expertise at about 20 per cent of the normal price, then clients would be queuing round the block for our services. But because of the positive results of the feasibility study and pilot, I underestimated the deep mistrust that existed between the for-profit and the non-profit sectors – something that continues to this day. Stereotypical attitudes and traditional roles are hardwired into the psyche of the international development sector. Businesses give money to charities. It's called 'corporate philanthropy'. If they're offering the time or expertise of their staff, then, of course, that would surely be free of charge, right? So here we were, flying in the face of these norms – asking charities to pay for something they'd traditionally got for free in the past. It led to a few interesting conversations on the phone as the team and I tried to sell our services.

'Oh, you're from Accenture... I see. Big consulting company, isn't it? Well, you're through to the wrong person. I head up our global finance, IT and operations. I'll put you through to someone in fundraising to discuss the amount of your donation.'

'Eh, no. It is actually you I wanted to speak to. I'm not calling to give you any money. Ironically, you may end up giving us money,' I'd say with a bit of a chuckle. The call would sometimes end abruptly at that point. If I was lucky, they'd want to hear more about this bizarre offer.

'Actually, I'd like to offer Accenture's services at a small fraction of our normal fees through a brand new business unit we've set up for this very purpose.'

'Yes, but when we've used consultants in the past from McKinsey, Deloitte or Ernst & Young, it's always been free of charge. We're a charity, after all.'

We were not only trying to change the business model of consulting, we were going to have to change paradigms and mindsets, too. Over time we would gradually manage to win over the trust of these charity clients. We'd explain the difference between what we were offering at a fee compared with what they would often get free or 'pro bono', to use the jargon. I'll state up front that I'm not a massive fan of such handouts – I'd sometimes glibly say, 'with pro bono, you tend to get what you pay for.' It was very normal for consultancy companies like ours to have people 'on the bench' from time to time. Namely, that between projects or during market downturns, they'd not have all their people out on projects earning juicy fees from the large business clients. It was fairly standard procedure to offer these consultants out to charities for a few days or weeks here and there to deliver some pet project or other. Fair enough, I suppose. I'm sure they did some good, although some of these under-utilised consultants might be second-rate performers who'd struggle to be staffed onto the normal fee-paying work.

With ADP we were trying to offer something fundamentally different. We would get into a contractual arrangement – committing Accenture to deliver a particular outcome for the charity client that would be of the same high quality that a corporate client would expect. We'd be offering some of our best people, who would be working on half their normal salary. They'd be based on the ground, at the coalface in a developing country, often side by side with client staff in a very complementary way – the local staff would provide the deep knowledge of that culture and of development issues, Accenture's staff would provide the technical expertise in areas such as technology, supply chain or strategy. The trick was to put these business capabilities into their specific context. For example, we could improve the interaction between a charity's headquarters and field offices through better use of IT. Or, the same supply chain skills that might get food efficiently onto supermarket shelves could equally be applied to the distribution of vaccines or essential medicines for the likes of UNICEF. We could offer to do their business strategies, re-design their global organisations or plan a change management programme – basically, the same skills but applied in a different context and for a very different kind of impact. A far cry from the usual mantra of 'shareholder value maximisation'.

For me, the most exciting work and the greatest potential for change was where we'd apply *new* technologies and *new* business thinking to the *old* problems of development – you know, health, water, education, poverty and the like. The kind of things people have been throwing cash at for years. Instead of giving money, we'd explore how to utilise the firm's e-learning capabilities to train doctors, nurses or teachers. How might a smart phone be used to provide banking services or perhaps affordable health insurance in sub-Saharan Africa? Could the same phone provide a digital option for birth registration or for storing health records? Even to this day, if such records exist, they tend to be paper based in too many countries, and if a tsunami or typhoon come along, then they'd be destroyed forever. In fact, some of the work I was most proud of was what we did in the aftermath of the dreadful Asian tsunami that struck on Boxing Day 2004.

At that time we'd been officially up and running for well over a year and were getting into our stride. Banda Aceh, on the northern tip of Indonesia, bore the brunt of the disaster, but Sri Lanka, southern Thailand and India were also impacted. Accenture had many local staff based in the Indonesian capital, Jakarta, and, like most big companies, we were very keen to try to help. In the immediate aftermath of a major disaster, there's a fairly chaotic relief phase that is best handled by the expert agencies such as MSF (often referred to as Doctors Without Borders), the UN or the Red Cross. The best that businesses can do to help then is give money, and that's what our firm did, both from employees and from the Foundation. If we'd sent business consultants with their laptops, then they'd no doubt have just got in the way. It was a few months down the line, when the 'relief' phase transitioned to 'reconstruction', that our capabilities really came into their own. By that time the world's media had lost interest and moved on to the next big story. Most corporations and their philanthropic dollars had moved on, too. That was when ADP moved in. There was still so much to be done.

So what kind of things did we do? Well, for example, many of the established charities had been forced to bring in huge numbers of extra staff to cope with the massive increase in demand for their services. Helping them improve their hiring and training processes was one area of need. We'd help with technology to improve coordination of various agencies on the ground, or to develop an early warning system for the next time a tsunami might hit. We worked with the likes of the UN and the World Bank to provide business support to local enterprises and startups. In fact, we'd find ourselves working on post-tsunami reconstruction across the region for the next three years.

At one point, we had multiple teams based at Banda Aceh working for a variety of different clients. I remember quite an unusual request came through for my approval at that time: a local religious ceremony was about to take place, where the tradition was for some poor cattle to be sacrificed and the meat given out to the poor. Many of the different NGOs and agencies were going to donate a sacrificial cow, which evidently had a price tag of 300 dollars. Andrew and Evelyn's training highlighted the importance of embracing local culture and our team wanted to donate a sacrificial cow from Accenture, just so as not to be the odd ones out. Each member had chipped in a bit of their own cash and come up with about 150 dollars so they asked if the firm might match this in order to buy a whole cow.

'Sure thing, just charge it in on expenses,' I replied.

'But Gib, there isn't a category called 'sacrificial cow' on the drop-down menu in the electronic expenses system.'

'Ah right, of course not. Well just charge it in as a steak dinner then, given that's what it'll end up being at some point.'

It's a silly story, but we got a laugh out of it at the time. It was also a symptom of the fact that we were stepping outside the norms of the system – improvising where there weren't rules and sometimes when there were rules, being forced to break them. Accenture was all geared up to work on a for-profit basis for very large businesses in developed countries where there was a high demand for our services. Our focus was 180 degrees in the opposite direction – trying to work without profit, for charities in the poorest and often most dangerous parts of the world. We found ourselves challenging the corporate machine and its policies head on. When we were small and operating under the radar, we could get away with it. As we grew in size and profile, our head was gradually rising above the parapet.

We were at risk of becoming victims of our own success.

NIGHT III – SCALING UP

*'I dream of painting
and then I paint my dream.'*

Vincent Van Gogh

Chapter 10 – The Empire Strikes Back

Thomson Psychiatric Ward, Saturday morning. November 2014

It was a very new experience for me. Doing nothing. That's what I'd been doing, or not doing, for most of the day since breakfast. Absolutely *nothing*. And it was really quite enjoyable. I had no computer. No phone. No diary crammed full of back-to-back meetings and calls. Nope, I had nothing to do and it felt great – even cathartic. The time had flown by as I lost myself in quiet thought in the spartan surroundings of the day room – a bit like the meditation I'd dabbled with in India a couple of weeks before I got ill. The day room was bright and airy with some comfy chairs and a couple of shelves of books that ranged from trashy novels to self-help books – neither genre appealed greatly. Hard to believe that I was already into my third day on the Thomson Ward and, to my surprise, I was beginning to settle in. *Was that a good sign or a bad sign?* I wondered.

I badly needed some fresh air. After three days in the warm, safe cocoon of care that the ward offered, it was time for a walk, and I ventured out into the little garden through the sliding glass doors leading out from the canteen. It was a bright, sunny morning, in contrast to the dreary, drizzly past few days. The garden was a wee bit drab (that's dull and uninteresting for those who don't speak Scottish) – we're talking the odd flimsy tree, mostly lawn with a couple of little paved paths running in different directions. I nodded and smiled as I walked past one or two fellow patients sitting on the benches beside the shelters. One elderly woman sat staring vacantly into space, puffing away on a cigarette, which hung from her fingers, on the verge of falling. On the ground around her feet, 20–30 cigarette butts lay in a small pile. I've no idea whether she'd smoked all of these while sitting there, but they certainly looked fairly fresh.

I followed the little path round the back of what seemed like a separate building. There, I stumbled across another grassy courtyard with more benches and shelters. On one bench, a young girl sat slowly rocking backwards and forwards. Her lips seemed to be mouthing something but no sound was coming out. Well, not that I could hear anyway. She saw me out of the corner of her eye and turned round and stared with an expression that was two-parts fear, one-part surprise.

'Hi, how are you doing?' I said with a smile, trying to reassure her. 'My name's Gib. Just arrived a couple of days ago. And you? What's your name?'

The young girl turned abruptly and caught me with a penetrating, slightly puzzled glare. Then stood up and walked off. *Well done, Gib, you've done it again*, I thought to myself. No, I'd not been trying to hit on a teenage girl in a psychiatric hospital. But it was a classic 'knock-back', reminiscent of asking girls to dance at the school disco aged 14. Or, indeed, if they'd like a drink in some club, aged 40-something. Slick one-liners and confident pick-ups were never my forte.

I retraced my steps and this time went along the path in the other direction. There was a grassy bank that led down to a car park and then what looked like the main road around the hospital complex. A mini-cab and a delivery truck were driving past. *WOT, no large perimeter fences?* I thought to myself. That's where the place differed from asylum scenes in films like *One Flew Over the Cuckoo's Nest*, where huge walls ensured patients didn't escape – or at least weren't meant to without the help of The Chief throwing the marble water fountain out of the window. Oops! Spoiler alert, but surely everyone's seen that film by now. If not, it's your own fault. Anyway, here it seemed like anyone could just saunter on out. *I wonder what would happen if I escaped from here?* I thought. It seemed, well, just too easy.

Caution got the better of me. I slowly wandered back round to where I'd come from, retracing my steps, and found myself back in the familiar little grassy courtyard with the same woman sitting on the same bench, still chain-smoking. As I came back into the canteen, I bumped into Christine, one of the friendly duty nurses who was passing through to grab a coffee.

'Got a quick moment, Christine?' I said.

She gave a smile that I took to mean, *not really, but go on.*

'So what's the score with going outside then? Are we allowed out whenever we want, for as long as we want, or what? I mean, what's to stop us?'

'Not quite, Gib. We have different rules for different patients depending on their condition,' she explained. 'For example, Jeannie over there can go out for several hours each day. She goes shopping or to visit friends, although she has to be back in here by the agreed time of 9pm. But she's an unusual case. For most people we lock the doors at 6pm.'

'And what are the rules for me then, Christine?'

'Right now, you're not allowed further than the end of the court-yard where we can still see you from the window, Gib.'

'Mmm, well I just accidently broke that rule,' I confessed. 'You see, nobody told me until now and I had a wee wander round the back towards that other building.'

'No problem, son, but do me a favour and don't venture further again, not for now at least.'

'OK, I won't. But there are no fences out there, Christine. What is there to stop anyone wandering off?'

'Well, I wouldn't advise trying it. Not that you would, I know,' she said. 'We'd know you were gone within five minutes and the surrounding area would be crawling with police all looking for you five minutes after that.'

This was a new experience – captivity. The first time in my life when I didn't feel truly free to go wherever I wanted whenever I wanted – well, not since I was a kid at least. Here I was, a grown man, yet confined to a specific place. Felt a bit weird.

'Good to know I'd be missed, I suppose, Christine,' I said with a sarcastic smile. 'Promise to be good and obey the rules.'

Obey the rules. The words rolled easily off my tongue. However, in my business life I'd done anything but obey rules, frankly. No, I'm not talking about breaking the law or getting involved in bad shit like bribery or corruption – Accenture was rightly fiendishly strict on all that kind of stuff. No, I'm talking about internal company policies and procedures. They were fair game as far as I was concerned, and in those early years the team and I often found our-selves off-piste and at odds with the corporate policy regime. After all, you can't aspire to *change* the system if you're not willing to *challenge* the system, right?

After a decidedly average lunch of ham, greasy chips and unidentified soggy veg, I wandered back through to the day room. No sooner had I sat down than Tony put his head round the door.

'Ah, there you are, Gib,' he said. 'The consultant psychiatrist has just arrived in the ward and is keen to see you. She's only in a few times each week and so it's great that you'll get a bit of time with her.'

'Woo hoo! Must be my lucky day.'

'Dr Ratner's her name. She's down in Room 3 on the left-hand side.'

Dr Ratner? The name made me think of Nurse Ratched, Jack Nicholson's nemesis in *One Flew Over the Cuckoo's Nest*. I walked down the corridor to Meeting Room 3 and knocked on the door.

'Come in,' said a commanding but friendly voice from within the room.

'You must be Gilbert, although I see from the notes that you prefer to be called Gib, is that right? Take a seat, Gib.'

Dr Ratner wasn't that dissimilar from the character in the film, in appearance at least. I'd put her at mid- to late-forties, long brown hair and a friendly, smiling face. She was softly spoken with a soothing 'shrink-type' voice – not that I'd ever spoken to a shrink before. Honest. I hoped she'd be a somewhat kinder person than the evil, manipulative Nurse Ratched.

'Morning,' I said in the friendliest voice I could muster. 'Yes, Gib would be great, thanks, Dr Ratner. It's only ever my bank manager or my mother when she's annoyed who calls be by the formal title.'

'Ah yes, I see,' she replied, with her head down in her notes so I couldn't make out if she'd even smiled at my rather weak attempt at humour. My desire to act *normal* hadn't started too well. I wanted to recover, but then there's that old problem again – how do you go about convincing a complete stranger you're not actually nuts? I mean, it's not exactly a level playing field when the encounter takes place inside a loony bin. A bit like someone trying to convince you of their altruism when you're sitting in the offices of a large Hedge Fund.

'So, Gib. I'm a senior consultant psychiatrist for Glendevon Hospital and have a lot of experience with business professionals like you, who are admitted to the Thomson Ward suffering from some kind of psychosis, manic episodes, or with other neurological issues,' Dr Ratner explained. 'Your case is an interesting one for me, given this appears to be your first mental health issue, if I'm not mistaken.'

'I believe so,' I responded, then couldn't resist adding, 'but others might feel differently.' Thankfully, she ignored me and carried on with the questioning.

'Good. So you're a fairly senior partner in the management consultancy firm Accenture according to your notes – a bit of a high flyer, by all accounts.'

'Well, I'm not too sure about that,' I interrupted. 'I plod along and…'

'Ah, no need to be modest, Gib,' she said. 'It's down in the notes and I've also had a chance to speak to your sister and she's spoken to the head of HR from your company who was very keen to make sure you were being properly looked after. The company leadership are evidently very concerned about you.'

'Oh really?' I said, vaguely remembering the dealings I'd had with the top brass in the days leading up to The Incident. 'Well that's good to know. And I'll be interested to hear what you've managed to glean from my sister.'

'Well, we'll come to that in due course, but what I was going to say is that with the business professionals I work with, in most cases they are suffering from some kind of stress-induced depression or anxiety. I suppose it goes with the territory in these high-powered jobs,' she continued. 'But according to my colleagues who were on duty at the time you were admitted to Thomson, you were anything but depressed. On the contrary, you were somewhat euphoric and felt that you had come up with some grand plan to change the world. Does that sound right?'

'Well, I am prone to a bit of exaggeration,' I admitted. 'But yes, this was a bit more than usual. Sorry about that.'

'Not at all. Help me understand more about what you were experiencing – what was going on inside your head?'

'Wish I knew.'

'Hadn't you been dictating lots of ideas and notes into your phone? That's what your two friends told the staff when you arrived.'

'Yeah. It was like a kind of flow of energy, creativity and ideas that lasted days. I'd barely slept in a week.'

'No wonder you were exhausted, Gib,' she said. 'We'll maybe come back to that, but for now I'm keen to know what makes you tick.'

'Sure, fire away,' I replied.

'Your file notes suggest you lead quite an interesting group in your firm. You work a lot with charities, which must be very fulfilling.'

'Yeah, I love it. It's a kind of internal not-for-profit group or social enterprise.'

'I'm not an expert in business, but would you say you worked in the area of Corporate Social Responsibility?'

'Well, yes and no.'

Dr Ratner had unwittingly hit a bit of a raw nerve. I'd always been a bit cynical about CSR programmes in general, and I'd no doubt made myself a bit of a pain in the arse in the eyes of Accenture's own CSR or Corporate Citizenship team as we called it.

To my mind, CSR departments were too often run as separate units, dislocated from the nerve centre of the business. Fig leaves of goodness plastered onto the rest of the business – much of which might be far from good. A bit like 'here's where we do business, and over here is the CSR department, where we do our good'. Ninety-nine per cent of a company's focus, investment and management attention would lie in the former, with a measly one per cent or less of the proceeds channelled towards the latter. I always believed that choosing between doing business or doing good was a false dichotomy – they had to converge. I'd deliberately positioned ADP within the core business and resisted attempts by the business to place us under the wing of the Corporate Citizenship team. We were creating a small-scale blueprint for a different kind of business – like a benign growth within the parent organisation that challenged conventional wisdom. My stubbornness and single-minded determination resulted in some heated debates, especially when the time came to creating a new Corporate Citizenship strategy for the firm. In one of the early workshops I jumped up and drew this diagram on a flipchart in an effort to make my case.

'Let's say this circle represents our firm's footprint in the world – the good, the bad and the ugly. The collective impact of all the internal work of our employees and the external influence we have through our global network of clients. Let's say some of what we do could be described as broadly "good" – our work in global health, clean energy or sustainable supply chains, for example. Other stuff might be considered less good or down right "bad", in the eyes of the public at least. I'm no fan of the work we do for Big Tobacco or the Arms Industry, for example. That's the stuff that lies below the horizontal line and, of course, we can debate where that line gets drawn. The vertical line divides our internal operations from the much greater sphere of influence we have externally. Our Corporate Citizenship agenda has been focused on this tiny little shaded section here.

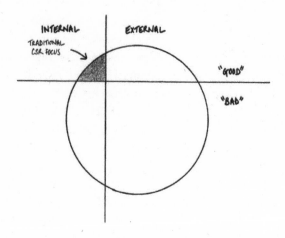

'Shouldn't our new strategy relate to the circle as a whole – seeking to attenuate the negative aspects of our business and accentuate the positives – we should communicate the impact of our business holistically. Talking about how much time or money we donate to good causes is only a fraction of the story.'

I scribbled on the diagram to show the horizontal line pushed much further down depicting how the 'good' aspects of our business could be accentuated and both internal and external impacts considered in an overall picture.

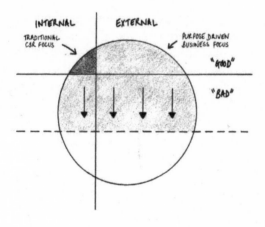

It made perfect sense to me. However, I failed to win the argument and the more conventional mindset prevailed. The new strategy had a catchy tagline and a focus on corporate giving combined with pro bono consulting thrown in. Rightly or wrongly, my response was to double down on what ADP was trying to achieve. But the more I tried to differentiate what we were doing from traditional Corporate Citizenship, the more they took it as implied criticism of what they were doing. Not my intention, but fairly inevitable, I suppose. I was accused of only focusing on the needs of ADP, ignoring the interests of the broader business. Fair criticism, if I'm honest.

'You need to solve for Accenture, Gib. Not just ADP,' I remember getting told by one boss during a lunch to discuss my annual appraisal.

'Solving for Accenture' was a phrase popularised by our CEO at the time, Bill Green, who was a master of the slick one-liner. He spoke with a slow, deep drawl and was charisma personified. Think Jack Nicholson in a business suit. When asked if he was worried about Accenture's competition on a quarterly earnings call with some of the 'Wolves of Wall Street,' he famously responded, 'Competition? They're either smashed on our windshield or choking on our exhaust'. Not your typical corporate speak, but it certainly dealt with one slightly impertinent young financial analyst. Like most senior executives in the firm, I had great respect for Bill, but 'solving for Accenture', I never really liked. It tended to get overused to justify any arbitrary decision. It certainly wasn't what got me out of bed in the morning.

I put down my knife and fork and looked up at my boss.

'Solve for Accenture? I'm first trying to solve for society, then Accenture,' I responded glibly.

I couldn't help but speak my mind. Leopards don't change their spots.

Chapter 11 – Inflexion Point

London. Mid-2000s

Make Poverty History. Boom! What a great campaign that was.

Yep, if you were to pick a golden era, a standout year for the International Development cause, it would undoubtedly be 2005. Make Poverty History in the UK and the One Campaign in the US, were organised by consortia of international NGOs. Both were lobbying for the same thing – to get governments to increase aid, promote free trade and drop the debt for the world's poorest countries. Simple, clear, unambiguous. It was also the year when the G8 was hosted in Gleneagles, Scotland, and had aid at the top of the agenda. It was a high watermark for anyone working in the field. The vibe even percolated into the corporate world. I vividly remember Sir Bob Geldof being invited to speak at the annual Away Day of Accenture's UK consulting practice in London. He'd no doubt given the same presentation a thousand times – how, in light of his response to the Ethiopian famine in 1985, he'd gone from second-rate failing pop star (his words, not mine) to heroic icon of the aid world, almost overnight. His talk was passionate and, true to form, spiced up with plenty of four-letter words. I loved it. Sir Bob diverted from his favoured text to talk about the role large businesses like Accenture could play in development. He'd done his homework on what the company was up to and even gave ADP a nice namecheck. Our team, sitting in the audience near the front of the hall, were all pretty chuffed. But it was his closing remarks that got me. Sir Bob claims to carry about a piece of paper everywhere he goes. On it is a scribbled quote from William Hutchinson Murray, which ends with a couplet attributed to Goethe. He pulled the scrap of paper from his pocket and read it out loud:

> Until one is committed, there is hesitancy, the chance to draw back. Concerning all acts of initiative (and creation), there is one elementary truth, the ignorance of which kills

countless ideas and splendid plans: that the moment one definitely commits oneself, then Providence moves too. All sorts of things occur to help one that would never otherwise have occurred. A whole stream of events issues from the decision, raising in one's favour all manner of unforeseen incidents, meetings and material assistance, which no man could have dreamed would have come his way. I have learned a deep respect for one of Goethe's couplets:
'Whatever you can do, or dream you can do, begin it.
Boldness has genius, power, and magic in it.'
Begin it now.

That really struck a chord. It mirrored the rollercoaster journey I'd been on trying to grow this unusual little startup, or some might say, *upstart* business, against the odds. I, too, felt I'd crossed a threshold – taken a leap of faith – followed gut instinct over logic. Then all sorts of unexpected help came my way. Doors opened up that had previously remained closed. The senior leadership got behind the idea, to the surprise of many. Over time, I found myself surrounded by a fabulous team of smart, committed professionals on our core team, who, like me, were prepared to commit their careers to the cause. There was something about that cause – something about our innate desire for meaning, which made ADP a lightning rod for attracting the brightest and best talent Accenture had to offer from all around the world. The ADP interest list was standing at over 40,000 by late 2016. I mean, show me another company anywhere that has so many employees virtually queuing up to halve their salary. We were also being featured in books about social innovation and the team and I were getting invited to speak at business schools and at conferences. We were winning awards for CSR (in spite of my valiant attempts to distance myself from the fluffier side of that movement). No, I could honestly say I had the best job in the whole company. There was no other job I'd have rather been doing, inside or outside Accenture.

From a career perspective, however, we were in uncharted territory. We remained dogged by misperceptions that our people were off on 'boondoggles' to exotic countries in Africa and Asia. (I love that word, which I learnt from my American colleagues – I think a 'jolly' is more commonly used in the UK, but *boondoggle* works far better for me). Maybe they thought we were painting schools or digging wells, a bit like some of the early corporate volunteering initiatives of the '90s. The reality couldn't have been more different. We discovered there's a counter-intuitive link between reducing someone's salary and increasing their effort levels. Yet this wasn't always recognised when they got back home six months later.

'Did you enjoy your vacation then?' one returning supply chain manager was asked. 'I hope you'll be ready to get back to some proper work now.'

'It was so demotivating,' she later told me, 'especially since I'd been working over 10 hours a day, six days per week for UNICEF for the previous six months, to improve the efficiency of their vaccines supply chain in Ghana.'

The problem wasn't new. I remember coming back from my year in the Balkans with VSO to be asked, 'So, have you got all that stuff out your system now?', as if I'd gone to be cured of some nasty bug called 'meaning' – or I'd been struck down with a heavy dose of 'purpose flu'. I explained to the rather bemused-looking partner that 'that stuff' was more in my system than ever. If purpose was a drug, then I was an addict-turned-drug-dealer. Yep, I was on a mission to get others hooked too.

It would be wrong to say that we didn't get support from Accenture's leadership – far from it. Those at the top were extremely supportive, but senior positions in any company are inherently transient. You can win over one leader only to find that they change roles, retire or get sacked for not 'hitting the numbers' and you have to start again with their successor. Groundhog Day. But we'll come to that in good time. No, it was actually the middle managers that were more often a challenge, particularly when it came to assessing someone's performance. I mean, all the old favourite performance metrics like sales, profit margin or 'chargeability' (now there's some classic consulting jargon for you) were wholly inappropriate in the non-profit world. It was like comparing apples with, well, orange-flavoured sausages.

I can now look back and laugh about my own end-of-year appraisal a few years after we first started. I was what we termed a senior manager at the time, and I remember clearly the meeting with two partners who were due to give me my end-of-year rating after what had been a terrific year of success for our team. They informed me that I'd been ranked near the top of the MEETS PER-FORMANCE group – average, in other words.

'Well, ADP has grown by over 90 per cent this past year – almost doubling in size. We've worked on 78 projects, delivering $25 million worth of services, in 45 of the poorest countries of the world. Employee engagement is through the roof and attrition down as a result. Oh, and I've had a letter of commendation for our work from the Head of the World Bank and ADP won Accenture the award for CSR at the Management Consulting Association's annual dinner,' I remember saying indignantly.

They both looked at each other with rather startled expressions.

'So what would you require for me to get an ABOVE PERFOR-MANCE rating next year? World Peace?' My sarcasm wasn't lost on them.

I really can't complain as I got more than fairly treated – certainly compared with some of my loyal team. There are upsides and down-sides of leadership, I discovered. The upside is that when you're the boss you get a disproportionate share of the credit for things going well, even stuff you've had little to do with directly. However, the converse is also true – you also have to take a disproportionate share of the shit when the same brown matter hits the fan. We'll come to all that in good time.

For many years, I enjoyed being the blue-eyed boy. I mean, who wouldn't? The less I seemed to care about my performance ratings, the more they took care of themselves. I think it was around 2005 when I got promoted to what was then called 'partner'. It was a major milestone, and with it came a bonus, pay rise and even some share options. Sweet. I might have been on a salary reduction, but by any standards I was doing very well. That said, I liken making partner to hill-walking or 'hiking', as our American friends call it. Just when you reach what you think is the summit and peer over the top, you discover you've only reached the foothills of a whole new mountain range. I was a very junior partner and had entered a whole new peer group to be measured against. The system would automatically generate a monthly performance report to each partner so that they could keep track of how they were doing against their targets. Each month, my report would be lines upon lines of great big *zeros*. Nada. Zilch. Sales: $0m. Yr/Yr Growth: 0.0 per cent. Controllable Income: $0.0m. You get the point. I found it hilarious, so much so that I have one framed on the wall of my apartment. All credit to the Accenture leadership, I thought. Would anyone else, in any other large corporation, manage to hang on to their job with a performance scorecard that looked like that? Don't get me wrong, it's not that I didn't have to report on what we did. Far from it. I was determined that ADP would be run like a business, with a profit and loss account, targets, you name it. The point is that these were a quite different, bespoke set of indicators from the standard ones used to operate in the 'business as usual' world.

By 2006/7, as we approached our fifth anniversary, ADP had reached a *point of inflection* – a fork in the road. We'd more or less doubled in size every year for these first few years, but now there were signs that growth was beginning to slow. It was almost like we were running to stand still with lots of small projects, for short durations and with relatively small teams. Even at about 20 per cent of normal rates, many NGOs still struggled to afford the amount of help they needed. But luck was on hand and we benefited massively from two key things: a new strategy and a new sponsor.

The new strategy was, in layman's terms, all around partnerships with private sector clients. Our existence had been fairly binary up until that point; Accenture worked with corporate clients on a (very) for-profit basis. ADP worked for large charities, foundations and NGOs on a not-for-profit basis. Pretty simple, right? There were very clear demarcation lines – never the twain would meet. But then the world moved on and so did the large corporates. The front-runners such as Unilever, DSM and GSK were starting to go way beyond the cheque-book charity CSR I've been rather scathing of and onto far more meaningful and sophisticated forms of engagement. A whole new lexicon was invented with terms such as 'sustainable business', 'inclusive business' and 'responsible business' – the cynics amongst you might say they've never seen so many oxymorons in a single sentence. Harvard Business Guru, Michael Porter, was starting to talk about 'Shared Value' as opposed to the Shareholder Value indoctrination he'd given me, and god only knows how many thousand others during our MBAs in the '90s. According to Porter, 'Companies should identify investment opportunities that provide shared value to the organisation and to society as a whole.' Well, maybe. It didn't go far enough for me. However, partnerships between businesses, NGOs and sometimes government institutions became the flavour of the month. So-called 'cross-sector partnerships' emerged as something of a panacea.

For ADP, they were like manna from heaven. We were extremely well placed to act as a broker and a convener of such partnerships. After all, by that time we had very strong, trust-based relationships built up with just about all of the largest NGOs, charities and foundations. Combine that with the fact that Accenture worked with about 6,000 of the largest global corporations, with relationships at the most senior levels. The firm viewed these relationships as business critical and, like most of our competitors, had a Senior Executive (Accenture's new speak for 'Partner', following the 2001 flotation) assigned to each. ADP became something of a secret weapon to enhance and extend these relationships. For example, Oxfam wanted to partner with Unilever to get more smallholder farmers in Tanzania into their supply chain of vegetables for Knorr soup, but lacked the business expertise around finance, business planning and quality control. Cue a team from ADP who worked on behalf of Oxfam to provide the necessary skills. Or when Barclays created a new 'village savings and loans programme' to bring microfinance to remote parts of sub-Saharan Africa – they lacked a presence outside the major cities, let alone a deep understanding of the needs of local communities. They partnered with two large NGOs, Care and Plan International, to get their new service the 'last mile' to those most in need. I'd describe the role ADP played as 'the glue' of these partnerships.

One of my favourites to this day remains an engagement we had with Coca Cola called Project Last Mile[1]. What on earth could a fizzy drink manufacturer have to do with the world of aid and development, you may well be wondering. Well, people often asked the age-old question: 'If you can get a bottle of Coke anywhere in the world, why is it kids in Africa are dying through lack of access to essential medicines and vaccines?' Fair question. Coca-Cola knew the answer wasn't to stick boxes of pills or temperature-sensitive vaccines onto the back of a Coca-Cola lorry and send it down a bumpy dirt track, stopping off at local clinics on the way to some little mom-and-pop shop in an African village. No, the challenge became how to transfer their expertise in logistics, inventory management and technology to what were mostly government-run health systems. We had a team of six consultants working in several African countries at the nexus of Coke's local bottler, the Ministry of Health and The Global Fund, with The Gates Foundation covering our fees. (Thanks, Bill Gates – I forgive all those times that Microsoft Word crashed, causing me to lose my work.) The result was dramatic savings in costs and a reduction in the lead-time for essential medicines from over 30 days to just three. Pretty cool, eh? Partnerships such as these played a pivotal role in a new phase of growth for ADP. We also got a credibility boost in the eyes of many within the leadership as we went from 'that cute little charity initiative' to something that might help to differentiate Accenture from its competitors in the eyes of their major corporate clients.

So, the second bit of luck we had was finding a new sponsor. Vernon Ellis provided great 'air cover' for many years, protecting us from too much unwanted attention from on high while we got established. He'd played a critical role in helping us get off the ground. However, it was clear that after more than 30 years in the business, he'd be retiring fairly soon.

The new sponsor emerged from a very serendipitous encounter I had in a lift at our London offices. Remember that Goethe quote about how 'providence moves too' when you've gone all-in on a cause? Well, I bumped into Mark Foster, a very tall man who was

---

1. http://www.coca-colacompany.com/project-last-mile

at the time heading up one of Accenture's largest global industry groups that covered everything from automotive and consumer goods to health and life sciences. He'd had an amazing career – youngest-ever manager promotion, youngest-ever partner promotion, youngest on the Executive Committee – you name it, Boy Wonder had achieved it. Unsurprisingly, Mark was heavily tipped to be Accenture's next Chief Executive. I knew Mark only by reputation at the time – and quite a reputation it was too. However, I decided to seize the moment and ask him a favour. I think they call this the classic 'elevator pitch', you know, where you've got about 30 seconds to grab someone's attention? Of course, most 'elevator pitches' don't take place in an actual elevator. But this one did. I went straight for the jugular and asked for a slot in his monthly *Noteworthy Newsletter* before the lift had even reached the first floor. *Noteworthy* wasn't your standard corporate bulletin, ghostwritten and then polished by Internal Comms. No, Mark had been writing his own monthly newsletter for years, detailing various client meetings, travel and leadership activities. Textbook HR stuff for leaders.

'Contact my assistant to set up a field visit. I want to see this for myself.'

'Erm… great. Thanks, Mark,' I stammered, knowing I'd completely lucked out.

I'd expected to be given one, maybe two days max on the back of another business trip, but Mark's assistant offered me one whole week! This was getting better and better.

Less than six months later I found myself with Mark, boarding a plane bound for Nairobi, Kenya. He walked down the airport walkway and turned left towards Business Class and, to his surprise, I turned right towards my usual 'Cattle Class'. Given ADP was self-funding from fees from non-profits, we had a policy to always fly Economy. That applied to all levels, including the boss – yes, *moi*. (No, don't worry, I'm not trying to evoke sympathy.) We planned a very full itinerary for Mark's trip that included client meetings and a big dinner with the half dozen ADP teams we had working in Nairobi at the time. They couldn't have been more excited that someone so senior – *the* Mark Foster – was coming to find out what they were up to. After a couple of days in Kenya we flew down to South Africa, stopping off in Johannesburg and then going on to see an eight-person team working for the United Nations Development Programme in South Africa's impoverished Eastern Cape. Mark took pity on me and used his air miles to upgrade me to Business Class on the flight from Nairobi to Johannesburg. It's not often you find yourself sitting right next to such a big cheese on a flight, but here I was, sitting beside the heir-apparent to Accenture's CEO, Bill Green. As Mark sank back in the large leather chair, I fumbled in my briefcase for the company-issued laptop, flipped it open and started feverishly typing away at my emails. It was important to make the right impression, I thought – important to show that even though I worked with non-profits, I was every bit as busy as my peers in the mainstream business. Yes, clearly I was carrying more 'baggage' than the suitcase I'd checked into the hold. Every now and again I'd sneak a glance to the side to check what he was up to. After about 30 minutes of shut-eye (or was it meditation, I'm not sure), Mark then reached into his own briefcase. 'Aha, he's no doubt got some very important work to do,' I thought to myself, 'about time too.'

I must have looked astonished, as instead of a laptop, Mark pulled out a thick novel and read it for the rest of the flight. It's a trivial detail, but it's one that strangely stuck in my mind as much as anything else from that fabulous, pivotal week in Africa. I'd had a rare glimpse into the world of senior leadership up close. We're programmed to believe that to get to the top requires more 'doing'. However, many of those at the very top have found a far better balance between the 'doing' and the 'being'. It's a lesson I learnt the hard way and, frankly, only with the benefit of hindsight years later.

Much earlier in this book, I explained my strong belief that it's the small, seemingly trivial events in life, and how one reacts to them, which define one's destiny. That chance encounter with Mark Foster in the lift would represent a significant turning point in ADP's fortunes and in my own career. It probably also marked a shift in his career, too, but perhaps not in the direction he'd anticipated or, indeed, aspired to at the time.

Chapter 12 – A Moment in the Sun

Thomson Ward, Glasgow, Saturday afternoon. November 2014

Warning: Asking me to talk about ADP is like asking someone to talk about their kids – you'll never get me to shut up. Poor Dr Ratner learnt that the hard way.

'Crumbs!' I said, glancing out of the window and realising it was beginning to get dark outside. 'I'm so sorry for going on and on, Dr Ratner. I completely lost track of time.'

'Don't worry, Gib,' she replied, closing her notepad as she looked up, 'I found it all fascinating. I'm actually back here tomorrow with a group of postgraduate psychiatry students. We could continue our discussion then, as long as you don't mind the students listening in.'

'Fine by me.'

'We'll focus on more recent events and some of the stress you might have been under at work.'

I got up, shook her hand and walked out of the meeting room. On reflection, I'd told her all about the good times, the exciting times, the glory days. Things had certainly got much harder in recent years. Yet, I'd always seemed to just about survive. I'd never felt even close to a breakdown, burnout or whatever the hell it was that landed me in a psychiatric hospital. Then again, I expect most previous inhabitants of Room 17 of the Thomson Ward would say the same.

I wandered down the corridor towards the day room to see if, by some small miracle, the lone desktop computer would be free. Of course it wasn't. As I turned to go back to my room, I came across Tony heading the other way towards the Supervisor's Office.

'Hey, Tony, you could really do with more computers in this place. You've got a snowball's chance in hell of getting to use that one ancient computer in there.'

'Budget cuts, Gib,' Tony explained. 'The only reason we have that computer or the PlayStation II in the TV room is because some generous past patient donated them.'

'Ah, I see,' I said, thinking about the many things I'd seen that were purely symptoms of budget restrictions in the NHS, from poor quality frozen food to flooding showers, not to mention the whiteboards and paper-based systems. I thought of the difference a day or two of pro bono time from some IT colleagues in Accenture could do to this whole department. It would be unrecognisable!

'I'm going to head off and find out what culinary delights are on the "austerity" dinner menu for tonight,' I continued, in a slightly sarcastic tone.

'You know, you can always order a takeaway. I've got a stack of menus in the office – Chinese, Indian, pizza, whatever you want. As long as you're willing to pay for it.'

'Really?' I said. 'What I wouldn't give for a Balti Chicken with some tarka dhaal and a wee naan bread on the side.'

'Stop it, you're making my stomach rumble! Follow me, Gib, and I'll give you the menu.'

I remembered that my parents had left me a bit of cash after their last visit – about 40 quid. The first 'pocket money' they'd given me since I was 14. It was all I had in the world at that moment, but it would certainly stretch to an Indian takeaway. I followed Tony down the corridor back to the staff office and phoned in the order, asking for it to be delivered about 5.30pm – my new dinner time. It arrived bang on time and I took the large brown paper bag into the canteen to unwrap it. The rich odours of cumin and coriander wafted around the room and I was starting to get a few envious glances.

Old Hughie, still with his straw hat on, had just finished his own dinner but was looking across at my curry longingly, almost drooling.

'Whit's that ye got there, pal? Smells pretty damn good tae me,' he said.

'It's a curry from the local Indian. Want to taste some?'

'Oh that wid be magic pal, just a teeny wee bit,' he said.

'Oh, is there enough for me tae get a wee taste, too?' came a voice from the table behind me. It was Tam, another of the older patients.

'Oh, could I have some, please?' said Jeannie. These were the first words she'd ever said to me.

As it happened, I'd ordered a mountain of food and could never finish it alone so was happy to share. What's more, my Indian take-away seemed to be the key to breaking down the barriers and build-ing a rapport with my fellow patients.

'Sure guys, just come and join me at this table,' I said. 'I'll get some more plates.'

I got a few clean plates from the counter and served small helpings of curry, rice and dhal onto each of them. It was becoming some-thing of a biblical scene, but instead of 5,000 sharing loaves and fish, it was just five of us sharing Balti Chicken. Oh, and to my knowl-edge, Jesus Christ wasn't around. That said, judging by the conver-sation, I'm sure some of my dinner companions may have begged to differ.

'Thanks very much. Yer a real gent,' said Hughie.

'No problem. There's plenty to go round,' I replied. 'So, tell me, Hughie, what were you doing before you ended up in here?'

'Oh, I've been in here for a very long time. I can't remember how long, to be honest. But I used to be in the movies, you know. I was an actor. Not always big roles, sometimes just walk-on parts like a kinda extra. But in the movies no less.'

'Really?' I said, no doubt with an air of disbelief.

'Aye, do ye no think he looks gist like George Clooney?' said Tam, sniggering into his tarka dhal.

'Shut yer face, you', said Hughie, 'Ah tell yeez all, it's true'.

The discussion continued with each of my new friends outdoing one another with ever more fanciful tales of past jobs, experiences and celebrity encounters. It was difficult to know what was real and what was illusion – the fanciful dreams of inhabitants of a mental hospital. Had Hughie really been an actor? Had Jimmy fought for the Cage Fighting World Championship? Was Andrea's father really the lead singer of a world-famous rock band who'd had a fling with her groupie mother after a concert in Paisley? Then again, did it even matter, as long as they believed it to be true? Perhaps we're all just illusionists of sorts, asking the world to view our lives through a Facebook lens, with Instagram-tinted spectacles.

Frankly, I'm one to talk about giving the illusion of a life that's different from reality. ADP had brought me many great experiences, including my own brushes with celebrities.

London. 2009

By 2009 ADP had become part of the fabric of the firm. We'd enjoyed our second wave of growth on the back of new forms of collaboration with big business, so-called 'cross-sector partnerships'. ADP was being used extensively in campaigns at universities and business schools as a recruitment differentiator for Accenture. Even the economic downturn was a blessing in disguise. Why? Because it meant that the business was willing to release more people to do ADP, when there was less demand from corporate clients. Makes sense, right? We'd also become far better known within the leadership ranks, amongst my fellow 'partner' peers, but still too many didn't really know what we were all about – what our teams *actually did* on the ground. I discovered that I'd developed a reputation as 'the charity guy', which I didn't particularly relish.

'So, do you do this ADP thing full time then?' I'd get asked quite often.

'Only 50–60 hours per week,' I'd reply, with a slightly indignant smile. When your job becomes your vocation, the standard nine-to-five day can feel more like five-to-nine. 'We've currently got 145 people on 58 projects in 42 different countries,' I continued, just to underline my point.

They'd look astounded. Sometimes I'd find myself being stopped in the corridor or in the canteen at lunchtime by someone wanting to tell me all about the great 'charidee' work they did in their spare time. Some worked with the homeless, the unemployed, old folk, young folk, birds, animals, the environment – you name it, someone did it. Moreover, they felt obliged to tell me, 'Mr Charity', *all* about it. I felt like saying that I was no Gandhi – just someone who gave a shit about the role business plays in our society.

Of course, when my Executive colleagues' desire to demonstrate their altruistic side involved supporting and supervising ADP projects in their spare time, I was only too happy to accept. Over time we developed a network of senior executives around the world, who were genuinely interested and engaged. They provided fabulous direction and support to our teams. Some would work on a one-off project, while others would work on many projects over several years. The poster child for the 'Supervisory Senior Exec' role (Client Partner in old speak) was Stephen Zatland from Accenture's Talent and Organisational Performance practice. Yep, consultancies do go in for fancy titles. Stephen was a bit of an adventure travel nut and so our projects in far-flung parts of the world were right up his street. Indeed, on several occasions he would go out and visit the teams and clients on the ground. A growing number of senior execs like Stephen were able to evangelise about the benefits that our teams were getting from their ADP experience. This really helped to develop a more level playing field during the performance appraisals. It was critically important that a growing number of the leadership ranks understood the complexity of the projects and the contribution teams were making.

However, when Stephen was given the job of planning and running the senior executive training in Chicago, his ADP involvement turned out to be far more of a chance lucky break than I'd originally anticipated. This brand new training programme ran two or three times each year, gathering 500 senior execs from all around the world, for a week's training in Accenture's massive centre in St Charles, a town on the outskirts of Chicago. The training involved a combination of plenary sessions, team breakouts and a selection of internal and external guest speakers. The main highlight was always some very big-name guest speaker who would give a keynote on the Friday lunchtime before people left for the airport. Stephen granted me a massive favour: a 20-minute slot to talk about ADP right before the keynote speaker would come on. The primary goal was to educate this important audience of global Accenture executives about what we were, what we did and, more importantly, what we did *not* do, e.g. digging wells and painting schools. So, thanks to Stephen, I found myself acting as the warm-up act for many big-name speakers including President Gorbachev, F.W. de Klerk, Mary Robinson and, several times, General Colin Powell. Senior guests and support staff had the privilege of having their photograph taken with each of these leaders in a rather undignified 'conveyor belt' fashion. I have a bizarre collection of posed celebrity portraits as a result, each with the same studio blue background and me sporting the same cheesy grin. Of course, my parents loved this as they provided considerable bragging rights in the local community – 'Look who Gib's just met,' no doubt. In fact, on one visit home I was shocked to find that my dad had created some kind of 'rogues' gallery' on the kitchen wall, alongside the large maps of my childhood. *Mortified* would be an understatement.

All of these big name Keynotes were of course very polished speakers, but General Powell was a particular favourite and was invited back on many occasions due to popular demand. When the time came for my short slot, I hadn't realised that he was sitting in a Green Room back stage waiting to go on, with a TV monitor allowing him to see everything that was happening in the hall. When he came on immediately after me and spent the first couple of minutes talking up ADP's work, I was blown away. A resounding endorsement from General Powell did no harm to our internal credibility, that's for sure. However, there was more to come.

I'd been waiting patiently in line for about 20 minutes to have my staged photograph taken with the great General. When I got to the front of the line he said, 'Great presentation, Gib. I love what you guys are doing. Have you heard of the IGD – the Initiative for Global Development?'

'Err... no, Colin... I mean, General Powell. I don't think I have.'

'I'm co-Chair with Madeline Albright. Think it could be relevant to what you guys are doing. If you've got a business card, then I'll send you some more information and would be keen to get your views.'

I fumbled around in my pocket and managed to find a rather grubby business card, which I handed over in astonishment.

'Thanks, that would be great, General Powell. Oh, and thanks for giving us a plug by the way.'

'You're welcome.'

About one week later, I found myself back on the Isle of Bute for the Easter Holiday. My sister, Looby, and her family had all come over from where they lived in Linlithgow, near Edinburgh, and we'd gone out to a local restaurant for a meal. It was about 9.30pm on the Saturday night when I felt that familiar buzz of the iPhone in my pocket and broke the family rule by having a quick peek under the table.

'Hoi, no technology at the table, Gib,' said Looby.

'Does the rule still count if it's an email from General Colin Powell?'

'Oh, will you stop your silly nonsense, my boy,' said Mum. 'That imagination of yours will land you in trouble one day.'

I was back in London on the Sunday night, sitting on my living room couch, carefully composing a response to General Powell's email. I read and re-read my short reply to make sure I wasn't saying anything ridiculous – then double-checked there were no silly typos or spelling mistakes, before plucking up the courage to hit 'send'. Then I lay back on the couch and let out a massive sigh of relief that I'd got that out of the way. Phew! Ten minutes later, a new email notification flashed up on the laptop – an instant reply from the General which read something like:

Thanks for these thoughts, Gib. I'll get back to you shortly. CP.

Crumbs, that was quick. I thought I'd better be equally responsive:

Thanks, General Powell. No rush. GB.

Forgive a bit of blatant namedropping here, but I'd have to say that lying on my couch at midnight, pinging backwards and forwards with the former US Secretary of State, remains one of the most surreal experiences of my life. It was capped only by a related incident a couple of years later when I was attending a conference in Washington, DC, that General Powell was chairing. I was engrossed in conversation with a prospective client, who was showing little interest in my sales pitch. Suddenly I felt a heavy hand slam down on my shoulder followed by a, 'Hey, Gib, how's it going, buddy?' It was, of course, the General, perhaps having a bit of fun. The prospective client's jaw-dropped expression was straight out of a *Tom & Jerry* cartoon, and no doubt amused General Powell just as much as it did me. A surreal experience.

Back in the real world, however, things were starting to get a bit tougher.

Chapter 13 – The Corporate Immune System

London. 2011–2012

Accenture Development Partnerships was approaching its tenth birthday – it had been quite a decade. Our little 'baby' was maturing from childhood into the commercial equivalent of adolescence and with it came all the usual pains and frustrations associated with growing up. But we'd had far more ups than downs along the way and it had been an incredibly exciting journey. I'd loved (almost) every minute of it.

In the same way that a child might have a birthday party each year, we'd always organised an annual 'Leadership Retreat' to reflect on where we'd got to and to plan the year ahead. In the early days, there were about three or four of us on the Management, or 'core team' as we called it, and these were very intimate gatherings. By the time we'd reached our fifth anniversary, we were still fewer than 10 people, and with budgets being tight, were struggling to find a venue. Lisa Jones, one of the longest serving and most loyal members of the team came to the rescue. Lisa is a smart, modest, understated girl, but we knew that her parents had several large houses – one of which sat not far from Royal St George's Golf Course in Sandwich, Kent. I reckon her family's wealth was from a time long before the term 'High Net Worth Individual' was invented. Personally, I've always hated the term – it loosely translates into Scottish as 'F****n' Rich Baaasterds'. However, I was never one to look a gift-horse in the mouth – we've already established my flagrant hypocrisy, after all.

These annual Leadership Retreats were always very special events – a powerful mixture of hard work, team building and yes, bonding. We had a marvellous time in Lisa's parents' house, although I fear they may have regretted making the offer, given the broken chair, couple of smashed plates and flipchart pen ink on the antique tablecloths. I think you can guess who the culprit was.

By our eighth and ninth annual retreats we'd outgrown any of Lisa's parents' houses and must have been about 30–40 people on the core team by then. These were our long-term staff with a further 100–150 consultants at any one point in time working on projects 'in the field', as we'd say, i.e. sub-Saharan Africa, Asia, etc. We managed to find a fairly cheap, self-catering conference centre not far outside London, which had been converted from an old farm. It had a great, large room for working during the day and a superb farmhouse kitchen where we worked in small teams to prepare the most amazing dinners. In the evening, we'd have the customary annual 'Fireside Chat', a chance to take stock of progress. We often took this once-in-a-year opportunity to go round the room hearing favourite experiences, proudest moments and funny anecdotes.

There were many. Over the years, ADP had all sorts of people on our teams with profiles which would have made our internal 'diversity police' very proud. Not only were we diverse in terms of gender and nationality – but also sexuality. We welcomed boyfriends with girlfriends, same-sex couples, married couples, accompanying babies and, of course, lots of singletons, too – some of whom would go on to become boyfriend/girlfriends, married couples and, no doubt, same-sex couples. ADP may have pre-dated Tinder, but it turned out to be every bit as powerful. At one point I feared that the employee appeal of our core mission, 'bringing business skills to development', might risk being overshadowed by the opportunities we offered for an exotic hook-up. After all, if you've got 20 young people working intensively for several months in challenging environments like Banda Aceh or Nairobi, then things happen, right? One of the team's highlights had been our first ever 'ADP Baby', born to an Accenture couple who had met on one of our projects in South Africa. That unexpected 'deliverable' hadn't appeared on anyone's performance targets. Pete and Lindsay are now happily married. Another person recalled the story of one male employee's badly broken arm, which had needed to be re-set and stitched up – rather poorly, I may add, with large, crisscrossed stitches like you'd see in a kid's cartoon. Before you get overly sympathetic, this accident had happened one drunken evening during an arm-wrestling contest.

So as we fast approached our tenth anniversary, we had, at long last, managed to shake off the albatross of being labelled 'just another fluffy CSR initiative'. However, descriptions as to what we actually were varied. Some called us a 'Corporate Social Enterprise', similar in concept to a Social Business, popularised by the Nobel Laureate Professor Muhammad Yunus from Bangladesh. Yunus created the Grameen Bank back in the 1970s, unleashing a whole new industry in microfinance, and went on to champion the notion that most social problems have a business solution. When I was invited to speak at conferences or at business schools, instead of saying that I headed Accenture's not-for-profit arm, I'd introduce us as a 'not-for-loss' business. That usually got a chuckle from the audience. However, my own personal favourite was an introduction given at Harvard Business School when I was due to speak on a panel moderated by David Gergen – one of CNN's political pundits – when ADP was described as a 'Guerrilla Movement' within Accenture. I have to admit that the notion of being some kind of business version of rebel leader Che Guevara did appeal to the ego, and 'maverick' was a label I was often given. I took it as a badge of honour, although I'm sure it was usually meant in the pejorative sense. I would discover that there was a growing number of other mavericks emerging in the business world.

It was around about this time that we were approached by INSEAD in Paris, one of the top-ranking business schools in Europe. They were keen to develop a 'Teaching Case' on ADP for their MBA class and wanted to ask Accenture's permission to do this. They also planned to interview some former participants, our management team and the Accenture leaders like Mark Foster and Vernon Ellis, who had played a pivotal role in helping us get off the ground. Teaching cases are standard teaching tools on most MBA courses and are used to get the students thinking about and discussing a particular business challenge or issue. It was, of course, very flattering to have a case study written on ADP, but what was of more interest to me was that it would be used by a professor who was running a course on 'Social Intrapreneurship'.

I had first been introduced to the concept of *social intrapreneurship* a number of years earlier by a UK based American woman called Maggie De Pree, who at the time was working for one of my big sustainable business heroes, John Elkington. John was, and remains, someone who is able to spot new business trends long before the mainstream – think eco-savvy Nostradamus with an MBA. He'd been a leader in the sustainability movement since the early '70s. John was writing a report on this new concept of Social Intrapreneurship and Maggie called me to ask if I would be willing to be interviewed.

'Social what?' I said, or words to that effect. 'Never heard of it.'

'I said "social intrapreneur". We think you're one of them, Gib,' she replied.

Now I've been called many things in my time, but this was a first. Yet while the label is not that important, I discovered I did buy into the concept, into the notion that when a business professional is seeking more purpose in their career, rather than changing job or company, you actually try to *change the company* you're in. As I've already mentioned, today's corporations are absolutely massive, gigantic behemoths. Believe it or not, if Apple were a country, it would just about knock Switzerland out of the G20. So if you use the analogue of a supertanker, changing course by even one degree can be slow and use a lot of energy, but results in a massive impact downstream. Yes, it may well have been easier to come back from Macedonia in 2001 and subsequently leave Accenture to create a consulting social enterprise. However, even the prospect of getting that one-degree shift in direction of the 400,000 person, $70 billion market cap Accenture supertanker, was worth staying for. I'm glad I did and I'm glad others did, too, within their own organisations.

Take, for example, the mobile phone industry. Near the beginning of ADP's life, I met Nick Hughes, a junior manager in Vodafone's Marketing department. Nick was a smart guy and he noticed that Vodafone's customers in Kenya were exchanging mobile phone airtime as a form of alternative currency, largely due to a lack of banking infrastructure. Nick is widely credited with sparking a mobile banking revolution in Africa, by coming up with the idea to create M-PESA in Kenya. Now over 80 per cent of the Kenyan economy flows through mobile money.

I somewhat serendipitously encountered a couple of other impressive people in these early days who, along with others, would go on to define the early social intrapreneurship movement. I met Roberto Bocca in London, when he was working for the oil giant, BP. Roberto had managed to create a startup business in India to provide 'clean' cooking stoves that would encourage people to stop cooking on open fires. I learnt that so-called 'indoor air pollution' is the fourth-biggest killer worldwide, through respiratory diseases. Roberto's business grew to over 500,000 customers in India alone – impressive.

It was around the same time that a mutual friend introduced me to Jo da Silva, who was an engineer within Arup, a company specialising in planning and technical design, but had worked extensively as a volunteer in the post-disaster emergency relief sector. Jo quizzed me on ADP's business model as she thought something similar could be done within Arup. She would go on to set up Arup International Development, a not-for-profit arm of Arup, focused on bringing their technical expertise in engineering design and construction to the humanitarian and development sector.

Pretty cool.

Nick, Roberto and Jo all had the option to quit their jobs and go out on their own – but, for whatever reason, they stayed put and sought to drive change from within the system rather than from the outside. That's not easy, as I knew only too well.

Maggie and I remained good friends since that first connection in 2007 and, along with a few other 'mavericks', she co-founded the League of Intrapreneurs. Its aim is to develop a movement of entrepreneurial change-makers willing to hack the system from within. Many will reside within these corporate supertankers, but there are also social intrapreneurs within NGOs and government agencies. The League of Intrapreneurs is trying to connect these people from within and across the sectors to try to drive change bottom up, inside out. No, you don't have to wait for a time when you might become CEO to drive change within your organisation. After all, for most people, that time will never come.

That said, there's a fine line between being a 'changemaker' and being branded a 'troublemaker', and intrapreneurs are no doubt a bit of both. That makes them something of an endangered species, certainly within the corporate world. It's almost as if a set of antibodies are unleashed by the parent organisation to try to attack anything that doesn't look like it's maximising short-term profit in the next quarter. I've often referred to this as the 'corporate immune system' – an invisible force made up of a combination of culture, risk management policies and inertia that can kill social innovation without even leaving any fingerprints.

Size does matter. When you're just starting out, you're often operating under the radar system or are not big enough to present a challenge to the host business. I'd often find good will from peers, or that ADP would be given the benefit of the doubt when we'd find ourselves breaching some corporate policy or other – as, indeed, we often did. For example, Accenture had rules about which countries were attractive markets for our services and which ones we were to avoid, for lots of legitimate reasons. However, we had senior friends in the legal, tax, commercial and asset security departments. They'd assess the true business risk, make a personal judgment call and then sign off a project in, say Zambia – a country not likely to be a commercial priority for Accenture for many years to come. As we grew, ADP's head gradually rose above the parapet and we became subject to the prevailing view that every project should be 100 per cent compliant with policy. On paper that makes sense – but businesses don't operate 'on paper', and if you apply the same controls that are applicable to a corporate behemoth to a small startup, let alone a social enterprise, then it's slow, painful suffocation – a death of a thousand cuts. We were bleeding, and it was starting to hurt.

Sometimes it can be a change of leadership in the upper echelons that presents the greatest risk to the intrapreneur – when one particularly supportive leadership sponsor leaves or retires and is replaced by someone less supportive. Jo remains in Arup, but both Nick and Roberto left their jobs at Vodafone and BP. Attrition within the intrapreneurship community is too high, and this is something the leadership need to address if they're to avoid haemorrhaging innovative talent[1].

---

1. 'Managing the Mavericks – Valuing the diversity of mindset as much as skillset', Gib Bulloch and Sarah Buckley, *Huffington Post*, 11 November 2017. https://www.huffington-post.com/entry/managing-the-mavericks_us_5a006d06e4b0d467d4c226c0

Port-au-Prince, Haiti. January 2011

Most of you will recall the dreadful earthquake that struck Haiti on 12 January 2010. Once the immediate relief and recovery phase was completed, the reconstruction phase was able to begin. We'd find ourselves working on the ground in Haiti for several years, just as we'd done after the 2004 tsunami in Indonesia. Mark Foster chose Haiti as the destination for his annual trip and wanted to see first hand what the ADP teams had been up to.

Now, Haiti didn't have a reputation as being the safest place in the world from either a crime or a health perspective. Indeed, there had just been a cholera outbreak that had rather controversially turned out to be caused by the UN. The trip had our friends in Global Asset Protection (GAP) freaking out. Like most companies, Accenture often claimed that, 'Our people are our greatest assets', and the job of GAP was to protect these precious 'assets' and keep them out of harm's way. They were a mixed bunch of ex-military types – marines, special forces, you name it, and had a language unto themselves. Conference calls would be timed at 'oh-six-hundred-hours' as opposed to 'six in the morning'. Certainly not a more civilised eight in the morning – sleeping late is clearly for wimps.

GAP decided to dispatch a support team to join Mark and me on the Haiti trip and there was an entourage of massive black Suburban SUVs awaiting us when we landed in Port-au-Prince, the country's capital. Frankly, I think the GAP guys were secretly delighted to have the opportunity to get up from behind their desks in Philadelphia and see some action. To most people, GAP is no doubt synonymous with middle-of-the-road high street fashion, but Accenture's version of GAP arrived resplendent in bullet-proof vests and combat fatigues. Let's face it: most grown men still love to play soldiers.

One of the big successes of the first year of reconstruction was the renovation of the famous Iron Market in Port-au-Prince, which had been completely flattened by the quake. A big ceremony was planned for the reopening and Bill Clinton was going to arrive as the guest of honour. Our teams had been working closely with the government and had managed to wangle VIP invitations for Mark and me. We set off in our large Suburban with an armed guard up front in another SUV and another following behind. Again, there was lots of military talk going over the radio – lots of acronyms. We had to be there by 'eleven hundred hours' sharp when Blue Dawn would be met by Operative 4. I'd heard the term 'Blue Dawn' mentioned a lot and my curiosity eventually got the better of me.

'What or who is Blue Dawn?' I asked Bart, the GAP Lead.

'It's the name we've assigned to the asset,' he replied. 'We always have code words when we travel with VIPs on trips to dangerous countries.'

'OK, I think I can guess who Blue Dawn is – it's MF, right?'

'Affirmative.'

'What's my codename?'

'We, er, we don't have one for you.'

Accenture's people may indeed be its greatest asset – but clearly some *assets* are more valuable than others.

They say that the worst thing about owning a superyacht is that no matter how big yours is, you'll always run into someone with a bigger one. I think the same goes for armed VIP convoys. There we were, driving down the centre of Port-au-Prince in our three armed SUVs, feeling like 'Very Important People', when, all of a sudden, we ground to a halt. President Clinton was arriving just ahead of us and he had no fewer than six Black Suburbans in his convoy. Don't you just hate it when that happens?

This trip with Mark would be memorable for a different reason: it was to be his last. As we boarded the flight to leave Haiti, Mark turned round to me and said, 'I've got some news I need to share with you, Gib. I'll be leaving Accenture in three months' time.'

ADP needed a new leadership sponsor – fast.

Chapter 14 – Strategy Reboot

Pierre Nanterme took over from Bill Green as CEO in 2011, while Bill transitioned to Chairman. Splitting the Chairman and CEO into two separate roles (a requirement in many countries), was quite a standard shuffle within Accenture, done to 'keep the market steady'. A CEO leaving can often have a big impact on a firm's value – just look at Apple when the inimitable Steve Jobs left. Well, 'left' is one way of putting it – just like you 'leave' the church after your funeral. In a box. Anyway, the old CEO staying on as Chairman for a couple of years allowed for a very smooth transition of power, and that's what Bill did. Pierre is a charismatic Frenchman, who was on a mission to bring greater focus (or 'fuck us' when said in Pierre's fairly strong French accent) to the business which he underpinned with a new strategy known as the Accenture Way. The quarterly Managing Director videoconferences were usually closed with a passionate appeal for focus from Pierre: 'I want you to *fuck us* the Accenture Way!' Always worth joining for that line alone.

It was commonly believed that my sponsor, Mark Foster, desperately wanted the top job and so his resignation hadn't come as a total shock – it was more the suddenness that snuck up and bit me on the arse. Were I a betting man, I'd have given you at least evens on him making it to the top. He was the heir apparent in the eyes of many, including the Wall Street investor community. Then again, promotion to the CEO of Fortune Global 500 multinational would never be a slam-dunk, and missing out must have hurt. Imagine you're running a marathon, which you've led from the starting gun and right through to the 26.1 mile marker. Then, on the last bend, with a mere 100 yards to go, a short Frenchman breaks from the chasing pack and beats you to the line. *C'est la vie* would probably be the appropriate term. However, with the share options Mark had, I expect he cried all the way to the bank.

Mark broke the news of his departure when we were together in Haiti. He had an enthusiastic senior leader in mind to take over the ADP sponsor reins, namely Sander van 't Noordende, a highly regarded, up-and-coming leader with a reputation for straight talking – goes with the territory if you're Dutch, right? What was more, well, unusual in the business world, was the fact that Sander was openly gay and living with his partner in New York. So I had a lot of respect for him from the outset, for one simple reason: he was authentic. Sadly, despite the rise of a whole industry dedicated to inclusion and diversity, too few at the top of business feel able to be transparent about their sexuality. I mean, until recently there was only one openly gay CEO in the Fortune 500, Tim Cook, the CEO of Apple. Statistically speaking, it's highly likely that there are close to 50 more still in the proverbial closet – OK, 'filing cabinet', given we're talking business executives. To its credit, Accenture took the whole issue of diversity very seriously and ran courses for its staff worldwide.

Sander lived up to his billing. He took a keen interest in ADP's work and helped us develop our thinking on how to take ADP from adolescence into adulthood. However, I knew that if ADP were to fulfil its latent potential, I needed to get Pierre interested. The opportunity would emerge sooner than I thought.

Davos.

Thud.

That's the sound of a name that's just been dropped from a great height. I doubt there are many other words in the business lexicon that carry more caché than *Davos*. A beautiful, sleepy little village perched on a mountain top in the Swiss Alps that one week each year undergoes a metamorphosis and hosts the annual meeting of the World Economic Forum. Around late January each year, I'd receive automated 'Out of Office' email responses saying something like:

Thanks for your email. Forgive a delayed response – I'm currently on business travel to DAVOS. I'll reply to you as soon as possible.

Such messages are right up there with the BA Gold Card luggage tags on my Crassometer.

So what's so special about Davos? Well, it's very exclusive for a start. Over 1500 of the global business elite pay an arm and a leg to mingle with each other, plus many heads of state. Oh, and a handful of celebrities to boot. They spend three to four days talking about major issues such as global inequality and climate change over copious glasses of champagne, before taking a helicopter back down the mountain, no doubt to an awaiting Learjet. They then spend the next 360 days of the year focused on maximising short-term profit for shareholders before it's time for, you've guessed it, Davos again. It was conspicuous consumption personified. Yep, Davos was amazing and I loved every minute of those annual trips to the Swiss Alps.

'They're your two best features,' my dad would say with a wink. 'Your standards.'

Like most of the big consultancies, Accenture sent a large delegation – five VIPs with coveted White Badges – and then a bunch of hangers-on like me. We even had our own film crew for the VIPs to record video messages that would be sent as internal postcards for the remaining 399,970 staff around the world who didn't happen to be in Davos.

Davos has a magnetic power. Most of the CEOs of my big NGO clients would turn up, and it was a great opportunity to set up meetings on the sidelines. On one particular occasion, I'd managed to get an interview lined up with the legendary Professor Muhammad Yunus – remember him, the godfather of microfinance?

I read somewhere that life sometimes presents a 'cubic centimetre of chance' which we have the option of ignoring or seizing. The outcome of such moments can be critical, sometimes even life changing. Pierre, sitting at his desk five minutes before my interview was due to start, was too good an opportunity to miss. I asked if he'd heard of Professor Muhammad Yunus, and whether he'd be prepared to join an interview I was doing with him. At that very moment, the unmistakable figure of the great Professor showed up at the door in his trademark flowing white Bangladeshi attire. Very dapper. My interview of this star duo on a Davos hotel balcony complete with snow capped peaks as a backdrop, lasted just seven minutes – no rehearsals, no preparation time, no second takes. Bang, it was in the can. Professor Yunus talked about the power of Social Business and

Pierre talked about Accenture's own version of a social business – namely, ADP. It couldn't have been better.

A few months later, Pierre told me that his teenage daughter never really took a lot of notice of what her dad did for a living, 'but that video of me being interviewed with Professor Yunus at Davos she shared with all her friends on Facebook,' he explained, smiling proudly.

I'd say that experience did wonders for cementing our relationship.

Dublin, Ireland. April 2013

After the Professor Yunus gig in Davos, Pierre had become my NBF – New Best Friend. OK, I'm prone to a bit of exaggeration, as you know. Let's just say that he was positively disposed to what we were doing. He felt it would be fitting for me to give a presentation to the Accenture Board on all that had been achieved so far on the ADP journey as we celebrated our tenth anniversary. Nice birthday present. I normally get socks.

You never know you've peaked until afterwards and with the benefit of hindsight. When you're in decline, you can look through the rear-view mirror and say, 'Yep, that was it'. Though I didn't know it at the time, 23 April 2013 would be ADP's peak. Well, under my leadership at least. This was the date of the Board meeting.

The venue was Dublin, Accenture's official domicile from a tax perspective. Ireland has a corporate tax rate of 12.5 per cent and a tax treaty within the US. But now's not the time for my sermon on the vagaries of the global corporate tax system.

I remember there being at least two prep calls with Pierre himself to review my draft slides and make sure I was 'on message'. I think my reputation as a maverick had preceded me and I expect he was keen to make sure the Board wouldn't get any surprises. Well, not nasty ones.

The team and I had been working with Sander to develop a new five-year strategy. It was all about taking our impact to the next level: scaling up by taking on fewer, bigger projects; how we'd harness the collective power of Accenture's commercial client base and ADP's NGO clients to really move the needle on the big issues of global development. Integration was the name of the game. Move from projects to large programmes. From silos to working on systems and solutions. We'd even have an innovation fund to unlock the potential of intrapreneurial talent inside our clients. It was a powerful new strategy and I was desperate to share our vision with the Board, but Pierre recommended that I focus on our achievements over the past ten years to 'put a smile on their faces'.

Kyboshed. For once, I did what I was told. There's a first time for everything. Putting a smile on their faces wasn't difficult – we had a powerful story to tell, something that I was very proud of and they as Board members could be proud of, too: the role that Accenture had played in nurturing our audacious little startup.

They say every slide deck needs one killer slide. This motto had served me well over my consulting career. My deck had been pruned and sanitised down to a punchy ten slides. But the *pièce de résistance* (a fitting description for a presentation to a Board with a French Chairman and CEO, *n'est-ce pas?*) was a one-page 'infographic'. An info-what? It's jargon for a page that combines pictures with facts and figures to make a more impactful slide.

'ADP 10 Year Update' was the last item on the agenda. That's OK – I was used to it. Whenever I'd be asked to give an ADP presentation to different business units or national offices, I'd always get the graveyard slot. The important stuff like year-on-year growth rates, client wins, business development targets, cost-cutting exercises, would all be up front. The feel-good 'charidee' update would be fitted in at the end, if there was time for it. I hated the do-gooder associations. We were doing business, just in a different way. I set myself the ambition of being given a speaking slot at the beginning of some agenda. Any agenda. I failed miserably.

Eventually, it was my turn. The meeting room table was large and oval – I was on one side with most of Board members spread across from me on the other. A few of Accenture's Executive Committee were on my side as if for moral support.

'Ladies and gentlemen. If you want to know what the team and I have been up to these past 10 years, then this page pretty much sums it up,' I said, handing out printed copies of the infographic in a triumphant gesture.

There were the obvious numbers – like the thousands of employees who'd provided their skills on hundreds of projects in about 80 of the poorest countries of the world. We'd worked extensively with all of the world's largest NGOs and so-called client satisfaction levels were through the roof. Overall, we'd delivered over a quarter of a billion dollars' worth of services to the sector. Not bad, eh? But it was the more unusual numbers that really captured their attention – like the thousands of consulting days that we'd spent reconstructing Banda Aceh in the wake of the tsunami or in Haiti after the devastating earthquake. My personal favourite? Between them, our consultants had foregone tens of millions of dollars in voluntary salary sacrifice. OK, you can always say consultants are overpaid, but imagine these were cash donations to charity – we'd actually managed to quantify the premium that employees will place on a job with purpose. Yes, you could say I was proud of what our team had achieved in ADP's first decade, all from a standing start in 2002.

The Board loved it. The leadership was suitably impressed, even those who weren't known for their warm appreciation of our efforts. Pierre was happy, and so was I. Well, to be honest, I was ecstatic. Over the fucking moon. It took a couple of pints of Dublin's finest draught *Guinness* to help me get off to sleep that night, no doubt with a smile on my face.

At about 3am I was wide-awake, sitting up in bed, thoughts racing through my mind. I tossed and turned in an effort to get back to sleep, but it was futile – the thoughts kept buzzing through my head. I had to write them down in case I'd not remember them in the morning. For the next 90 minutes, I sat writing at the hotel room desk. The top of the first page read:

Script for Board Presentation – 23 April 2023

Yes, it had been a great day – a milestone day, even. I knew we'd achieved a lot of great things in our first decade and touched the lives of possibly millions of people in many of the world's poorest countries. But for me it wasn't enough. All I could see was the potential we had to do so much more in the next decade. This ambition would end up costing me dearly.

NIGHT IV – AN EMERGING FOURTH SECTOR

'Leadership means finding a new direction, not simply putting yourself at the front of the herd that's heading toward the cliff.'

William Deresiewicz
Author, *Excellent Sheep*

Chapter 15 – An Accountant, a Banker and a Consultant Walked into a Room

Turn to Camera

So you get the picture. It had been a real roller coaster ride. Much of what I've shared so far is about how the original kernel of an idea morphed into something that went far beyond the original vision. Yet I was convinced there was latent potential to do so much more.

The team and I were starting to develop our own ideas around the world of possibilities that might exist when you fuse together social or development challenges and the latest business thinking, mixed with a sprinkling of innovation. In keeping with the consulting industry, we published a couple of 'Thought Leadership' papers, which were apparently well received in the sector. With the benefit of hindsight, I realize these papers had a limited audience within the business world and even internally within the firm. However, when shared in laymen's terms using more accessible language I tended to get much more traction. But I'm of course biased. Read on and judge for yourself.

Thomson Ward, Sunday Lunchtime. November 2014

'A bunch of wankers, isn't that what you said, Gib?'

An animated Danny was shouting at me from the other side of the canteen.

I wandered past and saw a few scattered souls sitting at tables in ones or twos, savouring the delights of an NHS lunch.

'You what? Someone been altering your medication, mate?'

Danny was sitting in the corner with another fairly young, dark-haired guy who I'd seen around but never spoken to.

'Gib, meet Gordon. Gordon, meet Gib. I know you'll both get on really well, given your love of banks and all things bankers, Gib,' he continued, with a mischievous smile on his face.

I walked across to their table and pulled up a chair, anticipating something of a setup. I'd gone off on one of my favourite anti-banker rants the day before and clearly Danny was seizing an opportunity for a bit of mischief.

'Gordon's an investment banker from Edinburgh,' said Danny.

Gordon. Gordon... The name seemed familiar.

'Gordon... Connor, perhaps?' I asked.

He gave a puzzled, kind of *how the fuck did you know that?* nod. Oh God, this was the guy from the room across the corridor from me. The name was marked on the whiteboard of his door. The guy who prays for 48 hours on end and has the nightshift guards parked outside his room. Gordon looked to be in his early thirties, had dark hair and appeared to be perfectly calm and relatively normal looking. Normal. There I go again. That said, his eyes did have that distant look of someone who was fairly heavily sedated.

'You must be the guy in the room just across the corridor from mine,' Gordon said, reaching out to shake my hand. 'Just arrived a day or two ago, right?'

'Correct. Pleased to meet you, Gordon.' I shook his hand.

'Don't believe everything 'Danny Big Mouth' has been telling about my love of bankers.'

'Oh, don't worry, I think it's a dreadful profession too and that's partly why I've ended up in here,' he said with a smile.

That broke the ice, thank God. A self-aware banker. *Rare breed indeed*, I thought to myself.

'But when you're part of it, in the midst of all these people working 80-hour weeks and focusing on making as much money as possible, it's very easy to get swept along, but it's certainly not what I plan to be doing for the rest of my life.'

'Yes, the pay structures are just something of an enigma,' I said.

'It's what's led to this culture of massive bonuses, greed and entitlement.'

Danny sat back and folded his arms, clearly chuffed at the discussion he'd provoked with his clumsy introduction.

'I knew I could get you going by introducing you to Gordon,' he chuckled.

As a management consultant, I shouldn't really be too judgmental about investment bankers. People in glass houses...

'I'm actually looking to get out. You know, to do something a bit more worthwhile,' said Gordon. 'Danny tells me that you have a really interesting job working with charities, social enterprises and the like. Do you think they have any need for a reformed banker like me?'

'They'd be biting your hand off, mate,' I said.

OK, put to one side the fact that the conversation was taking place in an asylum with someone whose mental health had recently been compromised. I actually meant what I'd said – financial wizardry could and should play a big role in the non-profit sector, to channel capital towards solving social issues. I'd written a bunch of papers and spoken at numerous conferences predicting that the world of international development was in for a period of radical change. New technology – this whole digital revolution – will be one of the big 'disrupters', just as it's disrupting every other industry. But the other major disruptor will be how the whole aid and development system is financed. Today it's largely funded through government aid budgets and private donations from the public, giving money to their favourite countries, projects, charities or thematic areas like health, education, nutrition, emergency relief – you name it. The so-called 'beneficiary' organisation will take the money and spend it as well as they can, reporting a year or two down the line on what they did with it. They hope that the donor, whether a government or an individual, is happy and keeps stumping up cash the next time they come asking. Don't get me wrong, I think these charities do great work and are full of hard-working, no doubt underpaid, people. But when they think of the effectiveness of their spend, too often it's claiming that they have a lower overhead percentage than the next charity and that 'more of your pound/dollar/euro goes to the cause'. Which, of course, means that they under-invest in training and developing their people, or in the likes of new technologies that could make their organisations slicker and more effective. We're as much to blame as we all love to see that our charitable donations result in nice pictures of healthy, smiling kids. A world-class IT system may be what's needed, but it's far less photogenic.

'It's ten tae wan lads, an' am goin' tae be clearing the food away very soon,' came Mary's dulcet Glaswegian tones from behind the counter. 'Yeez had bettur hurray if yeez want something tae eat.'

'Be right there, Mary,' I said, as the three of us each grabbed a tray and surveyed the delights on offer. The shepherd's pie looked the least offensive and I'd got used to tagging on a bowl of sponge and custard, in true school dinners fashion.

'It's not like I know anything about charities or Africa or diseases or any of that stuff,' said Gordon, his mouth half full of Mary's re-heated lasagne. 'So what kind of things could bankers like me be doing?'

'Yeah, or even business people in general, Gib,' said Danny. 'I'm thinking about a change of scene myself when they let me out of here.'

'If you get me talking on that subject I might never shut up!'

'Time is not something we are short of in here, Gib,' said Gordon. 'As it happens, I didn't have any fixed plans for the rest of the day, funnily enough. What about you, Danny?'

'Well, Shakira had asked me out on a date tonight doon the West End, but I'll follow up an' cancel it so that I can listen to you, Gib!' said Danny, with a sarcastic chuckle.

By the time of The Incident, I'd spent well over a decade working in the international development sector, with much of my time focused on rethinking the role that business can play in tackling the big challenges facing so many people around the world. For me, poverty isn't just about a lack of money. It's about a lack of choice as to how to live your life and a lack of access to the vital ingredients that allow individuals and societies to prosper. I'm talking about access to medicines, access to a quality education, access to nutritious food, to safe drinking water, affordable energy – and so on. It's a sector that is dominated by big international charities, aid agencies and the United Nations. Large corporations are still pretty much conspicuous by their absence, although this is beginning to change. Too many businesses still look at development through a CSR or philanthropic lens – they don't perceive there's any money to be made there. I couldn't disagree more. I'm of the, admittedly unconventional, view that there's actually quite a lot of money to be made in solving social problems – for individuals, companies and entrepreneurs. Of course, big business is treated with contempt by a sector populated by altruists. Bankers, management consultants, marketers and the like are made to feel about as welcome as a ginger stepchild at a wedding – unless they've got a big donation to make, of course! Terms like 'profit', 'return on investment', 'wealth creation' are considered quite toxic. Yet charities and governments alike must find ways of attracting *private* investment, capital, innovation and entrepreneurship into providing *public* goods and solving these big social problems.

How? Well, we first need to reframe these social problems – to think of them as business opportunities in disguise. Take access to energy. If money was made available and invested in electrifying rural villages in parts of Africa, then it could have a massive impact – lighting would allow kids to read and learn after dark or could power machines that would allow businesses to flourish. It would create more economic activity, provide access to the internet and perhaps access to markets or information. Solar energy could power pumps that could allow drip irrigation in fields. That, in turn, might improve agricultural productivity. So if a hectare of land that was producing, say, an average of 4 tonnes per hectare, could be made to produce 20, 30 or even 40 tonnes per hectare, then a lot of economic value can be created for communities and, indeed, governments, ultimately through tax revenues.

'So, you guys really want to put your business expertise to good use then?' I asked, pushing the plate of half-eaten shepherd's pie to one side.

'Convince us we can make a difference,' said Gordon.

'OK. Education.'

They both looked quite shocked – as if I was suggesting they should become teachers or something.

'I happen to believe that education and developing healthy talent might actually be one of the biggest untapped investment opportunities for business,' I said, getting into my stride. 'But we're thinking about the problem in the wrong way.'

I'd become quite obsessed by education in recent years. Perhaps it was something to do with the fact that my parents had both been teachers and my sister had re-trained as a teacher, too. You could say I had the ABCs as my DNA. But my interest was more about how education could and should be funded and delivered differently, on a global basis. I mean, take India as an example. Demographics mean that the global economy is going to be very reliant on India for the talent it will need to grow in the future. Like it or not, birth rates are falling in places like Europe, the US, Russia and Japan. Populations are ageing as a result. Where are the bulk of kids being born? In highly populous countries like Nigeria, Indonesia and India, which on its own is predicted to provide a quarter of the world's workforce as soon as about 2030... No, not next century, but just over 10 short years from now. Our friends in India, and Africa for that matter, should be benefitting from this so-called 'demographic dividend', but they're not. Why? Because too many kids in India are dying of easily treatable diseases before they're even five years old. Or, for the kids that are lucky enough to survive and make it into school, many will get a very poor quality education because of absenteeism – not amongst the pupils, but amongst teachers. In some states, up to 40 per cent of teachers don't even turn up to teach! There are many reasons for this – one being poor pay, which means they need to have a second job just to make ends meet. That comes down to the fact that the government doesn't have the money to invest in a high-quality education system. It's a vicious circle.

Think on the level of an individual child – let's say one that was born in India today. If you can ensure that that child is well nourished as an infant so that his or her little brain fully develops, survives past his or her fifth birthday, makes it into primary school, then secondary school, has a quality education, perhaps goes on to university, they can then become a productive economic asset for the country. That child might become an employee of a business like Accenture (who already have more than 180,000 employees in India and will no doubt need more in the future), earning profits for the company and paying taxes to the government. Or they could become a doctor, a nurse or a civil servant. Either way, it's better to be an economic asset than yet another child mortality statistic, isn't it?

Most people would agree with that, of course. But I was determined to try to put a number on the value. In 2013 ADP worked on a report with The Brookings Institute, which estimated that every dollar invested in that Indian child at birth would be worth 54 dollars if they made it into the workplace. It's an amazing statistic. The Accenture Brookings Report[1] estimated that India is losing about $100 billion every year as a result of under-developing its talent or through child mortality, morbidity, school drop-outs and the like. Instead of a demographic dividend, it's a demographic deficit, equivalent to about five per cent of the country's GDP each year! Drip, drip, drip – they're slowly losing the inherent value of their human capital. Now, if a country like Saudi Arabia were losing five per cent of its oil revenue through leaking pipes, they'd soon fix them. Surely the same should go for talent in India, or Africa.

OK, so now you understand that education was my favourite hobby-horse issue. I felt then, and still believe, it's where the investment expertise of people like Gordon could be harnessed. You see, there's lots of interest and excitement in the development sector about concepts such as 'impact investing' and innovative financing instruments like Social Impact Bonds. Now, I know this sounds like more management consultant jargon – maybe it is – but at its core is the notion of payment for results: outcomes and impacts as opposed to inputs. In terms of education, many development hacks talk about the need for X number of schools to be built, or Y number of teach-

1. 'Investment in Global Education – A Strategic Imperative for Business', Rebecca Winthrop, Gib Bulloch, Pooja Bhatt and Arthur Woods, 12 September 2013. https://www.brookings.edu/research/investment-in-global-education-a-strategic-imperative-for-business/

ers to be trained, Z more computers, etc. and then put a figure on the cost. However, what we should be talking about is the number of kids we want to educate to a specific level of literacy or numeracy, i.e. an outcome. Then you get governments or donors to place a value on that outcome and challenge organisations or, more likely, coalitions of organisations, to collaborate in delivering this common goal and, in turn, be paid in line with their contribution.

When I've shared these ideas with colleagues in the past, they usually ask where the upfront investment is going to come from. Well, there could be many answers to this. What about a 'Talent Tax' on corporates that could create a Global Fund for Education? After all, corporations, who need employees to grow, have a vested interest in developing talent in the emerging markets where they're increasingly shifting towards. I could imagine a scenario where these funds or 'impact bonds' would be co-funded between governments, business and donors.

'Solving the problems of the world are you, boys?' came a voice from the other side of the canteen. The three of us turned round in unison to see Tony, leaning into the room, balancing on the door handle.

'Actually, Gib, I was just wanting to let you know that Dr Ratner and her gang of students are gathered in Room 3 and ready whenever you are.'

'Oops, totally forgot I was seeing her again. Sorry, gents, Nurse Ratched needs me.'

'Let's pick up again later, eh Gib?' said Gordon.

'Yeah, I'm on for that too,' Danny added.

'What, you want me to spout off about my favourite topic? Not a chance.'

Both smiled. I could swear that Gordon's eyes looked less glazed than earlier – a little more alive. He'd clearly been engaged. Danny too.

'I have to say it's a far cry from my perception of the greedy business world that I've got used to,' said Gordon. 'You've certainly given me plenty of food for thought, my friend.'

'That'll be the only decent kinda food ye'll fine aroon here,' said Danny, giving Gordon a friendly pat on the back.

The 'greedy business world' – it's the standard narrative of our time. But it doesn't have to be that way. Business *has* the power to change, for the better. And if it does change, well, I'm convinced the results would be mind-blowing.

Chapter 16 – Bottom Up Leadership

Shrinks are like buses. You don't see one for 47 years and then five turn up at the same time.

'Come in.' It was the unmistakable, authoritative voice of Dr Ratner from within Meeting Room 3. Quite a welcoming committee awaited me. A semi-circle of student psychiatrists – two men and two women, none of whom could have been much over 25 years old. I made a beeline for the last remaining chair. The scene reminded me of the panel interviews that were commonplace on the University Milk Round when I was searching for my first job.

Dr Ratner was first to speak and clearly wanted to put me at ease.

'Good morning, Gib. A slightly less intimate setting this afternoon. I hope you don't mind if some of my PhD students join us.'

'Reminds me of the panel interview I had for my first job.' Damn, I'd done it again. Cracking stupid jokes would not be the best way to convince this 'panel' that it was time they were letting me get back home.

Thankfully, Dr Ratner chose to ignore me and continued on a round of introductions.

'We have on my right Claire and Robert, and to my left Alan and Rhona,' she said, gesturing at each student in turn.

The students gave a mumbled chorus of *good afternoons*. I nodded and smiled.

'Hi, everyone. Flattered by the turnout, to be honest.'

'Well, as I mentioned yesterday, these students are all doing postgraduate psychiatry degrees. They each have a keen interest in mental health in the workplace and are eager to hear a bit about your experiences first hand. We don't get too many senior business executives passing through Thomson and so we're seizing the opportunity that's presented itself.'

'Really? You surprise me. Perhaps they're just undiagnosed as yet,' I said with a bit of chuckle, 'or hiding it well from their employers.'

The students smiled at each other, but composed themselves again after a withering glance from Dr Ratner.

'You're referring to the stigma that still surrounds mental health in the workplace, Gib,' said Dr Ratner.

'Sort of. I sometimes think mild Asperger's could be an advantage to climbing the corporate ladder. God knows, I'm sure big business acts as something of a magnet for Asperger's sufferers.'

The students' scribbling paused as they exchanged glances, pens held static against their notebook pages. I was on a roll.

'I'm only half joking, actually. I mean, the ability to focus single-mindedly on the numbers, on the bottom line, on next quarter's results over and above just about everything and anything else'.

The scribbling began again, although I'd no way of reading anything they were writing – CYNICAL TENDENCIES, no doubt. One of the students, Claire, paused and was clearly gearing up to ask a question. A nod from Dr Ratner gave her the green light.

'It's not such an extreme view, to be honest,' she said. 'A recent book compared the brain scans of CEOs and psychopaths and discovered remarkable similarities.'

'Yeah, *The Psychopath Test*, right? Loved it. Who's the guy...?

'Ronson, wasn't it?' said Claire.

'Yeah, that's right – hilarious. Bet I have a few senior colleagues who could keep psychiatrists like you pretty busy!'

'You may well be right, Gib, but today we're focusing on you and your illness,' said Dr Ratner, cleverly swerving to avoid the pending rabbit hole. 'In fact, that's probably a good segue into what I wanted to cover this afternoon – the pressures you faced internally and whether you were under excessive stress. From our discussion, you'd spent many years trying to be, as I understand it, something of a change agent in your organisation.'

The students nodded knowingly, which made me think they'd been given a bit of reading homework to prep for this discussion.

'All right, no problem. So, pressures of the job? Well, I'd expect that most jobs in business nowadays come with their fair share of pressure. It goes with the territory, doesn't it? But it would be fair to say that the pressure I was experiencing in my role had gone up a notch or two after a reorganisation of the senior leadership ranks. Some of my biggest sponsors from the early days had either retired or left the company. Others got moved into different roles and no longer had any responsibility for our little not-for-profit startup. I got a new boss. A smart guy. He was nice and actually quite interested and supportive of what we were doing at first, but then got engrossed in his main role. He lacked the time to get to know and fully understand the specific quirks of our part of the organisation and the future potential for business to truly engage in the international development sector. I've found that trying to create and scale a startup social enterprise within a big company is a bit like playing snakes and ladders.'

'Ah'm no sure a follow yae, Gib,' said Alan, a beefy, red-haired chap and with an accent more Glaswegian than Billy Connolly.

'Well, in the early days it was all about getting buy-in and support for a big idea – a shared vision. The firm was great and I got huge interest and engagement from many of the top people, even though I was pretty junior at the time. It felt like landing on a square with a ladder that took me up a few rows. In the years that followed we made steady progress – rolled the dice, threw a few doubles – landed on a couple of snakes, which knocked us back a bit, but found more ladders than snakes. You know that exciting feeling when you think you're going to reach the final square first and win the game?'

'Makes sense,' said Alan, nodding. 'And then? Ye hit that dirty, great big snake that takes ye almost all the way back doon tae where ye started?'

'Exactly. Actually, it wasn't that bad, but it had got much, much, tougher. Each new reorganisation meant a new boss that had to be won over with arguments that I'd thought had been put to bed almost 10 years previously. I often joked that it felt a bit like we were fighting a corporate immune system.'

'Sounds like that film *Groundhog Day*,' said Robert, with a smile that soon morphed back into a more professional, serious expression.

'Indeed. I'd been focussing on climbing the biggest ladders I could find, but I seemed to be continually landing on snakes. No doubt this was taking its toll on me emotionally. Looking back, I'd not been at my happiest in the previous one to two years. Close friends would say I'd not really been my cheery, glass-half-full self.'

Dr Ratner walked to the window to half draw one of the dark blue NHS curtains. Some rare Glasgow sunshine was starting to dazzle her panel.

'I mentioned that your sister had been in contact with your HR Manager,' said Dr Ratner. 'Evidently, she's keen to know how you are doing. She wants me to probe as to whether you'd been under undue pressure at work or even felt bullied at any stage. Evidently your company has a strict code of conduct against that sort of behaviour.'

'Mmm... bullying. That's a tricky one to define, let alone prove. Bullying conjures up a traditional school playground context, where the bigger kid picks on smaller, more vulnerable kids. I was taught to stand up to bullies and would do, were it physical. I mean, I've practiced martial arts for over 20 years for Christ's sake. But emotional pressure is more difficult to deal with. There was this one guy, in particular. A tough, straight-talking German called Franck, who had a reputation for chewing people up. The "Executive Bullying Director," as I liked to call him. But to be fair, he probably wasn't that much more obnoxious than Donald Trump used to be in the average episode of *The Apprentice*.'

The students giggled to each other.

'Love that show,' said Alan, spontaneously, which earned him a scowl from Dr Ratner.

'You see, in the early years, our team was too small and insignificant to really matter all that much. We were working under the radar and also had the air cover of some very senior people in the firm, who were keen to see us succeed. We tended to get favours – the benefit of the doubt, you could say. In recent years, we'd grown much bigger and our head was above the proverbial parapet. We started to attract the attention of people like Franck, who is one of the top dogs in the firm. An internal reorganisation had meant we'd also lost some of that vital air cover and were exposed. It would be fair to say that Franck wasn't a massive fan of anything that didn't make profit. We had a couple of run-ins, which wasn't much fun, I have to admit.'

I paused and looked out of the window. For a moment, I wasn't in Thomson Psychiatric Ward, Glasgow. I was in Madrid.

Madrid, Spain. Six months previously

The plaque on the door says Room 5:34. I double-check the calendar invite in my diary before knocking on the door. Wait. I'm actually two minutes early. There is a small frosted-glass window on the door and through it I can just about make out a figure hunched over a laptop, head in his hands. Not a great omen for the half-hour slot I've got booked with Franck, the EBD – Executive Bullying Director. Franck was a small, wiry man with a brash manner – one of those 'doesn't suffer fools gladly' kind of people. The kind who make themselves feel big by making others feel small. Yes, arriving early would irritate Franck, but arriving late would be asking for his wrath. By the looks of it, he wouldn't need much of an excuse.

The iPhone tells me it's 11.15am sharp, so I knock firmly on the door.

'Yeah?'

'Hi, Franck. Is now still a good time for you?'

Franck doesn't look up or even budge. His gaze is fixed upon the laptop screen in front of him and his brow is furrowed. *This doesn't bode well for my short slot*, I think to myself.

'It's as bad a time as ever,' he replies in his usual gruff voice. 'Take a seat, but I've only got 10 minutes right now.'

Franck seems totally oblivious to my downcast expression at the news of our short meeting getting even shorter. He simply continues talking, although I'm not sure whether it was to himself, to me or to the computer screen.

'I just don't get it – we deliver seven per cent year-on-year growth and exceed the earnings guidance and still the share price dropped four per cent yesterday on close of trading. Bloody idiots.'

I sigh and shake my head, feigning empathy. After what seems like another couple of minutes, he eventually sits back in his chair and takes off his reading glasses, before placing both hands upon the desk.

'OK, Gib, I'm going to be very straight. That's how we Germans like to talk.'

Oh dear… this isn't going to be good. Brace yourself, Gib.

'Let me say up front that I love what you and your team do. Really, it's great.'

I've heard this kind of platitude from many of the senior leadership before – I wait for the 'but'.

'But…' Franck continued.

Here we go.

'I don't buy into this new strategy of yours; you have no mandate to implement it and you want to work in high-risk, non-strategic countries. To be perfectly honest, if I was an investor these past few years, I wouldn't have touched ADP with a barge pole.'

Imagine you've got a child, maybe 10 years old – the apple of your eye. Then some stranger turns round and says your kid's fat, ugly and will have zero life chances when they grow up. Sad as it may sound to all the loving parents amongst you, ADP was the closest thing I had to a child and I'd given everything to it for a large chunk of my career.

Franck sat back with his arms crossed. He was now awaiting my response – if I even dared. I slowly nodded my head and took a deep breath,

'Well, thanks for your honesty,' I said. 'At least we all know where we stand with you straight-talking Germans. The Scots also have a reputation for speaking their minds.'

Franck raised an eyebrow at what was clearly an unexpected show of defiance.

'We've built something that is unique in the consulting industry. Our clients are impressed; our competitors jealous,' I countered. If this sounds calm and brave, then don't be fooled – I was absolutely crapping myself.

Franck's eyes said it all. I could swear they'd turned a glowing, raging red. Business purpose, social impact, sustainability all seemed alien concepts. It was as if there was some Google Translate algorithm in Franck's brain that made him hear fluffy, do-goody, charity, bleeding-heart bullshit. I continued, regardless.

'Over 30,000 of our top performers are queuing up to work on our projects and, what's more, attrition rates are…'

'Am I speaking Chinese or something? You're not listening to me.'

'I'm listening, Franck. I'm just not agreeing with you.'

Ouch. Did I think that or say it? No, I actually *said* it. Unsurprisingly, the conversation went downhill from there. Maybe I should have kept my mouth shut and just nodded. How many other times had I not been sufficiently deferential to authority in my career? Would I be sitting in a fucking psychiatric hospital if I'd just played the game, toed the line, accepted the system and its protagonists the way it is?

But then, the way it is, quite simply, is wrong.

Silence would be compliance.

'You still with us, Gib?… Gib?'

Dr Ratner's voice jolted me from my daydream.

'Oops, sorry. Was a million miles away.'

'So how did Franck's behaviour make you feel?'

God, I thought, this line of questioning was straight out of the shrink–patient handbook. *Just go with it, Gib. They're only doing their job.*

'How did I feel? Pretty crap, to be honest. Disempowered. Frustrated by the fact that I seemed unable to convince him of the value of what we were doing.'

'Was Franck the main problem?' asked Rhona, the brunette with glasses.

'Yes and no. We also got confronted by legal, tax, compliance, security, you name it. My team bore the brunt of their endless checks, audits and bureaucracy. I remember having a very strong feeling that we were suffering a death of a thousand cuts and I was powerless to do anything. Good people were leaving our team out of sheer frustration or pressure. Much of the fun had gone out the job.'

There was a lengthy pause before Dr Ratner broke the silence.

'Anxiety, stress, depression and the impact of a really tough environment in the workplace are very real issues, Gib,' she said. 'We hear similar stories from many of the patients we see from the corporate world. These pressures can build up over time without you or anyone else realising it and it may have made you predisposed to some kind of incident like the one you had.'

I reckon I was in the meeting for about an hour, maybe more. The questions had continued. I'd tried to be as honest as I could, although I hadn't mentioned the fever I got in India and whether that could have triggered this whole episode. But we'll come to all that soon.

After the meeting I went straight to Room 17, kicked my shoes off and lay down on my small, single bed. I was exhausted, physically and mentally.

Am I speaking Chinese? ... speaking Chinese? ... Chinese? Chinese? Chinese?

Franck's words kept playing through my mind. Whether Chinese or not, something had been lost in translation. Franck was old school leadership. He'd climbed the ladder in the Business 1.0 world. He was programmed to have a single-minded focus on the business fundamentals – an entire career spent cutting cost, growing revenues, driving efficiency. What's the problem with that? you might ask. It certainly worked for him, and he'd reached the heady heights of the senior management ranks.

Both then and now, my strong sense, or at least hope, is that there's a new awareness, a new zeitgeist emerging amongst younger employees, bottom up, in large companies. They have grown up with far more exposure to issues such as the environment, climate change, chronic inequality and the like. They're far more engaged than previous generations – my generation, for example, who blindly followed the doctrine of business being solely about share price, cost reduction and revenue growth. Even today, challenging this received wisdom amounts to business heresy.

At its core, the problem is about leadership. Too many people believe leadership comes as the result of a promotion – or from a fancy job title on a business card. Not at all. Leadership is more of a mindset than a skillset. Leaders can emerge at all levels of an organisation, even low down. That's basically the whole thrust of the intrapreneurship movement – to inspire people towards purpose-driven innovation inside their organisation, regardless of their pay grade or whether they happen to be one of the lucky half dozen who sit within the CSR. Intrapreneurs can be anyone, anywhere.

I've heard people say, 'Oh, were I ever to become CEO, I'd of course make this change or that change.' Bullshit. Firstly, what percentage of us ever makes it to the very top? One per cent? More like 0.001 per cent if we're talking a Fortune Global 500 multinational. The second problem is what that 0.001 per cent do when they get there. Usually far too little, when it comes to moving the needle on sustainability, business ethics and purpose. No wonder trust in big business is at an all-time low. Granted, there are a few notable exceptions that prove the rule – not only Paul Polman of Unilever but also the likes Feike Sijbesma of DSM or Indra Nooyi of Pepsico, all of whom walk the talk on responsible business – but the fact remains that too many of today's CEOs are masquerading as COOs – Chief Operating Officers – each presiding over a very fiscally tight ship that they'll go to great lengths to avoid rocking or feel is simply too big to rock. They're ensuring quarterly earnings targets are met or, if that's failing, organising large share buy-backs to maintain share price, which in turn keeps them in their role. Premiership football managers are perhaps the one profession that has a higher turnover than a Fortune 500 CEO. No wonder they're paranoid.

I have learnt a lot about leadership from those above me, as well as many below me. Often it was through my mistakes from which I'd learn the most – god knows, there were plenty of them.

Chapter 17 – The Fourth Sector

Thomson Ward, Sunday evening. November 2014

How do you think the UN would go about building a Tesla? Or, put it another way, how do you think the UN would be run if Elon Musk, Tesla's entrepreneurial founder, took over as Secretary General? *Differently* is probably the best answer. Granted, it's a highly unlikely scenario, but these are the kinds of questions that go through your head when you've had four days of enforced digital detox.

Danny, Gordon and I had reconvened in the canteen for dinner and, after a quick debrief on the Dr Ratner meeting, I'd got us back onto my same favourite hobby-horse – rethinking the role of business in development. They seemed genuinely interested in the work I'd been doing and the relevance of their business knowledge to a more worthy cause than investment banking or accountancy. It was as if they were planning their next career move. Me? I was in my element. I decided to 'road test' my thinking on Elon Musk running the UN.

'Yeah, I've heard of Elon Musk and Tesla,' said Gordon. 'They've just opened a dealership near Edinburgh and one of my mates from the Bank has one. They go like shit off a shovel these electric cars.'

'So, go on, I'm sure you're going tae tell us how the UN would build a Tesla,' said Danny.

'Not very well, would be my opinion. They'd probably develop a bunch of goals with 15-year targets and hundreds of indicators that they'd fail to achieve.'

My sarcastic reference was to the Sustainable Development Goals created by the UN in 2015. There are 17 broad goals, 169 targets for these goals and 304 indicators that will measure compliance – all relating to Health, Education, Poverty, Peace and all the other things you'd expect would make the world a better place. Complex, right? But it's not a UN-specific problem – my issue is more with the way the whole aid and development sector is organised. It's been constructed to work in silos, whereas the issues tend to be in systems, or interconnected. Can you achieve success in education without having one eye on health or nutrition, for example? The current aid world is not dissimilar to the Command Economy of the Soviet Union in the 1980s. Central planners telling factories to make widgets of dubious quality and not in line with the needs, wants and preferences of consumers and the market – 'consumers', in the case of the UN, being poor and vulnerable citizens in developing countries. One NGO may be working on early childhood development in one country – another focused on tackling HIV/AIDS – different organisations will be looking at energy access, nutrition or rural livelihoods and so on. All too often they're not collaborating effectively, yet these issues are inextricably linked to one another. OK, I accept it's a complex arena, but I've long believed there has to be a better way of harnessing the benign power of market forces and channelling them for the public good.

'I'm still not sure how these UN goals link to your sports car analogy, mate,' said Danny, dunking yet another digestive biscuit into a cup of milky tea.

'My point is that if they used the same approach to make a Tesla, they'd no doubt set up a bunch of independent projects to make the wheels and the drivetrain; another set of projects to make tyres, the engine – and so on. How much these projects make of each would be determined, not by what was needed to make a good quality vehicle, but by which particular donor government was giving the money. And that will depend on whether they have a geo-political preference for wheels, tyres or engines.'

'Or, more likely, which of these helps to drive their foreign policy objectives in a particular region,' said Gordon, with a cynical smile.

'Right – sadly that's all too true. You can see that happening right now with the aid budgets in the UK and the US. The fundamental issue is that it's completely in the absence of what the overall "solution" or end result should be – and by "solution" I'm meaning the final design and business case for a completed electric car. Are you still with me?'

Silent nods gave me the green light to continue.

'Musk used a market-based model to achieve his dream of creating a high-end electric car as a practical business approach to addressing the issue of climate change. That was and is his mission. All electric cars at that point had been pretty crap and could only travel twice round the block on a single battery charge. Nobody wanted them. Musk's real skill was to innovate in line with the perceived needs of high-end customers for a better experience as they go from A to B, faster, more quietly, more ecologically. He knew they'd never fork out for an ugly box on wheels. So he went to the best designers to create a pleasing shape. His techies and engineers no doubt defined exactly the engine it needed, specs for the tyres, the wheels, the chassis, and then Musk integrated it all to produce a nice, gleaming new car. The result is the Tesla. All the way along that whole process of making his fancy new Tesla, there are literally thousands of little suppliers making bits and pieces that go into the car. One will make the door handles, another might make instrument gauges, steering wheels, all sorts of stuff. They're all part of the broader automotive ecosystem. Then, of course, the acid test is whether anyone buys your product or not. If they do, like Gordon's banker mate, the car company survives and perhaps even thrives. If people don't like what you've made, they don't buy it. What happens then? The company goes out of business of course. End of story, unlike the UN, the World Bank and co, who are able to continue indefinitely irrespective of the results achieved.'

'A bit like the nationalised British Leyland in the '70s who made crap cars that nobody wanted tae buy, but were kept afloat by government subsidy from the taxpayer,' said Danny.

'Exactly, and look what happened to them!' I agreed, 'OK, I admit to being a bit hard on the poor old UN, the World Bank and big NGOs. It's not their passion, values or commitment I'm questioning, just their execution ability.'

I took my tray and placed it on the rack before grabbing an instant coffee to take back to our table.

'So where are you going with all this building a Tesla stuff, Gib?' asked Gordon.

'Well, let's swap the word Tesla for that child in India that we discussed at lunchtime.'

'The five per cent of GDP that India is losing annually through kids dying or dropping out of school and the like?'

'Exactly, so how might Elon Musk tackle this challenge of educating the next generation in India, when there's a clear lack of state funding?'

'Beats me. An electric school bus, perhaps?' quipped Danny.

'Glad you've been really listening, Danny,'

'Daft twat,' said Gordon, punching his arm.

'Gimme a break, guys, I'm only joking with ye... It's interesting, really. So the answer is that he'd adopt a market-based approach, right?'

'Correct. Take a gold star.'

'Smartest kid in the loony bin. Well done, Danny.'

'Fuck off, Gordon! I'm not hearing any bright ideas from you.'

'Give me a chance, I think I get it now,' said Gordon, poised to continue as if a light bulb had just gone on in his head. 'So the $100 billion that India's losing could in effect be a market incentive for organisations to solve the problem?'

'Precisely,' I said, slamming my hand down on the table triumphantly.

'... and tools such as social impact bonds would be the financial instrument to turn that market incentive into an investment opportunity?'

'Very good.'

'But how would the bonds provide returns to investors?'

'Well, based on a set of indicators being achieved by a diverse ecosystem of players such as social enterprises, NGOs are everyday businesses – each would be contributing something to the goal of taking the child from birth to a healthy economically productive citizen 20 years in the future. It's analogous to the ecosystem of suppliers that Tesla works within. An independent assessment body like the UN or an NGO would determine if target indicators had been reached – you know, things like literacy rates, numeracy rates and so on. That's where the skills that auditors like you have could come in very useful, Danny.'

'I think I just about get it, but it's complex,' Danny said, leaning back in his chair and folding his arms.

Danny was right. It is complex. Not only do we need to radically rethink the way kids are educated in these countries and how it's funded, but the whole paradigm around globalisation needs a fresh pair of eyes. How can we continue to adopt national approaches to challenges that are inherently global in nature? Like ensuring India does have the resources to provide the world with the skills it will require in the future. To my mind, we need to fundamentally rethink how we educate the kids of tomorrow and explore the creation of a global talent pool in what has become a very interconnected, interdependent world. Can this realistically be achieved if we remain wedded to national budgets, national curriculums and a token bit of aid money? Or, take global health: America might spend $14k per capita annually on healthcare, whereas a country like Eritrea spends the equivalent of around 20 dollars on each of its poor citizens. In the past, we've never really cared much, or even known. It was *their* problem, not ours. But if a SARS or Ebola outbreak originates in Eritrea and their health system lacks the basic capacity to constrain it, then we're all fucked. I'm convinced we must open our minds to an entirely different way of thinking about these problems. Creating a new breed of 'hybrid' organisation tasked with solving social problems would be a noble future ambition of a recalibrated, redefined private sector. If they make a bit cash at the same time, that's fine by me. In fact, it's more like a whole new sector that's needed – one that blends the best of capabilities, approaches and know-how of business, government and NGOs (often referred to as the third sector). In ADP we coined the term 'The Fourth Sector'[1].

'Look, at the end of the day it's all about integrating different capabilities, from different organisations, into a common outcome.

1. 'Convergence Continuum: Towards a '4th Sector' in global development?', Gib Bulloch and Louise James, https://www.accenture.com/t20150523T022417__w__/us-en/_acn-media/Accenture/Conversion-Assets/DotCom/Documents/Global/PDF/Dualpub_1/Accenture-Convergence-Continuum-Global-Development.pdf

Very different from the current situation of a pilot here and a project there, effectively with all the players doing their own thing.'

'And the role of we financial services folks would be?' asked Gordon.

'To find new financial instruments such as social impact bonds to attract private investment, entrepreneurship and innovation into delivering what are essentially public goods.'

'Good luck with that, Gordon,' said Danny.

Don't get me wrong, I'm no free market fundamentalist. Nor do I see the private sector as being a panacea for all the world's problems. God knows, business, particularly the big guys, have a lot to answer for in terms of what's caused some of the problems in the first place. But I have been an unashamed advocate of a very different role for business and that it could and should be part of the solution – the notion that social challenges could be business opportunities in disguise. However new thinking, new business models and a new purpose-driven sub-economy would be required to achieve them – that's what we meant by this term 'The Fourth Sector'.

NGO X Global Leadership Meeting, Berkshire, UK. Sometime around 2011

I'd quite often be asked to give talks to the management of different international development charities. The brief tended to be 'challenge our thinking and be a bit provocative'. All credit to some of these progressive CEOs who invited me along to speak to their teams. At times I felt like a bit like Daniel in the Lion's Den. But I'd like to think I'd earnt their trust – that they felt I was on their side. Maybe also a thorn *in* their side. Challenging them to engage with the private sector in new and different ways – beyond just taking passive donations.

On one such occasion, I'd been invited to speak to the top 100 managers of a large international NGO who'd come into the UK from all around the world. I was on my standard script about the size and scale of multinationals.

How many customers does Nestlé serve each day? Answer: a staggering 1.4 billion.

How many litres of water does it take to produce a single litre of Coca-Cola? Answer: 253 litres. Three litres for the liquid and a further 250 litres to grow the sugar cane to make it sweet. Intriguing, don't you think?

I'd offer multiple-choice answers and usually most would guess wrongly and be suitably surprised by the correct answer. My basic point was that these multinationals are a bit like supertankers – even a small nudge in the right direction can have a massive impact downstream. I'd end with a slightly impertinent question.

'Who has had the biggest impact on poverty in Kenya over the past five years?'

a) The United Nations

b) NGO X (My pseudonym for the well known global charity I was speaking to)

c) Vodafone

'Let's have a show of hands for A. No one. Poor old United Nations. OK, what about B?'

Two hands went up, sheepishly.

'Really? Am I in the wrong place? I thought you all worked for NGO X? Is ending poverty not a big part of your stated mission?'

Some nervous laughter in the audience.

'OK, hands up for C, Vodafone?'

Of course, 98 other hands went up.

'Why do you believe that?'

'For all their work on mobile banking and "mHealth",' came a voice from the middle of the audience.

'OK, fair enough. Well the answer is…'

I'd give a bit of a pause before clicking to transition to the next slide – a great big question mark symbol!

'To be honest, I have absolutely no idea which of these organisations has had the greatest impact on poverty in Kenya. But I'm interested that almost all of you believe that it's Vodafone.'

This would be greeted by a mixture of groans and smiles from the audience.

'My point is this: how might that influence the way you partner with corporates like Vodafone in the future?'

Yes, I know what you're thinking. Nobody likes a smart arse and sure, I'd definitely risked appearing like one. But I felt it was worth it to make the point that innovative partnerships with the private sector could drive new breakthroughs in their important work on the ground.

To be fair, in ADP we also tried to practise what we were preaching. Remember me mentioning one of our flagship projects with African NGO AMREF in Kenya – the one that used eLearning to train thousands of nurses faster and cheaper than could be done in the traditional classroom? Well, a spin-off project was launched with Vodafone's subsidiary in Kenya, Safaricom. The gist of it was to extend the nurses' training programme to many thousands of Community Health Workers (CHWs) in rural parts of sub-Saharan Africa. We helped create a new mobile platform – think WhatsApp but dedicated to sending health messages. Using Safaricom's mobile network, we were able to get vital health information out to CHWs in the field and receive back all kinds of data on patients and their symptom. Pretty cool, eh?

We chose AMREF / Safaricom as one of our flagship projects when Bill Green decided he wanted to see our work on the ground.

'Maybe you and me should go on a road trip sometime, Gib,' said Bill in his Jack Nicholson–esque drawl.

'Would love to, Bill. But there might not be roads in the places I'd like to take you.'

'A road trip without roads. I like that.'

I suspect he had more time on his hands since taking on the role of Chairman, and he started to take a keen interest in ADP. Within six months, Bill and a small entourage of his Executive staff were bound for Kenya – on his Learjet. Yes, I know, not really in keeping with the development sector. Sander van 't Noordende came too, and for a moment it seemed like we were undergoing a new renaissance of leadership support. Visits to a couple of projects in neighbouring Tanzania proved to be a great success, and the finale was a meeting with the AMREF leadership team in Nairobi, to see first hand the success of the eLearning programme. An impromptu practical demonstration of the nurses' newly acquired gynaecological prowess involving a prosthetic torso proved almost too much for poor Bill. His face was a picture.

However, he subsequently said it had been one of the best and most interesting business trips of his 30-plus-years Accenture career. Then, almost in the same breath, he told me that he'd be retiring from the firm at the end of the year. Damn. Another one bites the dust. There was something about the nature of ADP's work that seemed to attract senior leadership as they entered the twilight of their careers. People often want to 'give back' when they've reached the top. I've always disliked the term 'giving back'. Begs the question what they stole in the first place, don't you think? Yes, leadership epiphanies amongst the 50- and 60-somethings are commonplace in many businesses. We need more epiphanies to take place amongst the 20- and 30-somethings: the so-called 'Millennials'. That's the demographic who have the most productive and influential years of their career lying *ahead* of them as opposed to clinging to the laurels of past glories. They've got the least to lose and the most to gain from a profound change in the role of the corporation in society. It just takes a bit of courage to take that first step away from the herd.

Personally, I could never have imagined the bizarre and surreal encounters I would have on my own intrapreneurial journey. None more so than the one I'm about to share with you.

Chapter 18 – Tipping Point

Sofitel Hotel, Haymarket, London. July 2013

Think of the most bizarre meeting of your career. Then double it.

ADP had been approached by a senior figure in Tony Blair's Africa Governance Initiative (one of the former UK Prime Minister's business and charitable activities that is now part of the Tony Blair Institute for Global Change). He was keen to explore ways in which we might help the Myanmar government's transition towards democracy, by strengthening the capabilities of a very inexperienced civil service.

I came to London for what I thought was a routine planning meeting in a Piccadilly hotel basement and found myself sitting opposite the entire government of Myanmar (Burma). Blair and President Thein Sein of Myanmar sat in throne-like armchairs on a platform at one end of the room. Down one wall sat two rows of the Myanmar Cabinet – all men and, no doubt, former Generals. Three lonely figures sat opposite them: Blair's Chief of Staff, her deputy and, you guessed it, *moi*.

'I'm delighted to have Gib Bulloch from Accenture, the large management consulting business, with me, who is kindly donating his services on a pro bono basis,' said Blair.

I smiled and nodded. No, ADP weren't about handouts or giving stuff away. However, on this occasion I'd made an exception, given the mouth-watering prospect of playing an impactful role at such a critical stage in Myanmar's transition to democracy. It was a decision that, in time, would have far-reaching and unforeseen consequences for ADP's future.

Back in 2013, Myanmar was a rich country full of poor people. It was at ground zero when it came to economic development – three quarters of the population didn't even have access to electricity and less than 10 per cent had a mobile phone. I saw it as a blank canvas to pilot some of our more innovative ideas. Could the base stations for a new mobile phone network be used to generate electricity in off-grid rural areas? What new possibilities would emerge for rural health and education. I even wondered if we might take the learnings from our health logistics project with Coca-Cola, or the Community Health Worker training in Africa, into Myanmar. The possibilities seemed endless and, what's more, we had a team working on the ground in Yangon, the capital of Myanmar, to develop the strategy. It was about that time that the proverbial wheels came off. An email landed in my inbox, which read something like this:

Gib.

What the hell are we doing in Myanmar? Why are we there working for free? That's not your mandate. Call me.

Franck

Short and to the point. That was Franck's preferred style. However, this time he seemed to be really pissed off. It was serious. Ordinarily, a former head of state putting a call in to your CEO to praise the work your team's been doing would be a good thing. However, Mr Blair's call with Pierre sent hares running left, right and centre, as he'd no idea we were doing anything in Myanmar. Suddenly we got a lot of unwanted attention. We were exposed, and I knew it.

The canteen door opened with a bang.

'Ah, there yeez are. Might have known yood all be gabbing away in here,' said Agnes, one of the night supervisors. 'I need yoozlot doon at the dispensary counter for yer pills. Ye shid ha' been there ten minutes ago.'

'Oops, sorry Agnes. Totally lost track of time.'

'Yeah and after that, I'm heading off to ma bed,' said Danny.

'You're right, Danny-boy, it's getting late,' I said, leaning back in the chair and stretching my arms wide behind my head.

'It's pretty interesting stuff, to be honest, Gib', said Gordon. 'Certainly plenty to reflect on.'

The three of us wandered down the corridor to the open space and went through the standard ritual of visiting the counter one by one. I then said goodnight to the boys and some of the other patients in the TV room before going back to my bedroom.

I really hoped I hadn't completely bored the boys with my lofty ideas and *ideals* on how to transform the development sector. It had been quite cathartic to have an engaged audience actually willing to listen. I'd spent more time in one evening with these relative strangers explaining my ideas than I'd spent with my new boss in almost a year. Ironic really, given he'd have probably been interested, had he not had too many things on his plate.

Myanmar had given the team and me a lot of headaches – but it was just a symptom of a far deeper, underlying problem. The fact that I seemed to have lost my ability to persuade a new crop of leaders of ADP's full potential – that the inherent risks of working collaboratively with our clients in such places were manageable and worth the rewards. I felt like I was being stretched like a giant elastic band – pulling upwards was the latent potential for Accenture, with and through our clients, to really move the needle on some of these big ideas and impact the lives of millions. Pulling downwards was my frustration at the lack of engagement and support. It wasn't a sustainable position. I was losing my confidence and losing some of the best members of my team simultaneously. Something had to change, and fast.

NIGHT V

Mental Break~~down~~through

'Here's to the ones who dream,
Foolish as they may seem'
Mia, The Audition, *La-La Land*

Chapter 19 – Time to Retreat

Kota Kinabalu, Borneo. Late October 2014

I'd never really seen myself as a workaholic. But then, that's no doubt true of most workaholics and, indeed, alcoholics too. The first step of the cure is to admit you have a problem, right? In hindsight, the retreat in India with Leaders' Quest couldn't have come at a better time for me. I was knackered, frustrated and badly in need of a break. As luck would have it, I'd managed to take two weeks off prior to the retreat so that I'd have a chance to unwind – to recharge the proverbial batteries. Well, that was the plan. The first week I spent in the Philippines with my mate Yunus for some R&R – more Rowdy & Raucous than Rest & Relaxation, but hey, it was fun. The second week, spent on my own in Borneo, was a chance for some proper rest before heading off to Jaipur, India, for the Retreat.

Turn to Camera

Yunus Jaleel is a good friend of mine who I met during my MBA year in Glasgow back in 1992. He's a second generation Indian who grew up in North London – not to be confused of course with Professor Muhammad Yunus, who I mentioned earlier during the Davos encounter. I can't resist sharing a story of the time when Yunus (Jaleel) visited me in Geneva. I mentioned to a young couple I know, who also worked in international development, that Yunus was in town. Would they like to join us for a dinner?

Unbeknown to me and by complete coincidence, Professor *Muhammad* Yunus happened to be paying a visit to Geneva at exactly the same time. My friends had heard about this in the news and showed up in

---

their smartest clothes, excited about the prospect of an intimate private dinner with the famous Nobel Laureate. To say they looked a bit downcast at the sight of my Indian friend from Dollis Hill would be an understatement.

So what was this Leadership Retreat all about? Well, I'd describe Leaders' Quest as providing an immersion experience for senior executives – to unplug them, literally and metaphorically, from their day jobs. It's a social enterprise founded by the charismatic Lindsay Levin – a woman on a mission to change attitudes in the boardroom. She and her small team organise retreats in different parts of the world; many in India, but also in China, Africa and even the Middle East. The aim is not to teach per se. More to take business leaders out of their normal day-to-day cocoons and expose them to another side of life. Meetings with senior politicians, heads of NGOs, trade union leaders and the like, would be interspersed with moments of personal reflection and discussions with peers. I'd experienced one of their Quests several years previously, travelling from South Africa to Mozambique, and found it to be a powerful model – but the Indian gig was going to be a much bigger affair. There would be about 100 of us attending from all around the globe.

So, back to Borneo. I'd managed to unplug from work and email for most of the break. There's a macho bullshit culture in much of big business that dictates that one should always check in for urgent emails, even when on a break. And we wonder why burnouts are now endemic? No, fuck that! I worked hard enough the rest of the year and was a strong advocate for people taking proper breaks. That said, I'd scheduled a prep call with Gene Early from Leaders' Quest who was leading the cohort I'd been assigned to. He wanted to have a one-on-one check-in with each of the 10 members of his group in advance of the retreat, to understand where they were at in their lives and careers. I took the call lying flat on my back on a king-size bed in my hotel in Kota Kinabalu, on the northwest tip of Borneo.

'So, what is it you want to get out of this retreat?' said the warm and inviting voice on the other end of the phone. 'Help me under-stand more about where you're at in your career and life in general, Gib.'

I have to say, there's something very cathartic about pouring your heart out to an inquisitive, empathetic stranger. Poor Gene got both barrels. He got the history of our little startup – all the stuff I've been sharing with you. I gave him the motivations, the elations and the frustrations, together with an ambitious vision for the future, a vision that had become very clear in my mind – like a blurred image in a camera lens gradually shifting into sharp focus. Gene seemed to like the story, but I also explained to him that I'd had less success con-vincing some of Accenture's leadership – how I felt I'd lost my mojo.

Gene was insightful with his feedback and suggestions.

'Have you read *The Hero's Journey* by Joseph Campbell?' he asked.

I'd never heard of it. It's evidently a seminal book on leadership and he recommended it highly. My challenges and frustrations were not that unique. He'd encountered plenty of people over the years who'd been in a similar place in their careers and in their life jour-neys. I should use the time in India to speak to others and develop my plan of action. Sound advice.

Rajasthan Desert, India. Early November 2014

I flew to Jaipur via Singapore on the Saturday night and was met by my driver holding up a handwritten sign that read 'Bullucks' in large letters. Well, near enough, I suppose. I've had worse. The taxi journey was about one-and-a-half hours to the retreat venue – an amazing former Maharaja's Palace set high in the hills of the Thar Desert in Rajasthan. The last few kilometres saw us wind up through small villages and the road became ever bumpier with kamikaze scooter riders swerving to avoid us, or a stray cow meandering along the middle of the road. When we finally arrived, it was a surreal, almost magical experience. There had been a wedding on earlier and so there were dancers adorned in flowing saris and men from the village in traditional dress riding elephants out through the large entrance gates to the palace. It felt like I'd just rocked up at a casting for the next Bollywood Blockbuster.

Then there were the steps. An endless set of wide, stone steps covered in candles and rose petals stretched all the way up to the flood-lit palace, a bit like Disney's Magic Kingdom. This felt like a special place. A spiritual place. This was going to be an interesting week.

The next morning, over breakfast, we were handed our itineraries for the coming week. The days would start with optional mindfulness sessions or yoga, lots of time in group discussions, then feasts and music in the evenings. I've always been a bit cynical about the whole yogi spiritual thing, but I was determined to go with the flow and venture outside my comfort zone. To be honest, I'd been cruising along there for far too long and was, in fact, open to a good kick in the backside.

After breakfast, it was time for the first breakout session in our groups and an opportunity to meet Gene in person. He turned out to be a tall man with piercing blue eyes and a friendly smile, who greeted me with a bear hug, just like a long-lost friend. Gene assembled our ten-person cohort into a circle and invited us to all hold hands and close our eyes to create the energy of the circle. I was certainly out of my comfort zone, but I stuck with it.

That first evening, as special entertainment, we were taken on a short bus ride to an open-air venue set out in the enchanting desert wilderness of Rajasthan, with majestic mountains, trees and rocky cliffs as a backdrop. There were numerous fire pits that took the chill out of the cool evening and lots of fabulous food. An Indian band provided the musical score and then a traditional Indian Sufi dancer, whose very special performance promising a fusion of music, dance and Rumi poetry, strode majestically onto the stage. As her finale, the dancer began to rotate gracefully, arms aloft, in a traditional whirling dervish spin – she whirled at great speed for 10 solid minutes. I was totally mesmerised and by the time she eventually stopped, I thought I was going to throw up on her behalf. But she calmly walked down some steps and off stage without a hint of dizziness. Truly mind-blowing[1].

For the Monday, we'd been given a choice of different day trips ranging from social enterprises combatting child trafficking through to rural livelihood programmes. I signed up to visit a small village, half a day's drive into the foothills of the Aravalli Range. Most of the men from the village are migrant workers – off building the World Cup stadium in Qatar, or the latest monolith in Dubai, earning a few dollars a day for their efforts, no doubt. As a result, the women have taken things into their own hands where education for their kids is concerned and improving livelihoods to feed them. I could never have anticipated the welcome we'd receive on arrival. I mean, I'd like to think that we know a little about hospitality in my native Scotland and give a warm welcome to visitors, but this was on a different scale. Over 300 of the village women and a handful of the remaining men came out to greet us, all dancing, beating drums and showering us in rose petals and garlands. We were celebrities, and it was quite overwhelming. I felt a tug at my arm from behind me and turned to catch a glimpse of a grey haired old woman smiling as the frenzied crowd jostled all around. As I pulled my hand back I discovered a bright orange thread had been tied around my wrist. We then gathered in the shade of a large tree on the outskirts of the village and the men amongst us, including me, had turbans wrapped around our heads. Women were given saris and garlands of flowers. We sat and listened to some of the village women and young girls talk about the progress they'd made in improving the yields of their crops and milk production from the cows. And how they'd invested much of the proceeds into improving the local school and the quality of teaching. It was really inspiring stuff.

After a bit of dancing, we split into smaller groups of two or three people and were taken into some of the homes to jointly cook a meal. This really was biblical stuff, worthy of any Charlton Heston film. Mud floors, open fires, grain from the store ground on an ancient millstone before being fashioned into chapattis and cooked on an open wood fire. This was genuine hospitality from people

---

1. 'Realms of DanceTM – Leaders Quest', performance by Zia Nath, Samode, Rajasthan. https://www.youtube.com/watch?v=pok_XoWHG1s#action=share

who had so very little but were willing to give so much. So when it came to eating the vegetable curry that they'd prepared, I couldn't bring myself to refuse. Looking back, I wonder if that was the decision that would lead to the worst fever of my life. Who knows.

The rest of the retreat was a mixture of uplifting plenaries and some interesting breakout groups. I even attended a couple of the mindfulness sessions and learnt, to my surprise, that my feet were rooted deep into Mother Earth, or 'Gaia' as they called her, and my head was attached by a long chord pulling it up to the sky. Well, who'd have thought it, eh? Perhaps it was the idyllic surroundings, or perhaps the mindfulness was having an effect on me, but I've seldom felt so close to nature – its true magnificence. I've since learnt they call this 'Oneness'.

If I were to single out the one thing that had the most profound effect on me, it would be the Sufi dancing workshop run by Zia Nath, the traditional dancer we'd watched on the first night. There had been a list of options to choose from; new approaches to climate change, impact investing or *Stillness through Motion – Introduction to Sufism Workshop*. Well, it was a no-brainer for me and apparently for others, too, given the popularity of the class. It's not often you see a bunch of middle-aged (mostly) blokes sitting around cross-legged in a circle, eager to learn how to dance!

We heard a bit more about the Sufi philosophy, which is basically the mystic side of Islam, based on the teachings of Rumi, a 13th-century Persian poet, scholar and theologian. He and his followers evidently spent decades reading philosophy, writing poetry and whirling themselves into a state of transcendent consciousness until they ultimately saw 'the face of God'. Well, we're all entitled to believe what we want, aren't we? Theory over, it was now time to put it all into practice. Zia explained the preparatory rituals – a deep bow, then arms rise up in the air, before being lowered slowly to the horizontal, palms facing inwards like mirrors. The trick was to focus your gaze directly at the palm of your hand and, given that it was turning at the same speed as your body, you'd avoid dizziness – in theory. Zia started the music and invited us to try it for ourselves, just slowly to begin with. We could stop and sit at the side if we got tired or dizzy. I started quite gingerly, left foot over right, fixing my gaze and my concentration into my palm. I'm no dancer, but I've done a lot of martial arts in the past[2] and this meant I'd got pretty good balance. Slowly the room started turning, becoming increasingly blurred as I picked up speed. The outstretched arms acted as counterweights for one another and seemed to give increased momentum to my spin. Faster and faster I went, eyes still focused on the surface of my right palm, surrounded by a blur of other bodies and walls blended into one. What if I spun into someone and knocked them out? How do I actually stop myself whirling? I was starting to feel like I was going into a trance, arms flowing slowly up and down as the music ebbed and flowed, meanwhile my body spinning faster and faster, yet with that stillness at the core. Just like a spinning top or coin: when it's spinning at its fastest it appears almost stationary. Faster, faster. Arms out, head back. OK, this was getting a bit scary. I wanted to stop but my mind seemed unable to tell my body how to do that. In the end, I threw myself to the floor and landed with a loud thud. I'd been the last man standing and was told by one of my colleagues afterwards that he'd seen me spin twice as fast and for twice as long as anyone else. It had been a profound sensation and, judging by the murmurings as we left the hall, others had found the same.

So, all in all, the Retreat had been time well spent and I was glad I went. I left with many good memories, lots of food for thought and a whole load of fascinating new friends. Gene had given me another bear hug as we left and we both promised to keep in touch. However, it was the Sufi spinning that really stuck in my mind and the weird feeling I had as I left the workshop. I hadn't experienced anything quite like it before. No, I hadn't seen the face of God, but I may have unwittingly set in motion a sequence of events that would rapidly spin out of control.

2. Zhuan Shu Kuan Chinese Kickboxing, Gib's home club in London for many years. http://www.zsk-chinesekickboxing.com

Geneva, Switzerland. Mid-November 2014

I had the weekend to recover before returning to work. Within just two short days, reality would set in and I'd be up to by neck in emails and fighting fires once again. But I felt, well... if you'll excuse the expression... 'energised' by the whole retreat experience. For most people it had been a journey to find one's personal purpose in life. But for me it was a little different. I feel like I've known my own purpose for many years now. I know that the rest of my career will be spent challenging the role of business in society – to do everything in my power to change a broken capitalist system, from the inside out. What the Leaders' Quest folks had given me was the strength and energy to tackle the current challenges I was facing head on; to raise my game and aspire to be the leader that my team deserved. Whether I liked it or not, I knew in my heart that one way or another, things would have to come to a head soon. But I hadn't quite realised just how soon.

I'd relocated from London to Geneva, Switzerland, in January 2011 as part of an effort to grow our business with the Swiss-based international organisations like the Red Cross and The Global Fund. If you've ever flown into Geneva airport, you'll have no doubt been exposed to a gauntlet of advertising on either side of the moving walkways which lead to the baggage reclaim. From my experience, the illuminated hoardings promote only two things – private banking and wealth management services or exclusive watches. 'You never actually own a Patek Philippe. You merely take care of it for the next generation,' is one of my favourites. You're damn right I won't own one – I'm not paying 30 grand for a watch!

Each time I pass through the airport I reflect on how Red Cross or World Health Organization employers must feel returning form a war zone to be met by these adverts. The juxtaposition is a stark reminder of the inequality in today's world – as if one were needed.

As it turned out, I'd returned from India with a bit more than happy memories and a renewed sense of purpose. I'd felt a little unwell, a little feverish for a few days, but told myself it was nothing more than a minor dose of the flu. But it got progressively worse. I'd hardly eaten in three days and when I sat in one client meeting with a shirt that was soaked through with sweat, it did occur to me that I probably shouldn't have made the trip to the office.

By 11pm that evening I was feeling like death warmed up – oh, and then cooled down again, warmed up again and so on. The fever oscillated between sweats and severe shivers. In sheer desperation, I called the emergency paramedic and a young Swiss doctor showed up within half an hour. He took my temperature then turned the electronic thermometer screen to face me with a pensive smile: 40 degrees C... That's over 106 Fahrenheit in old money. He gave me a few tablets to take and helped me to bed. I can honestly say that the eight hours that followed were probably about the worst in my life. I tried to sleep, but given I was lying in sweat-soaked bed sheets, duvet and pillows, sleep just wasn't happening. And then there were the cold shivers. I've never before experienced uncontrollable spasms in my body like it. Legs and arms were shaking violently. Even my teeth were chattering. I was counting down the minutes until the next paramedic visit at 8am, which felt like a lifetime away. There I was, all 90kg of fat, bone and muscle (in that order), reduced to a quivering lump of grease on the bed. I was a sorry sight.

I survived to tell the tale, obviously. But though the fever had subsided, my brain was still on fire. Something had changed. Something had awoken within me.

And then it all started, just a few days later. Exactly what I don't know, but I would describe it as an energy; some kind of creative flow. The darkness in my bedroom told me it was nowhere near time to get up. It was 4.05am and I was wide awake. Indecision and hesitancy had been replaced by a feeling of absolute single-minded clarity and resolve. I started to voice my thoughts out loud. Throughout the night and for the next several days, as if in a trance, I would record my ideas, dictating them into my iPhone. My first thought came in a flash of clarity. Now was the time. I needed to go directly to the top – to write to Pierre, the French CEO, and ask him to help save our precious little business that was slowly dying. Going over the heads of my direct bosses would be dangerous and could put me in some trouble. *Grow a pair, Gib. You have no choice*, said my conscience.

With barely any hesitation, I spoke for 10 minutes into the phone – then switched it off and rolled onto my side to make another attempt at sleep. But it was to no avail. The second thought that flooded over me was equally bold and clear: I would have to be prepared to resign if I couldn't get the backing for our new vision. My hand fumbled in the dark until it found the iPhone again, then I began to dictate my own resignation letter. No, I didn't want to resign. But the very fact that I was willing to walk away was cathartic. As if someone had just taken a sledgehammer to the chains that were binding my feet.

I'm not sure just how little I slept that night. One hour, maybe two max? Yet in the morning I didn't feel tired in the slightest. I plugged my headset into my iPhone and typed up the note to Pierre on my laptop while munching some muesli. I'd promised myself I wouldn't leave home until I'd sent it. But when it came to the crunch, I was hesitating. I sat in front of the screen with my finger poised nervously over the 'send' key. Then my phone rang. Saved by the bell.

It was Bjorn, my Norwegian career counsellor who was calling to give me my annual performance rating for last year. With all the holiday, illness and insomnia of the last few days and weeks, it had completely slipped my mind that it was 'that time of year again'. These were never good conversations. I got on fine with Bjorn on a personal level. He was a decent bloke. But I knew he had no idea of what I got up to on a day-to-day basis. I doubt anyone in the firm really had, come to think of it.

'Hey, Gib, it's Bjorn. How are you? I just wanted to let you know your rating for last year.'

I had known what my rating would be before the year had even begun, but I played along.

'Oh, really, Bjorn. Tell me, what might it be this year?'

'You're, er, well, a three-minus again, Gib. I fought for you as hard as I could in the ratings meeting but, you know, it's a very high-calibre peer group that you're up against.'

That was just the gentle nudge that I needed. With a wry smile, I hit 'send'. I had gone straight to the top – over both my career counsellor and boss's heads in a game of high-stakes poker. My fate was now out of my hands.

Whoosh – Message Sent.

Chapter 20 – Pandora's Laptop

Ever had someone give you a piece of good news that should have made you very happy but instead made you a little sad and unsettled? Well that's the feeling I had when Tony approached me at breakfast to let me know that this would be my last day in the Thomson Ward. He'd asked if I could come to see him in the staff office after I'd finished my plate of cold, soggy toast and drunk my tea. The wink was a bit of a giveaway, to be honest.

'So, Gib, do you want the good news or the good news?' he said, smiling like the Cheshire Cat.

'Just the good news would be fine, thanks, Tony.'

'Well, Dr Ratner thinks you're making such good progress that she's recommended you be let out tomorrow.'

'You mean I've got to leave this place and all you guys? No way!'

Tony's face froze for a moment and then the smile came right back when he realised I was being my usual sarcastic self.

'Ah, always the joker,' he said, playfully punching my arm. 'You had me going for a minute there. I've already contacted your parents and they'll be driving from Bute to pick you up tomorrow morning.'

'Seriously, Tony, that's great news. I mean, thank God I'm getting out. I really appreciate everything you've done for me.'

I tried to sound sincere, but my voice betrayed the feelings of a boy trying to feign gratitude for an unwanted Christmas present. Don't get me wrong – I had no great desire to hang around any longer than I needed to in a psychiatric ward – yet I'd found the experience incredibly therapeutic, in a bizarre way. I hadn't had to think about anything. All my meals were prepared for me; I'd met some interesting people – in all senses of the word. Most of all, I'd been forced to completely unplug from the world of email, Twitter, Facebook and WhatsApp. I can see now how people can easily become institutionalised.

But my newly discovered Zen peacefulness would be shattered sooner than I thought.

'The other bit of good news is that I'm allowed to give you back your briefcase and mobile phone.'

'Really? In here?'

'Yeah, when a patient has been deemed fit for release, then they're deemed fit to use their phone, too. So, here you go,' Tony said, handing my briefcase and iPhone over the desk.

Now this was indeed big news. My enforced digital detox hadn't done me any harm, but I knew that my iPhone and computer held important information about what I'd been experiencing in the days leading up to being hospitalised. Memories that were a bit hazy, no doubt due to the copious quantities of Diazepam they'd been giving me. I thanked Tony and quickly scurried back to Room 17, reunited with my possessions, like a lion dragging its prey back to its den. A quick press of the magic thumbprint and then *whoosh*, the screen sprang to life with the message, 'Warning: Low Battery Charge'. My hand scrambled around the bottom of my briefcase until I found the charger – my 'life support machine'. Then went straight into the 'voice recorder' app and, sure enough, there they were. A comprehensive audit trail of my thoughts, ideas, hopes and dreams recorded at all times of day and night, spanning a period of about a week. Some recordings lasted only five or six minutes, others much longer. Was I really ready to revisit what were probably the weirdest few days of my life? What if I discovered some uncomfortable truths, like that I had indeed really lost the plot? Could I handle that?

I kicked off my shoes, lay back on my bed and plugged in my headphones. It was time to find out.

Turn to Camera

If you've stayed with me this far in my little story, then let me thank you for your perseverance. What I've shared with you until now is pretty much my recol-

---

lection of events as they happened. From childhood, to adulthood, I've tried to represent the facts as I saw them.

This next section is different. It was the hardest part of the book to write. Why? Because I wasn't really myself. Believe me, revisiting a manic episode where you apparently lose the plot is actually quite scary. Some bits of the phone recordings I recognised – others were like it was someone else talking, using my voice. Whatever it was that I was experiencing, it felt very, very real. I want you to feel what I felt – what I thought – what I did and why. As much as possible. I'm sharing the series of events in the few days leading up to going into hospital as accurately as possible, recognising that I'm piecing together the jigsaw puzzle as much for myself as I am for you. So, if you're sitting comfortably, then we'll begin. Here's my best guess at what was going through my head at the time.

So what did I uncover in this little treasure trove of recordings? A whole mixture of things, actually. Some recordings were dictations – notes that I'd intended to type up and send to colleagues, clients, friends or family. Others captured ideas, observations, thoughts, hopes or dreams that I'd found inspiring at the time. There were a few 'notes to self' – like *Spend more time visiting the Wrinklies as they're not getting any younger. Phone your friends more often.* The recordings had started in Geneva and continued night and day throughout a trip back to my parents' home on the Isle of Bute, which accounts for the fact that I was lying in a psychiatric hospital in Scotland, not in Switzerland. Now *that* would have been even more weird.

As I've mentioned, the Scottish trip was triggered by the death of Mowatti's dad on the Friday. Mowatti called close friends to break the news, and I got on the plane the next day. It was a perfect opportunity to visit my parents. Perhaps I was becoming increasingly aware of their mortality. Guilt is never a good motive. But I'm getting ahead of myself. We'll come to all of that.

As I lay in the solitude of Room 17 of the Thomson Ward, I started listening to the recordings in chronological order, piecing together some kind of sequence of events leading up to being hospitalised. The first night's recordings had been my resignation letter and the cry for help to Pierre. I opened my computer and checked MS Word and sure enough, there was the file *resignation.doc* sitting in 'recently opened'. I re-read it for amusement. Quite a plaintive missive, I have to admit – a bit like a jilted boyfriend writing a breakup note. It's not you, it's me – that sort of thing. Come on, we've all been there. Now here's a worrying statistic – my relationship with Accenture had lasted many times that of my longest relationship with any woman. Probably because every woman I'd ever known had felt she'd played second fiddle to my work and, of course, my little baby, ADP. They had a fair point and admitting that here, now, is, I suppose, my way of saying sorry.

I then checked my Outlook mailbox sent folder and sure enough, there was that email to Pierre. From memory, there were three paragraphs of digital Semtex that went something like this:

Pierre,

I need to ask your help and I know you will listen, as you have done before. It should only take 2 mins of your time, when you have the time.

We're at a critical phase in ADP's 12-year evolution – an inflexion point to use the jargon… and frankly the trajectory is downwards. I badly need your help to flip the switch if we possibly can. I'm haemorrhaging some of my most talented staff – amongst the very best in the firm – through sheer frustration in their roles or for more attractive opportunities outside the firm… there's a belief that elements of the leadership do not share our vision and are not up for backing us on the next stage of our journey. We are dying a slow death of a thousand cuts and it breaks my heart to watch something which I've invested most of my Accenture career into building, fall apart around about me… and I can't go on like that. Something needs to change.

So all I'm asking for is a 30-minute slot – 60 mins if you feel generous, to include a chance for discussion. If you want more detail one-on-one then I'll jump on the train to Paris any day, any time and share my thoughts. I hope you will grant me some time, Pierre. I know I can make it worth your while.

Gib
Executive Director
Accenture Development Partnerships

Of course, I knew hitting *Send* was risky but I could never have imagined that within five days of sending it I'd find myself in a loony bin. To his credit, Pierre had replied to my email within a couple of hours on the Friday, offering to speak by phone the following Monday. The excitement of finally feeling listened to was starting to show through audibly in the pace and tone of my recordings. The fact I was becoming a bit hyper didn't go unnoticed by my parents when I phoned home to tell them I'd be paying them a visit at the weekend. My mother's natural default setting is 'worried'. As a Latin scholar, her advice that evening had been *festina lente*, which she explained meant 'to hasten slowly'. In simple terms, you can go faster if you don't rush. Mum was always quick to give advice during our chats on the phone. You know the kind of well-meant stuff: 'Be careful,' 'Drive safely now, won't you,' or, 'You're burning the candle at both ends, my boy,' were some of her favourites. This, of course, tended to go 'in one ear and out the other'. Her words, not mine.

However, *festina lente* was a new and rather interesting piece of advice. I travelled on planes every other week and usually found myself rushing through security or running to the gate to get on board just in time. No wonder my brilliant assistant, Mina, called me Last Minute Larry. She had a point. However, this time I'd decided to adopt a *festina lente* attitude. I set off from home well in advance. I decided that I wouldn't run or even walk too briskly within the airport.

It might sound strange, sharing this with you now, but forcing myself to slow down made me start to question the nature of my own consciousness and reality itself. What was *real* life, what was fake or an illusion? Try it some time. It's a bit like watching a video in slow motion. You see so many new things. This heightened consciousness seemed to start shortly after taking off on the first BA flight out of Geneva on the Saturday morning, flying to Glasgow via London. I remember vividly how the dawn sun poured in through the aeroplane windows as we soared on up through the low clouds, almost as if travelling into another world. With the benefit of hindsight, perhaps I was... Even on the plane, I continued to capture my thoughts and feelings in the 'voice recorder' app on the iPhone. I'll share this excerpt to give you a feel for what was going through my head. Polite request: don't judge – not yet.

 iPhone Voice Recording

---

c:\data\voicefiles\IceCaps.wav
Saturday 22.11.14 7:55am 08m:34s

'I've just opened the window blind a fraction and see the red light of the dawn from 37,000ft... A bright fireball set against a perfect Azure-blue sky with the fluffy cotton wool layer of cloud base down below. If I didn't know better, I could imagine that we were flying over the polar ice caps... I'd then believe that white layer to be solid snow and ice, that the plane could land on and I could step out onto it... What a mistake that would be... I know it's nothing more than vapour. I know that much. Or do I? Really? Beyond all doubt. What is reality, after all?'

No, of course I didn't *really* believe that the layers of fluffy clouds were polar ice caps – I was just testing the underlying assumptions of everything I believed in. Another recording went further:

 iPhone Voice Recording

---

c:\data\voicefiles\IllusionofLife.wav
   Saturday 22.11.14 8:14am 02m:54s

'I mean, we're living in this crazy Facebook, YouTube world of 24/7 connectivity. If it's not posted online it didn't happen. Are our online posts a true representation of the lives we're actually living? No way. Most photo and video uploads have the sole purpose of creating an illusion – an attempt to convince others of what marvellous lives we all lead. We create our own personal Nirvanas by carefully selecting the one per cent we share and filtering out the 99 per cent that represents the mundane reality of everyday life. Real life is the illusion we lead when we go offline for five minutes.'

I admit it's a bit out there. But you'd surely agree that the illusion of our Facebook lives is a fair point, right?

I remember getting my laptop out on the plane. It was a semi-automatic ritual that followed the seatbelt sign being turned off. But this time I wasn't catching up on work emails. I'd downloaded an article on Joseph Campbell and *The Hero's Journey*[1] that Gene Early had mentioned to me during my prep call for the Leaders' Quest Retreat in India. I wanted to know what was so special about this guy Campbell and why Gene had felt it so relevant to the successes and challenges I'd been experiencing with my own journey within ADP.

Perhaps it was the state of mind I found myself in. Perhaps it was something to do with the aftermath of the fever. I've no idea. What I do know is that I was mesmerised by what I read. It's not easy to summarise a topic which has inspired numerous films, books and even song lyrics, but in essence, Campbell's *Hero's Journey* is an archetype of the change process that humans and organisations go through. Campbell drew on a combination of ancient mythology and more recent Jungian psychology to assert that we each have an innate destiny, something that is bigger than us, more than we can comprehend. The journey of life is all about developing the wisdom, power and resources of character needed to follow this path or adventure, in service of others and in keeping with our own truths.

Campbell describes three broad phases or acts of the journey:

Departure involves a calling to adventure – a call to become what we are *meant* to become. The hero within us must transcend the usual fears of inadequacy or of losing everything we've built and step across the 'threshold' into the field of adventure.

The second phase, *Initiation*, involves a 'Road of Trials' where the hero has to overcome a series of tests, trials or ordeals, sometimes with the supernatural aid of helpers and mentors. In mythology, this supernatural element might be the magic bow and arrow, or the light sabre in *Star Wars*, that allows scary creatures and dragons to be slain. It's a land of both terror and opportunity and, if successful, the hero will then enter the third and final phase:

Return. This is when he or she passes from the supernatural world back to day-to-day life, bringing back some gift or boon to the society they left.

Heady stuff, right?

---

1. https://en.wikipedia.org/wiki/Hero%27s_journey#/media/File:Heroesjourney.svg

That article had a profound effect on me. It's not that I had a messianic complex or saw myself as the all-conquering hero – well, at least I doubt any more than the next person. It's just that it resonated so strongly with what I'd been experiencing. A calling to a cause bigger than oneself – a sense of purpose so strong that you feel you have no option but to heed the call. Since returning from India and overcoming the extreme fever, I'd been feeling this flow of energy rise up within me. Sending that cry for help to our CEO had felt like crossing a threshold, and maybe I was now finding myself in the 'field of adventure'? Or had I crossed that threshold years earlier when I'd left for that transformative year in Macedonia? Had I been in the field of adventure ever since? Gene Early had, it seemed clear to me, been one of these mentors. He'd opened my mind to the power of myth, metaphors and illusions, to convey important messages and influence hearts and minds. Might there be some way to use that same power to influence the world of business and people's perceptions of it? As I write, I'm fully aware this may come across as sanctimonious bullshit, but I'm just trying to be open and honest about how I felt.

I had almost two hours of transit time to kill in Heathrow Terminal 5 and decided to put Joseph Campbell's concepts and Mum's *festina lente* advice into action. Wit and cunning would matter just as much as brute strength on this journey. So, instead of reacting impulsively or emotionally when something happened, I deliberately delayed my response, then thought about what the mirror or opposite response would be to the situation and tried to react in line with that.

I had the chance to test out the new strategy at the airport transit security. My bag was stopped for searching, as was the suitcase of the man in front of me. For frequent flyers there is only one thing more frustrating than having your bag searched by airport security, and that is having a backlog of fellow passengers' bags waiting to be checked before your own. There was a distinguished-looking, old Italian bloke in front of me, probably late-sixties, who wasn't taking it very well and started to be quite abusive. I felt quite sorry for the staff, who remained calm, polite and professional.

After a wait of almost 10 minutes, it was my turn. My natural response would have been frustration or agitation. Instead, I thanked the security staff for keeping my fellow passengers and me safe.

I took their smiles as a sign of encouragement for my new approach and decided to test it again when I went for a quick shoeshine – another favourite airport activity of mine. Yes, I'm a lazy git and never get round to cleaning my own shoes at home. Normally I'd sit and do my emails on my iPhone while the poor shoeshine guy vigorously polished my shoes. It's pretty obnoxious, I'd agree, but this time I put the phone down and actually spoke to him. I discovered his name was Musa and that he was a devout Muslim. In these 10 short minutes I learnt more about that religion than I'd done in the previous 30 years. I walked slowly and calmly towards the gate, while so many others were rushing past me, sweating or panting. It seems so ridiculous when you pause to observe the pace we're all living at.

On the second leg of my journey from Heathrow to Glasgow, I decided that I wouldn't crunch away at my email on the laptop for a change, rather I spoke to the passenger next to me. That's something I never tended to do – not because I didn't want to be friendly – it's just that I always seemed to have too much to do and didn't want to waste valuable time on small talk with a stranger. This time was different, and I discovered I was sitting next to a well-known Scottish entrepreneur who'd made millions creating his own food business. I wondered how many other interesting people I'd sat next to on planes over the years without ever saying a word to them. If these were trials or ordeals, then they were relatively minor ones, but I still felt that I'd dealt with them successfully and was preparing myself mentally for tougher tests that might be in store.

A tingle of excitement always comes over me as I board the ferry to the Isle of Bute. On business trips, I craved the peace and anonymity – but going home was more of a pleasant stroll down memory lane. I'd never quite know which faces I'd see on such trips, and this time I was in for a treat. There had been a farming event on the Ayrshire coast and I discovered a whole group of former classmates from school were on the boat as well as some customers of Willie McFie's Bute Tools shop where I'd worked in my youth. We reminisced over a couple of drinks during the short half-hour crossing and then it was time for *la pièce de résistance* – a rendezvous with my dad and his mates in the local pub, The Black Bull. I often deliberately scheduled my arrival on Bute to coincide with the weekly ritual of 'a pint and a wee dram'. The pub is conveniently located at the end of the pier and the boat arrived in perfect time for me to walk down the gangplank and join them.

The Black Bull Pub, Isle of Bute. Late November 2014

'Oh, crumbs, Gib! Look at the time,' said Dad looking at his watch on one hand while gulping his last drop of whisky from the other.

'I promised your mother we'd be home by seven and it's almost half past.'

We quickly said our goodbyes to the lads and headed for home. It wouldn't be the first time we'd been late, but we knew we'd be facing the wrath of Wee Marj and the prospect of *burnt*, as opposed to '*baked* white rat'.

Chapter 21 – Two-Faced Reality

'Well, well, well. What sort of time do you boys call this?' said Mum, standing in the hallway, scowling with her arms crossed.

'Sorry, Mum, it was my fault,' I said sheepishly. 'I was probably doing most of the talking and we lost track of the time.'

'You're both smelling of drink. Come on, own up, how many did you have?'

'Just the one pint, dear,' said Dad, 'and maybe a wee Lagavulin.'

'Or two by the looks of it,' she said, making a tutting sound. 'Both your livers will be frazzled.'

I hadn't seen Mum in a couple of months and she couldn't feign anger any longer. She ran up the hallway and jumped into my arms for a big hug.

'How's my boy, then?'

'*Festina lente*, Mum. I've been hastening slowly, just like you suggested.'

A roll of her eyes said it all.

In keeping with tradition, we sat by the warm coal fire and chatted over a pre-dinner dram. The 'burnt white rat' turned out to be haggis, neeps and tatties, something Mum would make me as a special treat. (That's traditional Scottish haggis with mashed potatoes and mashed swede on the side. If you've never tasted it, I suggest you try it *before* you ask what it's made of.) We talked about my trip to India, the fever and my apparent recovery, and I shared with them the exciting news about the call with Pierre that I'd arranged for Monday morning. They reciprocated with stories of the various goings-on within the island community, their choir rehearsals, how bad the weather had been, Mum's dismal golf and Dad's work with the Bute Arts Society. They led busy lives. Just a usual evening in the Bulloch household – well, nearly. Despite trying to contain myself, I was more excited, more animated than normal. The manic state that had begun when the fever subsided kept me up all night again.

The flow carried on over the weekend on the island and I captured more ideas on my iPhone. It was almost as if I were journalling this 'Road of Trials', capturing any lessons or ideas that might come in handy down the line. I'd go out for long walks to my favourite beaches, and some of the recordings have the scrunching noise of my feet walking over pebbles on them, or the splashing of the waves on the shore. I even made a rare appearance at Trinity Church on the Sunday morning – no, not for God, but to hear my dad play the organ and feel immersed in the local community, to catch up briefly with figures I'd known since childhood. In my frame of mind at the time, these larger-than-life figures took on a kind of mytho-logical presence. My dad rewarded my presence at church with a rousing rendition of Widor's Toccata, a fanfare in my honour at the end of the service. He knew it was a childhood favourite of mine. Of course, like so many things over the past few days, I captured it on video, earning myself a bit of a scowl from the minister as he strode down the aisle to the church door to say his farewells to the ageing and dwindling congregation. Each time I returned home it seemed like one or two members of the community were missing, a feeling that was confirmed by a cursory glance at the Obituary column of the local paper, *The Buteman*[1].

No, I couldn't claim to be religious, but whether it was a spiritual awakening or something more mundane and chemical going on in my brain, it was as if I were experiencing a different level of con-sciousness, where life itself had switched from black and white into glorious High Definition Technicolour. A bit like Dorothy stepping out of her monochrome world into a colourful dream in *The Wizard of Oz*, I, too, was transitioning into my own supernatural world of adventure. There everything made perfect sense, to me at least. To others, however, I was clearly going nuts. Either way, I'd never felt more alive in my life.

---

1. https://www.buteman.co.uk

Parents' Home, Isle of Bute. Monday morning, late November 2014

Here's a question for you: if you had a really important call scheduled with the Chief Exec of your company at 10am on a Monday morning, wouldn't you want to be well prepared, well rested and at the top of your game? Staying up until about 6am and getting less than two hours' sleep would seem like a schoolboy error. Yet, that's apparently what I'd done the night before the call with Pierre. I'd sat up in front of the coal fire, thinking, still capturing ideas on the phone and writing an email to Gene to tell him that I now understood what he'd been trying to tell me about Joseph Campbell's *Hero's Journey*. My dad had paid me a slightly exasperated visit just before 2am, suggesting I go to my bed.

'Yes, I'll be right up very soon, Dad. Just finishing something off.'

My digital audit trail betrayed me. I'd sent a lengthy email to Gene at 4.16am and the last voice recording was marked 5.52am.

Despite my chronic lack of sleep, when the time came for my call with Pierre, I'd felt wide-awake. Buzzing even. At least that's how I'd described my feelings in the summary of the call I'd written up. This would be my greatest test yet, and the fact that the sun shone brightly into the living room throughout the call, I took to be some kind of affirmative sign from the universe. I'm sure it had been a rather unusual discussion. I'd reached the end of my tether and this was my last chance to convince the CEO of the latent potential of Accenture to change the world, and the power he had, as an individual, to harness and shape that future direction. I laid it on thick: the business world, the world of our large, multinational clients was 'like a symphony orchestra warming up before a great performance'. Fragmented, with lots of ad hoc noises and disharmonies. What the orchestra needed was a conductor, someone who could interpret the musical score and harness the power of each diverse instrument to create the harmonies. 'You're holding that baton, Pierre.' It was colourful language, to say the least. But I knew this was my last roll of the dice and I was giving it everything. What mattered to him most in the world? Was it money? The status that came with heading up one of the largest companies in the world? Perhaps it was Accenture's shareholders? Or was it his legacy? Pierre told me that he cared little about money or ego. For him, family came first. To him, they were the most important thing in the world – his wife and his teenage daughter. I reminded him of what he'd told me after that memorable interview with Professor Muhammad Yunus in Davos – that this had been the thing that had made his daughter really proud. She and her generation were what mattered.

I told him that he could become the first business leader to win the Nobel Peace Prize. OK, I admit, as someone prone to a bit of hyperbole, even I felt I was going a bit overboard. But I remember making a similar predication about Paul Polman, CEO of Unilever a couple of years prior to that, while allegedly of sane mind. Perhaps we should launch a social media campaign – something like Paul Polman for Peace Prize: #PPPP?

I'm still of the view that it's only a matter of time, assuming the will of the right business leader is there. Of course, their actions would have to match their lofty rhetoric.

The call had been scheduled to last 30 minutes, but it drifted towards a full hour. All credit to Pierre for giving me that time. It may have been out of pity; it may have been a ploy to get me off the phone; or it may have been because he was intrigued by what I was trying to say. It doesn't really matter. What does matter is that he agreed to give me a slot at the next Global Executive Committee meeting in Paris in January. He wanted them to hear first hand about my ideas and to 'make up their own minds' about their merits.

I remained calm and thanked Pierre for giving me this opportunity. Then, I hung up and let rip.

'YEEEEEEEESSSSSSSS!!!' I screamed, jumping out of the chair and starting to dance around the lounge. My screaming had caused a bit of unnecessary alarm for my parents, who were, no doubt, already a bit on edge from my erratic behaviour.

'What on earth's wrong?' shouted my dad as he ran down the stairs, almost colliding with my mum as she dashed through from the kitchen.

'Oh, sorry. No, nothing's wrong,' I said. 'Pierre just offered me a slot at the next Global Executive Committee meeting in January!'

My parents looked more relieved than excited on my behalf. They'd always been incredibly supportive of my work, but there's no way they could possibly understand the significance of what I'd just been given.

This was a turning point. I was beginning to spin out of control. But you've sensed that already, I'm sure. Events were taking on a kind of surreal, or supernatural, context. The Pierre call had far and away exceeded expectations. I'd got more than even I had hoped for – a presentation to the most powerful decision-making body in the firm. What a coup. It would be the most important presentation of my life. I'd be very intrigued to hear Pierre's take on that pivotal call.

As I lay in bed on the Monday evening, wide awake in spite of the lack of sleep the night before, my mind went back to the Facebook pseudo-reality of our online lives. I was in the same bed that I'd used to drift off to sleep in, 40 years before, listening to the faint melodies of the piano in the living room below. For a moment I was back in my childhood again, as an eight-year-old child, remembering how my dad had shown me an image he'd taught in his art class that day.

Rothesay, Isle of Bute. Autumn 1975

'What do you see in the picture, son?' asked Dad.

   'It's a woman, of course, silly.'

   'Do you see a young woman or an old woman?'

   'A very young woman, wearing a hat, with long hair,' I said.

'You're sure about that? I can see a very old woman. She looks like a witch.'

'You're being stupid, Dad. Of course she's not a witch. She's young and beautiful.'

'Really?' said Dad with a smile, pointing to the features of the old woman.

'Woah… I've just seen the witch too! Weird…'

'There are often two sides to every story. Even when you're convinced you're right, you might not be seeing what the other person's seeing. You might not be seeing the whole picture. It's possible for two people to see the same thing differently, to have completely opposite views but both can be right at the same time.'

Both can be right at the same time… right at the same time… both can be right at the same time… same time… time… right at same time…

The words were coming deep from within my subconscious. Then my thoughts drifted back to that fake *FT* article I'd written after coming back to Macedonia. I'd effectively created an illusion of a different reality, a different vision of the future. I'd unlocked the second image buried within the picture – an image of a thriving business that put people before profit. How could I create something similar, 13 years on, to bring to life the future for ADP that I saw so clearly, but couldn't convince others of? I'd need to think of something different, go one step further. Then a thought hit me like a punch to the head.

The answer is a film.

To harness the power of film.

A movie about how a corporation might change the world. Here's the raw idea, as it came out in the middle of the night:

 iPhone Voice Recording

---

c:\data\voicefiles\IceCaps.wav
   Tuesday 25.11.14 4:05am 06m:27s

'Yes, this is a ridiculous time of the morning. But, I've just had what I think could be termed a "eureka moment" (laughing). Campbell's *Hero's Journey* had a profound effect on me... I'm not yet able to understand why... but it feels like... like my whole life, all 47 years of it have been a rehearsal for this moment... and I think I'm now ready for the show to begin.'

(silence... slow breathing...)

'Campbell inspired George Lucas to make one of the most popular films of all time – *Star Wars*. So the answer to the question that's been perplexing me for so long – how to win over hearts and minds about a different role for business in society – is a film. It's pretty obvious, now that I think of it. No, not some weird Sci-Fi film but instead... it's a film about business... Big fucking business. This wouldn't be your everyday business film. I'm talking about a living film. Yeah, that's right... a film co-created with its audience, with infinite potential plot twists and outcomes.'

(Long pause... breathing deeply...)

'The audience gets to go deep inside a real, live global corporation, to really understand what it can do, where it invests, where it innovates... and here's the best bit... they get to influence the outcome of the film through simple 'Likes' and 'Dislikes'. Thumbs up or Thumbs down. The viewing public get to engage in the firm's business strategy and have a direct impact on it... through the movie itself. A crowd-sourced business strategy no less... a more democratic corporation governed by the 'wisdom of the crowd'. Now, wouldn't that be interesting?'

The next day, I was still buzzing from this film idea. We've all been brought up in a world of heroes and villains or cops and robbers. Who doesn't love a good story where Good triumphs over Evil? In some ways, we're all the heroes in our own life stories and, in some strange way, I felt I was living out mine on screen – every thought, word or deed could have an influence on the plot – on whether my life story, my life's purpose, has a happy or a sad ending. I mean, we can all think of so many cinematic moments from our lives with ourselves cast as the hero figure. That break-up after the Ashburn Disco aged 19 and watching Janice McDermott walk out into the rain, ignoring my pleas for her to wait, was right up there with *Gone with the Wind*, the stuff of Oscars. My mind was coolly saying, *Frankly my dear, I don't give a damn,* but my face was blubbering like a little baby. Now the broken-hearted lad of the Ashburn Hotel Discotheque had become the hero of a David against Goliath movie blockbuster. I revelled in the notion of being the underdog, taking on the might of a big business and somehow winning against the odds.

However, there was still a significant cloud on the horizon. Pierre agreeing to the presentation meant that the Holy Grail was within my grasp, but there was still a fire-breathing dragon standing on guard at the sacred crypt – my nemesis, Franck. I feared he would kybosh the whole thing – surely there must be a way to get him on board. I remember Gene telling me that the hero sometimes uses wit and cunning rather than brute force to slay dragons or monsters. I had only been seeing the young woman in the picture all these years; Franck could only see the old woman. We could both be right at the same time, yet from completely different perspectives. There was common ground to be found. I quickly emailed Franck's assistant to ask if he'd have time for a brief chat.

The call lasted about 20 minutes, most of the time was spent with me telling Franck how I hadn't fully appreciated the great role he'd played in making the company profitable and efficient. He'd created the stable platform from which ADP could be launched. I'd only been seeing my side of the story, but from now on I would see his, too. 'Let's draw a line under the past and look only to the future,' I said. The conversation had the same kind of effect as a tranquiliser dart fired at a wild animal. Franck thanked me for a very constructive conversation and looked forward to seeing ADP doing great things in the future.

A week with barely any sleep would have an impact on most people's state of mind – I was no exception. As I stepped on to the boat to leave the island, I was less than 24 hours away from being taken into a psychiatric hospital. Of course, I had no idea of this at the time. I was so hyper that I'd lost my grip on what was real and what was an illusion, a result of having transcended into Campbell's supernatural world. It was intoxicating.

I was in my living movie and, as we set sail across the Clyde to the mainland, the scene was reminiscent of Jim Carrey in *The Truman Show*. You know, the infamous scene where poor Truman escapes the grasp of his game show controllers by setting sail on a yacht, only to hit up against the limits of the giant ocean in the film studio in which he's lived his entire life? As I looked at the horizon where the sky met the River Clyde estuary, it did cross my mind that I could be living in some kind of artificial game show studio with the world watching my every move. Completely nuts? Yeah, maybe, but it's not such a far cry from the media spotlight we put celebrities under, who don't have the luxury of the selective Facebook filter we put on our own lives. Surely that must feel like living your life in a reality TV show.

I went up to the top deck of the car ferry, and made a very blustery recording:

🍎 *iPhone Voice Recording*

c:\data\voicefiles\IceCaps.wav
   Wednesday 26.11.14 5:47pm 07m:51s

'I mean, it's not so far out there to think that we might all be on video... God knows how many selfies are taken every second... How many million YouTube videos are uploaded every day... It's like we're living the videos of our own lives. I mean, these big-name celebrities must feel as if they're in a living film... Everywhere they turn, everywhere they go, everything they say might be captured by one of the paparazzi or, more like a thousand adoring fans, hoping to catch a smartphone-enabled photo of their superheroes... But what if we all lived that way? What if our every action, our every deed, were to be judged in the court of public opinion? How would you like it if 50 million *Hello!* magazine online readers were judge, jury and executioner of the morality or worthiness of your entire life? Would you still fake that taxi receipt or insurance claim? Would you still do that insider trade or fix the Libor rates, Mr Banker? Would you still offer or accept that bribe, if millions of people were going to pass real-time judgment on your actions? I–don't–think–so.'

It occurred to me that perhaps the organisational transformation I'd been fighting for all these years might have to start at the level of the individual – that corporations are nothing more than an amalgam of the individuals that work within them and the decisions they make. How would these decisions be impacted, if you thought 100 million people might be watching you? Like an online 'court of public opinion'.

West End, Glasgow. Wednesday evening, late November 2014

I'd arranged to stay with Johnny in Glasgow the night before the funeral. Such visits were always enjoyable and tended to involve a few beers and a late-night curry. From the boat I'd taken the train to Glasgow and then it was a short taxi journey out to Johnny and Liz's flat in the West End, where they lived with their son, Joe. I remember the taxi driver offering me a few blank receipts, as many of them do in most big cities. They think they're doing you a favour – but it's exactly the kind of low-level corruption that my 'court of public opinion' would take a dim view of. Rather sanctimoniously, I refused the blank receipts and offered to pay an extra tenner if he'd promise not to hand them out to other people. He no doubt thought I was quite mad (and given where I ended up the next day, he'd feel quite vindicated in that belief) but was happy to take the extra tenner that I gave him on trust. In my world, I'd lost a tenner but got thousands of likes from the online community within the virtual world, and that more than made up for it.

I even filmed my arrival at Johnny and Liz's flat on my phone, which they found more amusing at the time than concerning. I told them it was part of a special project that I was working on, something to do with online education – a MOOC no less. It was possible that their parenting skills could be of interest to others as we harnessed the 'wisdom of the crowd' to decide on best practice parenting. Not such a crazy idea, is it?

Johnny and I sat up late into the night, putting a large dent in a bottle of 12-year-old Talisker Single Malt. He listened and questioned while I tried to share with him what I'd been experiencing. What if our lives were exposed to the scrutiny of public opinion? What if we all had an innate purpose in life? What if we're all effectively living out our own versions of Joseph Campbell's *monomyth* as the heroes and heroines of our own lives' stories? What if we could extend this to the business world? Is it inconceivable that we could create a corporation whose business strategy was determined by the society in which it operated? Yes, my brain felt ready to explode.

It was after 3am when Johnny eventually managed to coax me to go to bed. It would be my last night of freedom as my old self. My old life as I knew it would soon be coming to an end. Nothing would ever be the same again.

Chapter 22 – Dear Jeff

'I hear yer leavin' us, Gib,' came the voice of old Hughie from the Medicines queue. I'd spent the entire day holed up in my tiny bedroom, listening to hours and hours of recordings I'd made over the week post fever. Tony had knocked on my door just after 9.30pm to make sure I remembered to visit the dispensary kiosk. Even though I was getting out the next morning, I'd still have to be very disciplined about taking my medication.

Word of my pending 'release' had clearly spread amongst my fellow patients and I got quite a few pats on the back, handshakes and good luck wishes. Danny came across to wish me all the very best and told me he'd miss our chats.

'I reckon I'll be oot right behind you. Maybe a day or two more for me, that's all.'

Perhaps he was right; I just don't know. He seemed pretty fine to me, but then, what would I know? Gordon was nowhere to be seen. I reckon he'd have a bit of a longer wait and, as for the likes of Hughie, well, he'd no doubt become resigned to the fact that he was one of Thomson's semi-permanent residents. I said my goodbyes and wished them all the very best, before heading back down the corridor to Room 17.

Was it really almost a week since my arrival in Thomson? My memories of what happened that particular day are a little hazy and that's where the digital audit trail stops. My last message from Johnny's flat on Thursday morning was fairly frantic – but I seemed aware of what was going on. I knew I'd reached an impasse and would have to submit to my friends' demands. Instead of driving south to the funeral, we'd walk together down the road to the Royal Infirmary so that a doctor could confirm my protestations that I was 'absolutely fine'.

I remember walking between Johnny and Carlo, all three of us dressed in dark suits and black ties in preparation for the funeral. It must have been quite a sight for any passers-by – a bit like that great Tarantino scene in *Reservoir Dogs* when the gangsters are walking down the road and all you see is their legs. The whole way down the road I continued trying to convince them that this really wasn't necessary. They were right to ignore me, of course.

On arrival at the hospital, my overriding memory is of finding the whole experience quite funny, actually. Not least the expression on the face of the poor woman at the reception desk, as three large bald men in black suits and ties strode up the hospital steps. Once we'd gone inside, I'd been asked to give a urine sample into some enormous cardboard receptacle, which made for some school-boy humour. I still had my two mates present as a gallery to play to, but the two poor shrinks who were assessing me were clearly less amused and, no doubt, a bit more concerned by my erratic behaviour.

Perhaps that swung their decision, and I was soon put into an ambulance and taken down to the specialist Thomson Ward at Glendevon Hospital, I assume for further assessments. I was still finding the whole experience amusing and remember cracking jokes with the ambulance drivers and the staff. Some poor young nurse brought me a tray of lunch complete with a drink of apple juice, which I rejected on the grounds that it looked too much like the urine sample I'd just given. Hardly hilarious, I'd admit, but at the time I simply didn't care. I was still obsessed by the fine line between reality and illusion (and that context is everything). Like the master illusionists, we can convince anybody of anything if we have asymmetric access to information. Just ask Derren Brown or David Blane, who've both made fortunes by playing with 'reality'. So in this surreal hospital scene in the movie I was living in, I decided that the apple juice tasted of piss and they'd given me back my urine sample by mistake and therefore that was my new reality.

The last thing I remember doing before the tranquilisers must have kicked in was trying to scribble a 17-syllable Haiku onto the back of a BA boarding card. Clearly, the whole Rumi Sufi spinning experience was playing on my mind. I remember the Indian dancer, Zia, explaining that Rumi's followers would go off to the mountains for decades of solitary spinning and meditation and then have to summarise their enlightenment experience in just 17 short syllables. Had I discovered Enlightenment, or had I simply lost the plot – had a good old-fashioned breakdown? The jury was out on that, and, frankly, remains out to this day.

I lay back on my bed in Room 17, folded my hands behind my head and let out a long, deep sigh. Could there really be anything in this crazy film idea? I no longer believed I was living in my own version of *The Truman Show*. But I was intrigued by the notion of a living film that shaped business strategy through the wisdom of the so-called crowd. I've always been interested in the work of Jeff Skoll, the Canadian philanthropist, and how he'd used the power of film to send a social message. Having made a fortune as the co-founder of eBay, he then invested lots of his money into creating The Skoll Foundation, to support social entrepreneurs. In 2004 Skoll created a production company called Participant Media, which makes films designed to inspire social change. He was the guy behind *An Inconvenient Truth*, Al Gore's seminal warning on climate change, but Skoll has also done many other powerful films like *Spotlight* and *Contagion*.

Let's face it: every film that's ever been made about business has followed the standard narrative of 'Big Bad Business': the nasty mining company's pursuit of blood diamonds; giant pharmaceutical companies manipulating markets in vital drugs. Then, who can forget *The Wolf of Wall Street*? It exposed the obscene greed of these immoral investment bankers. OK, it was set in the 1980s before I even went to business school, but far too many are still at it, every bit as bad 30 years on – just arguably less conspicuous than they were back then. Yes, *arguably*. But I bet they're cast as the villains in most of your life movies, too.

I lay on my bed, pondering whether Mr Skoll might contemplate making a film portraying big business in a positive light – to help people re-imagine its potential to do good in the world. Then a horrible thought occurred to me: what if all of these ideas, recordings and calls just hadn't happened, or had only happened in my head. Part of me wanted to believe everything was true and that the excitement I'd felt was genuine. My heart wanted to believe it, but my head, the rational side of my brain, started questioning whether my mind had been playing tricks on me. Was it some kind of weird dream or hallucination resulting from the fever? The call with Pierre had felt *so* real, but where was the proof that it happened? Where was the proof he'd promised me a slot to present to the Global Executive Committee in Paris? How would I know?

It hadn't even occurred to me to check the diary – idiot. I mean, if he'd given me dates I'd have surely entered them. I opened up January and scanned each day. Sure enough, there it was on 15 January – 'Paris: Presentation to Global Executive Committee'. Bingo! The call must have actually happened and Pierre had agreed to the date, after all. I could feel the adrenalin starting to run through my veins, no doubt fighting against the sedentary effects of the Diazepam. Could I really bring this dream to reality and get my ideas across on the Big Screen? I began to wonder again if Jeff Skoll might be interested in taking on such a project – he'd at least deserve first refusal on the deal. I googled him to find out a bit more about his background and what makes him tick. Born on 16 January 1965. Shit. His 50th birthday was going to be the day after my presentation in Paris. This was yet another *Truman Show* moment. Destiny was speaking to me with a very clear sign. I'd have to be bold. I'd write and offer him a most unusual 50th birthday present. As I thought about it, I remembered that I actually knew one of the senior VPs at the Skoll Foundation quite well. I'm sure if I asked Angie nicely and explained the situation, she could pass on a message to Jeff. I'd go out to visit him in San Francisco and convince him of the power of this idea.

There was no time to waste. I hurriedly opened my laptop and fired off an email to Mina, asking her to check out flights to San Francisco in early January. I told her that I couldn't explain why right then, but to trust me as it was really important. Then I started to craft my 'Dear Jeff' note for Mr Skoll on some paper I'd found in the day room.

Jeff Skoll
CEO

Participant Media
Los Angeles
CA

30 November 2014

Dear Jeff,

We've never met before, but I'm a huge fan of your work. I'm writing with a rather unusual proposal for you – in essence, to create a different kind of movie to bring democracy to multinational corporations and harness their power for social good. Let me explain what I mean in more detail.

Firstly, some context. In the past three decades, global corporations have seen unparalleled growth and now represent more than half of the largest economies of the world. Yet, they are amongst the most highly undemocratic institutions in existence. Sure, they're accountable to shareholders and Boards of Directors. But that's a very tiny proportion of society and many of these shareholders are and should be part of the solution, rather than always being perceived as the source of the problem.

I'm passionate about the latent potential for these enormous global organisations to have a massive benefit on society as a whole, but they're currently simply wrongly calibrated to do that and, moreover, they've lost the trust of society that would allow them to. It's as if there was an election where the wealthiest one per cent of society got 1000 votes each and the rest only one. No democratic society would put up with that, right? Yet we have for too long and we can't continue in the same way. There needs to be rebalancing – a fundamental shift in focus from profit to purpose.

This is where you and the power of film could play an

important role. To open hearts and minds as to what a reimagined private sector could achieve in the world, solving some of our biggest social challenges where governments have too often failed. Quarterly earnings statements, sanitised Annual Reports and glossy CSR brochures would be replaced by the power of social innovations, brought to life on the big screen and evaluated by the wisdom of the crowd. Employees, customers, students and normal citizens would have as much of a say as investors.

There's far more detail to this idea than I can possibly share in a letter. However, in mid-January, I have an opportunity to pitch the concept to the global leadership of one of the most powerful global organisations in the world. Getting their support and buy-in to this idea is what I'd like to offer you as a 50th birthday present.

However, to do so, I'll need your help. I'll be more than happy to come to California to share more details with you in person.

I look forward to hearing your thoughts.

Yours sincerely,

Gib
Executive Director
Accenture Development Partnerships

A NEW DAWN

'It's good to be idealistic. But be prepared to be misunderstood. Anyone working on a big vision will get called crazy, even if you end up right.'

Mark Zuckerberg
CEO Facebook
Harvard Commencement Address

Chapter 23 – High Noon

Breathe in... two... three... four...

Breathe out... two... three... fou...

Breathe in... two... three... fo...

The knock on the door jolted me out of my deep, meditative state and I opened my eyes to see the smiling face of Veronique, Pierre's assistant. They were ready for me.

I got to my feet, buttoned up my jacket and checked I had both envelopes. In the left-hand breast pocket I had a signed copy of my resignation letter hardly changed from the version I'd dictated into my iPhone in the middle of the night, but dated for that day. In my right-hand breast pocket I had an envelope containing something altogether more exciting – the spoils of my trip to San Francisco earlier in the week. But it would have to stay sealed. For now, at least. The time wasn't right.

'*Merci*, Veronique,' I said with a smile as I left my small office and started to walk down the corridor towards the main Board Room.

'*Et bon courage*, Jib,' came Veronique's voice from behind me. I looked back and gave her a friendly wave. For these last few steps I wanted to focus my mind entirely on the job at hand. I'd only arrived in Paris the day before, off the overnight flight from San Francisco, and had barely slept. I knew this was it. The biggest and most important presentation of my life – bigger even than the gigs Stephen Zatland had given me in Chicago to be the warm-up act for a swathe of former US presidents. This was the real biggie. This was High Noon.

Pierre welcomed me into the room, giving me a friendly pat on the back. 'I think you'll recognise many of the faces round the table.'

I glanced around the room at the 25 or so men and women who were assembled – the so-called Global Executive Committee. Several were typing away on laptops and barely looked up. Others were checking messages on their phones – sadly, the fashion for multitasking is now the accepted norm in the majority of large companies, meaning that most topics seldom get anyone's *full* attention. However, a few, thank god, nodded and smiled.

'Good morning,' I said, clearing my throat nervously. *Oh, you'll need to do a bit better than that, Gib, if you're going to win this lot over,* said the voice in my head. *Get a grip.*

Pierre sat back in his chair at the far end of the boardroom. I turned to him and nodded. Then looked around the room slowly, took a deep breath and tried to ignore the fact that my heart was pounding so hard that my ribcage was starting to hurt.

Good morning, ladies and gentlemen. I've got 15 minutes, no PowerPoint slides and one simple message: that the men and women gathered in this room have the opportunity to profoundly re-shape the world we live in and impact the lives of millions of people for the better. If you're expecting this to be the feel-good charity or Corporate Social Responsibility presentation, then I'm likely to disappoint you. Issues, which may have once been considered *social* for business in the past, are now highly *strategic* for business, and we, as a major global corporation, must respond. Let me first provide some brief context.

Fifteen years into the new millennium, you don't need me to tell you that the world is not a particularly happy place. Poverty, mass migration, conflict, climate change and growing inequality are just a few of the challenges you'll read about in the news. Indeed, according to the charity Oxfam, 62 individuals – 53 men and nine women – have more wealth than the poorest 3.6 billion people on the planet. That's just not sustainable economically, socially or, indeed, morally.

So, whose problems are these to fix? We business people have traditionally said that it's certainly not our role. We provide the goods and services the world craves, create value for shareholders, work within the law, pay our corporation tax – well, we could debate that point.

I couldn't resist that little quip and noticed the CIO looking up from his screen and smiling.

Surely these issues of global development are the job of national governments, the UN or international charities such as Oxfam or Save the Children? Besides, we've created Corporate Social Responsibility programmes and Corporate Foundations that give away proportions of our profit to such worthy causes. Isn't all that enough?

The simple answer is no. CSR won't cut it. Global Corporations like us can no longer separate the 'Doing Business' agenda from the 'Doing Good' agenda. We must ask ourselves, what is the true purpose of our organisation? What problem is it seeking to address? What benefit is it providing to society? Surely we're about more than just selling stuff to clients and employing lots of people.

If this is all sounding a bit like the 'do-gooder' agenda, then let me tell you the good news: I don't want to tug on your heart strings, but instead appeal to your commercial business instincts. It's my strong belief that some of the biggest challenges we face in both the developing and the developed world are, in fact, business opportunities in disguise. Electrifying rural Africa, educating the next billion kids, feeding and nourishing those at the base of the pyramid, or providing access to healthcare, finance and insurance to those in need. Each of these has a 'business' solution waiting to emerge.

But it will require significant change – a change of heart, of mind and, most of all, a change of will. If we, as business leaders, remain suppressed by the drumbeat of short-term quarterly earnings to meet market expectations, we'll never get there. Instead, we will need to strike a better balance between people, planet, profit and, perhaps most importantly, purpose. This new paradigm will mean profound change for each sector – public, private and civil society, the so-called third sector. Today we are witnessing not just a blurring of the boundaries, but a fundamental redefinition of where these boundaries actually lie. Business will drift into new territory that was once the domain of the UN and NGOs and government. We may even see the emergence of a new 'fourth sector' – an ecosystem of hybrid organisations enabled by new technology platforms, funded by innovative financing mechanisms and driven by a new breed of employee passionate about improving the world in which they live and work.

What do I mean? Well, let me take each of these points in turn.

I knew I had to give it my very best shot, muster every ounce of passion I could. Round the table, the typing away on smartphones had all but stopped; laptops shut as my audience began to sit up and take notice. I was on a roll.

Firstly, technology. From a business point of view, the digital phenomenon has revolutionised every industry and organisation in the world. Accenture are helping to shape this transformation. From a development point of view, new technologies will allow old challenges to be tackled in new and different ways.

To illustrate what I mean, let me pose this question to each of you: What single word links the following three things?

One: Fighting poverty in Kenya

Two: Exposing corruption in Afghanistan

Three: Tackling Obstetric Fistula in Tanzanian women?

There was a somewhat bemused silence, which thankfully didn't last more than a few seconds.

'The UN,' came the first guess from a guy who I think was the Group CEO for Financial Services. Then other random guesses were called out. I was encouraged. They seemed to be, dare I say, engaged.

'Oxfam.'

'UNICEF.'

'Religion.'

I shook my head to each.

'Accenture.'

This suggestion was greeted with laughter around the room.

'Accenture? Sadly, not yet,' I said, 'but it's a good guess and I'll be coming to our role very shortly. No, the word I'm actually looking for is in fact, a different company – Vodafone.'

There were a few raised eyebrows, and murmurings of surprise rippled across the room.

Why? Well, Kenya was the birthplace of the mobile banking revolution which Vodafone pioneered and which has provided access to banking services for over half of the Kenyan population.

Secondly, a mobile banking platform was used to pay police in Afghanistan through Vodafone's local operator. The frontline police thought they'd been given a 30 per cent pay rise when their salaries were paid electronically into their digital wallets, but they were in fact being paid correctly for the first time, without the corrupt hands of their superiors taking their cut first.

As for fistula in Tanzania, Vodafone's Foundation discovered that very few women were coming forward for corrective surgery, despite an availability of trained medical staff and facilities. This was due partly to the stigma associated with the condition and to a lack of awareness, but also to the prohibitive travel costs to reach the clinics from remote parts of rural Tanzania. Mobile technology was used to drive awareness of the availability of corrective surgery amongst women – then their mobile banking platform was able to send funds electronically to reimburse travel expenses. The net result was a 424 per cent increase in fistula operations in just eight years. Pretty impressive,

I'm sure you'll agree, and a solution that might lend itself to other taboo issues such as mental health.

As I surveyed the room, I could see nods of agreement and expressions of surprise.

> This takes us to the second driver of change I cited: innovative financing. We need to adopt a mindset that asks, how might we solve a social problem profitably – perhaps not profit maximisation but profit optimisation. We're seeing rapid growth in impact investing. New sources of capital are emerging that seek a dual or triple bottom-line return – not just a quick buck. Companies such as Danone in France have created a fund to invest in social innovation within their supply chains. Barclays and Deloitte have set up funds to support social entrepreneurs inside their organisations – an emerging breed of so called intrapreneurs. It's interesting to think that Vodafone's mobile banking innovation was not conceived in the R&D department or indeed the boardroom, but instead by an 'intrapreneurial' mid-level employee.
>
> Which leads me to my third driver: the power of people – of employees. According to our friends in Deloitte, 75 per cent of the workforce will be millennial by 2025. As you're no doubt aware, Accenture's workforce is almost at that number already. They want fundamentally different things from their careers – very different from what we wanted at their age. They're less interested in making a fortune and more interested in making a difference. Just look at what Unilever managed to achieve by putting sustainability at the heart of their strategy with their Unilever Sustainable Living Plan. The company went from about 80th to being inside the top 10 on the rankings of most desirable employers. I actually believe the views of these so-called 'millennials', and who they choose to work for, could be the biggest driver of business strategy over the next 10 years.

So what does all this mean for us in Accenture?

I joined the company in 1996 when we had the bold and somewhat audacious mission statement: 'To Bring Innovations to Change the Way the World Works and Lives.'

It was strong, inspiring and aspirational. The right vision, but perhaps at the wrong time. Now, more than ever before, is the time that we can do justice to that aspiration. Almost two decades later, we're now an organisation valued at over $70 billion, we have thousands of the world's largest corporations as our clients, we work in most of the developed and developing countries around the world and are leading the digital revolution. What's more, we have access to the world-class expertise of almost 400,000 employees globally, the vast majority of whom are of the millennial generation. Think what we might do if we got all of these resources working in harmony to 'bring innovations to change the way the world works and lives'. If the world of business were an orchestra, we're extremely well placed to step up to play the role of conductor. If not us, then before too long, one of our competitors will.

Are we prepared to take hold of the baton?

Are we ready to unleash the entrepreneurial and innovative power of our own employees and those of our clients, to create the new products, services and innovative business models to solve some of the biggest problems on the planet?

I was still on a roll, but got stopped in my stride by Janice Ford, who headed up the US business.

'How exactly would you propose we do that, Gib, in concrete terms?'

We run a global competition within our clients to find the best ideas and innovations amongst their employees and, indeed, amongst our own. We seek out the social intrapreneurs who reside deep undercover within these massive organisations. People like Nick Hughes at Vodafone, who drove their mobile banking concept, or Jo da Silva, a junior engineer from Arup, who created a new business to provide expertise in engineering design and construction to the humanitarian sector. I'm convinced there are countless other latent intrapreneurs among our clients who feel ignored, unloved and frustrated by the fact that they struggle to engage senior decision-makers in their company. We'll drive awareness of the competition amongst our clients to uncover the best ideas with the greatest potential impact for both the parent company and society. Through Accenture Development Partnerships, we could provide the business, technology and consulting expertise on a not-for-profit basis to implement these ideas and thereby have a direct influence not just on the strategy of dozens of our clients in which these intrapreneurs worked – some of the biggest global corporations – but have a positive impact on the world as a whole.

I was interrupted by a slow handclap from the far side of the room.

'This all sounds a bit too good to be true, Gib, but I have two quite basic questions,' said a portly, stern-looking man with a thick American accent. He wasn't someone I recognised.

'Who decides on which are the best ideas and where will you get the funding for all this implementation work through ADP? Accenture's not a charity, you know; we're a commercial business.'

The large American sat back and folded his arms with a kind of smug, 'gotcha' look on his face – clearly delighting in having had the opportunity to grandstand in front of his peers. But I was ready for him.

'Great question – and this is the best bit of all,' I countered, confidently. 'The public will decide. The viewing public.'

'Viewing?' said Pierre with a frown.

Yes. We bring the best ideas to life firstly on the big screen. Short video vignettes that will help people re-imagine how large corporations might play a different role in society and

234

help build trust in global business – trust that is currently, let's face it, pretty much at rock bottom.

Murmurs went round the room as I reached into my right-hand breast pocket. It was time to play my ace card. I pulled out an envelope and held up the letter inside.

This is a Letter of Intent signed by Jeff Skoll, the Canadian businessman-turned-social entrepreneur, who founded eBay and subsequently created Participant Media to harness the power of film for social change. Mr Skoll is willing to put up $100 million towards bringing this concept to life. Instead of a film, it might be numerous short films – more of a mini-series on Netflix where each episode would highlight a different insider story – a bit like a *House of Cards* for business.

'"House of Business Cards" perhaps?' quipped Geoff, the CIO.

That certainly has a ring to it, Geoff. Each short film would depict different scenarios and the viewers would get to choose the outcome. Like *The X Factor* or *America's Got Talent*, but instead of votes launching somebody's singing career, it's re-launching their business career and harnessing the intrapreneurial talent of employees. Through this pioneering new initiative, Accenture would at last be providing a voice for all those people who are sitting on the outside of business but are impacted by its behaviour. It's also, a voice for those on the inside, too, who are frustrated or inhibited by the 'corporate immune system'. Entire workforces would get to vote and help to create the kind of company they aspire to work for. We'd be creating more democratic global corporations and, as for Accenture, we'd effectively be the first multinational to crowd-source a major portion of our business strategy. A strategy driven more by the will of citizens and employees and less by the short-term commercial interests of our clients' shareholders.

Now that really would be 'bringing innovations to change the way the world works and lives'. Thank you for listening.

There was something of a stunned silence as I gazed around the room. Then some hushed murmurings started around the table.

I think it's best that I give you some time to talk this through amongst yourselves. I'll leave the room and will return in 10 minutes. No doubt you'll have many questions on the detail – those can be worked through in due course – I'm really simply looking for a vote of confidence to proceed, a Yes/No decision that I can report back to Jeff Skoll at Participant Media. The Letter of Intent has a deadline of noon, Pacific Standard Time, tomorrow, 16 January, which just happens to be Mr Skoll's 50th birthday. I hope we can jointly give him a very special gift.

I turned and left the room. I could feel my heart pounding in my chest and the sweat literally dripping off my hands. But I was buzzing – never once, in my entire career, had I felt so alive, so convinced by what I was doing.

Ten minutes later

This was High Noon. I took one last deep breath before clearing my throat, knocking on the boardroom door and walking on in. Pierre broke the silence.

'Gib, thanks for a very provocative and bold presentation. We've come to our decision.'

Chapter 24 – Full Circle

Parents' home, Isle of Bute, Scotland. Early December 2014

'Our top priority is for you to get well again, Gib,' said Lisa, the HR Director for Accenture Strategy. 'Maybe you want to take a bit of time off? Three months, six months, even take a whole year. You decide, Gib.'

This was my first call with Liz since being released from Thomson the previous week. However, she'd been in regular contact with my sister and parents and had gone out of her way to help. They'd been singing her praises and I liked and trusted her.

'No, I'm keen to get back at the beginning of January at the latest, Liz,' I said, assertively. 'I've got a big presentation to the GEC mid-January and I'll need to prepare for it.'

'That presentation won't be happening, Gib. You've been quite unwell and now need to take the time to fully recover.'

'You don't understand, Liz. Pierre promised me a slot at the GEC in January. It'll be the biggest presentation of my career.'

'I've spoken to Pierre. His priority is the same as all of ours in the leadership – that you take time to get fully well again. I'm sorry, but you need to understand that the presentation will not be happening.'

Turn to Camera

Totally confused? I know what you're thinking.

'Haven't I just read a full chapter about a presentation in Paris and a big idea to bring intrapreneurship to the silver screen?'

Well, what's that old saying? If something sounds too good to be true, then it means it's usually not true.

Yep, I'm ashamed to say that I made up that entire last chapter. Complete and utter fiction, every bit of it. Sorry. But you'd have to admit, it would have been really cool if things had turned out that way, right? I mean, it wasn't a completely implausible scenario and in my defence, everything up until that chapter was pretty much true. Yes, including writing a letter to Jeff Skoll while in a psychiatric hospital and the fact that I had been offered a slot to present to the Global Executive Committee, ironically the day before Skoll's actual 50th birthday. But that presentation sadly never happened. I can understand you feeling a little cheated right now – even my editor said she felt let down. 'You feel let down?' I said to her. 'Well how the hell do you think it felt for me when I got the news that the presentation wouldn't be happening?' 'Gutted' would be an understatement. I'd even written my presentation script. So I've fought hard to keep this admittedly frustrating ending, even if only to share with you how I'd rehearsed for events to turn out, 1,000 times in my own mind, before reality got in the way.

Thud.

I felt like someone had just cut off my legs and I'd dropped to the ground. All the excitement of the past couple of weeks, the sense that something big was about to happen just vanished into thin air in the space of that short conversation with Liz. I felt flat. Empty. Defeated. Most of all, I felt totally frustrated. But there was nothing I could do. Well, not at the time at least. Liz was my single point of contact back into the firm. I had to accept what she was telling me.

Over the next few weeks I would spend more time with my parents than I'd done in the entire previous decade – one whole month on the island. I began to learn their new little routines that creep into daily life as you grow older – 8.30am for breakfast at the bedroom window overlooking the fields and trees towards Loch Fad. Evenings by the fire, where nightly TV quizzes would take priority over anything that I might have found remotely interesting to watch. Regular portions of 'baked white rat' would manifest themselves in the form of childhood dishes. The Prodigal Son had returned from five days in a psychiatric hospital. Bring out the fatted calf – but no one mention mad cow disease.

I went for long walks along my favourite beaches, taking the time to think. What could I have done differently? How could I have avoided all this anguish for friends and family? Even then, the events of the previous couple of weeks still felt somewhat surreal in my mind. Having an empty diary and nothing much to do during the daytime was equally surreal. There were no late night email sessions as I was barred from doing any work. Besides, my email account had been blocked by the company's IT guys. I even went to two Christmas Carol concerts to watch my parents perform. Of course, locals stopped to interrogate me about my long stay on the island.

'He got a nasty fever in India,' my mum would explain, lying by omission. 'He's been working a bit too hard recently and is under doctor's orders to take some rest.'

Friends thoughtfully came to visit, including Gordon and Sarah, two of my oldest Bute friends, who'd travelled up from London. It's understandable that they'd worry as the news of my illness slowly spread out.

I was actually enjoying the downtime and being a bit pampered. One of the highlights of spending a month back home was that I was able to join the boys for a pint in The Black Bull on Tuesday and Friday nights. I was becoming one of the regulars. Besides my dad, these intimate gatherings always included his best friend and former teacher colleague 'Big Bert' Alexander, or 'Uncle Bert' as I'd known him throughout my childhood. He's another one of these larger-than-life characters from the local community and was one of my childhood heroes – the closest thing I'd ever had to a real uncle.

Graeme is a relative newcomer to the island and, having been a frequent visitor to The Bull, fell in with my dad's crowd, despite their being at least 20 years older. He's a fascinating guy – one of the best read and most intellectual people I've ever met, who has an interesting and seemingly informed opinion on just about any subject that comes up. While he's the human face of what government statistics would refer to coldly as 'the long-term unemployed' and never has any money, for me he's just Graeme. The long hair and scruffy appearance don't go down too well at job interviews – not that there's anything available on the island that would challenge him intellectually. He's too proud to stack shelves, cut grass or whatever other options the local job centre has offered him, which means he doesn't even get unemployment benefit. He seems to get by doing bits and pieces of IT-related work and, he's confessed, lives pretty much from hand to mouth on about £50 per week. He's a real character, and I've grown to like him a lot as I've got to know him over recent years. He's a rampant socialist but despite the fact that I've been operating on what he'd refer to as 'the dark side' – a management consultant to big business no less – I think he likes me, too, no doubt much to his own surprise.

These sessions in the pub are somewhat analogous to a meeting of the UN Security Council, although I suspect a lot less dysfunctional. They all sit there and discuss the issues of the day over a pint of real ale and a single malt chaser and come up with their own solutions to how we might solve the problems of the world. This week's dilemma had clearly been, 'What the fuck happened to Gib?' As a former social worker and the most tech literate of the gang, Graeme had taken it upon himself to do some internet research. He found an article about a rare condition called 'Post-Dengue Mania'[1], which had occurred in India. Admittedly, the symptoms did sound identical to those I'd experienced – lack of sleep, rapid speech, excitement, euphoria, the lot. The only problem was that the blood tests had ruled out both malaria and its cousin, dengue fever. Nevertheless, my parents both became convinced that this was what I'd had. This had to be the reason. Certainly, it was much more palatable within the local community to say that I'd had a bad fever than to

1. 'Late Onset Mania in Dengue Fever', ShailenMohan Tripathi and Neeti Mishra, Immunology and Infectious Diseases 2, 1–3. DOI: 10.13189/iid.2014.020101. http://www.hrpub.org/download/20140105/IID1-16701785.pdf

contemplate the fact that their happy, easy-going, high-flying businessman son had gone a bit nuts.

Over the years, these sessions in The Black Bull had become very precious to me. I felt they brought me back to my roots, kept me grounded in how 'normal people' think and live, the issues they face on a day-to-day basis, many just getting by. I often wondered if one day I would leave my cocooned existence of the jet-set lifestyle and home in a cosmopolitan, international city and return to this little island of my birth – this place I loved more than anywhere else in the world.

The only other activity during that long, cold December was bi-weekly meetings with Mary, the local Community Psychiatric Nurse. The more alert readers amongst you will remember the irony of the fact these encounters took place in my old primary school on Union Street, Rothesay. So, friends, I suppose this means that we've come full circle in our little story. Back to standing outside that large wooden entrance-door, pondering the almost surreal events of the previous few weeks and, indeed, the life I'd been living until that point.

Union Street, Rothesay, Isle of Bute. 20 December 2014

I stood at the top of the steps and gazed out over the playground in front of me, surrounded by grey stone walls that had once seemed so high. As I did, my mind took me back 40 years to the young six-year-old in short trousers, standing on these very same steps. I had a vivid image in my head of that innocent little fair-haired boy standing in his school uniform: blazer, yellow, red and black school tie and a small brown leather school bag worn like a rucksack on his back. Could he ever have imagined he'd be back on these same steps four decades later, and would he be content with the life he'd led and the thousands of decisions he'd made that had somehow navigated him back to that same step? I pressed Fast Forward and the movie image in my head began to morph, like one of these animated identikit figures. First the trousers grew longer, then I grew a bit taller and the hair disappeared. The school uniform became a business suit; the school bag a briefcase. Then the tie went and the pinstripe trousers became chinos. My waistline appeared to ebb and flow as the wrinkles on my forehead slowly grew longer and deeper. Eventually, the animation stopped at the 47-year-old man I am today, standing in jeans and a thick woollen coat. Then the strangest thought went through my mind: what would I look like in 40 years' time? Would this good old school building still be standing? Would *I* still be standing, for that matter, as an elderly man approaching 90 years old? What advice would that bent old man with a walking stick give his younger self? How would he want to have used the experience of the past few weeks to shape the years to come and convince him that there had been some small element of purpose to his nine decades on Earth?

A deep sigh rose as a cloud of vapour into the bitterly cold morning. I took the hat and gloves out of my pockets, buttoned up my coat and started to walk back home with the words of that old man still ringing in my ears.

Epilogue

'Travellers, there is no path, paths are made by walking.'

Antonio Machado
Spanish Poet
1875–1939

Eat, Pray, Love... In A Business Suit

Imagine you were told out of the blue that you had between one and three more years to live. How would you react? What would you do with the time you had left?

I met Garmt van Soest for the first time in October 2013. It was a meeting that would profoundly change my life. I'd agreed to teach a module on Communications in the C-suite (yes, still an awful term) at a senior manager training course in Accenture's massive training campus in St Charles, just outside Chicago. The group consisted of about 25 male and female senior managers, most of whom were aspiring partners. I was sharing my experience working with senior clients, some dos and don'ts and probably one or two horror stories. At the end of the session on the penultimate day, I was approached by a tall, heavily built Dutchman who asked if he could have five minutes of my time. He wanted to tell me that what sounded like a minor speech impediment was in fact the early stages of motor neurone disease, or ALS. He went on to explain that just two months earlier he'd effectively been given a death sentence. There is no cure and he'd been told to expect to live for between one and three more years. The five minutes turned into an hour. Here was I, thinking that this group of young bright professionals were learning skills that would last them a lifetime. Where would the motivation come from when you have but 12 more months to live? A week-long business communications course certainly wouldn't be on my bucket list.

Why was Garmt here? Well, to their credit, Accenture's Netherlands Office had been marvellous. He'd been told that he'd continue to be paid his full salary but could choose to do whatever he wanted with his time. He could come and go as he pleased. What's more, his wife Iris would be taken care of financially in the event of his death. All credit to them for that.

So how should you react when a stranger shares such tragic news? Sympathy, pity, words of comfort? He'd have those in abundance. I chose instead to ask him a challenging question. How might he, a smart, tech-savvy senior manager in one of the largest consultancies in the world, harness its power and that of its clients to confront this disease head on? It was tough love. Looking back some four years later, I had absolutely no idea of the depth of character of the man I was speaking to and what he would achieve against all the odds. I'm a firm believer in the fact that we cannot choose what happens to us in life. But we can choose how we react.

Since that first encounter, I visited Garmt regularly in Utrecht and we became close friends. His physical condition deteriorated rapidly in the first 18 months following his diagnosis. He was soon confined to a wheelchair, on a ventilator, unable to move any part of his body except his eyeballs, which he used to move a cursor and type on a screen in front of him. It was his only means of communication with the outside world. He was fed through a tube in his stomach, shaved, bathed and nursed by a team of carers who lived in 24/7. Yet his spirit and wicked sense of humour remained undiminished. He wrote short blogs each day from his initial diagnosis and turned them into not one, but two books[1], which have helped countless ALS sufferers and their loved ones come to terms with this most debilitating of diseases. Books that he wrote with only the power of his eyeballs. Garmt was one of a group of ALS sufferers who were behind the ALS #IceBucketChallenge. This innovative campaign went viral, as I'm sure many of you remember – with a shiver. He inspired hundreds of Accenture employees around the world to do charity fundraising swims. He worked with Accenture's technology labs and clients like Philips to pioneer new technologies to improve the quality of life for ALS sufferers. And perhaps most impressive of all, he led a team that created an innovative, multi-million-dollar venture fund which injects funding into early stage biotech ventures, seeking to accelerate cures for the disease. Pretty good for an able-bodied person, but when you consider all of this was achieved by someone who could only move his eyeballs, it's quite unbelievable.

I bet you're wondering why am I telling you all of this and what's it got to do with the story you've just read? Well, for me, Garmt is the

---

1. Even with ALS, Garmt van Soest (Lucht BV, 2016). https://www.amazon.com/s/ref=dp_byline_sr_ebooks_1?ie=UTF8&text=Garmt+van+Soest&search-alias=digital-text&field-author=Garmt+van+Soest&sort=relevancerank

epitome of the social *intrapreneur* – smart, creative and, above all, bold and determined. He managed to fuse together his own passion and capabilities with those of Accenture and its clients in pursuit of a social purpose – a purpose that he didn't have to go in search of. It came to him quite unexpectedly, like a punch in the teeth from Tyson Fury. He chose to '*ask* for forgiveness' instead of '*begging* for permission' in all that he did. My favourite, if rather trivial, example was when he decided to change the job title on his email footer and business card to:

Garmt van Soest

'*Kicking ALS in the Balls*'

Accenture, Netherlands

Do you think he asked if he could do that? Of course not. He knew what the answer would have been. If I sound like I hero-worship this guy, then that's good. Because I do. Quite unashamedly.

Coming back to my book and The Incident that took place back in late November 2014. You're perhaps wondering what's happened since then – to my precious baby Accenture Development Partnerships, to some of the other characters I've introduced you to and indeed, to me.

The outside world has changed dramatically since 2014. The US has elected a climate change-denying President while, as I write this epilogue, its shores are lashed by hurricanes of biblical ferocity. Daily terrorist outrages vie for media coverage with yet another nuclear test by a trigger-happy Kim Jong-un in North Korea. Not to mention scaremongering by the right-wing media, fuelling fears around immigration that helped in no small way to push the UK electorate to vote for Brexit. Yes, if anything, the world out there has become even crazier than when I was observing it from the unique vantage point of a psychiatric ward.

Despite all of this craziness, I'm pleased to say that ADP is alive and well within Accenture. Much of the loyal and capable management team I had the privilege to work with are continuing to channel Accenture's business and technology expertise to the world of international development. The baby became an adolescent and the adolescent grew into an adult that will find its own way in the world. I look on with vicarious pleasure and pride at the fascinating and often ground-breaking work they're doing.

More broadly, I'm pleased to see that the business world is starting to engage seriously with the UN's Sustainable Development Goals (SDGs). Throughout this book, I have shared my firm belief that these global goals or challenges are, in fact, business opportunities in disguise – a point of view that was vindicated in a report by the UN's Business Commission in January 2017[2], which valued the potential opportunity at $13 trillion. However, accessing this hidden commercial value will require new thinking around business models, new forms of collaboration, and for the business community to move beyond a singular focus on short-term profit maximisation. To even suggest this is tantamount to heresy in business circles and flies in the face of the received wisdom being passed down to MBA students in business schools all across the world. I say, bring on the heretics and change the curriculum. The world needs you!

That's my take on ADP and the goings on in the outside world. As for me? I can honestly say that the last three years have been the most incredible of my life. The most significant black mark during that period was the passing of my dear father, Lyn Bulloch, in March 2016. Having now read the book, you will begin to understand the scale of loss for our family – my mother, Marj, in particular, and, of course, the local Bute community. He is sorely missed and I feel blessed to have had him as a father for almost 50 years.

You may be wondering what I've been up to during the three years since getting out of hospital. Well, after taking a short sabbatical, I returned to work on a part-time basis, but formally left Accenture in January 2016. It was time. Then, with the 'pause button' pressed on my career, I took the opportunity to travel to lots of fabulous coun-

2. UN Business Commission for Sustainable Development. http://report.businesscommission.org

tries, meet some amazing people and read lots of books that I'd never even heard of. The travelling took me out of my comfort zone both physically and metaphorically, and culminated in 10 days at the Burning Man festival in the Nevada Desert in late August 2017. Indeed, much of this epilogue was written there. I feel very fortunate to have had the luxury of taking some time to myself, to better understand the profound experience I went through in November 2014. Was the cause medical, mental or spiritual? I still have no clear idea, but quite possibly it was a combination of all three. Whatever the cause, I now exercise more, drink less, eat better and have seldom felt healthier and happier. Mindfulness certainly beats madness hands down. Every cloud, as they say...

My *Eat, Pray, Love* sabbatical also gave me some space to decide what I'd like to do in the next phase of my life – and to be a little introspective on what I could have done differently in my role in ADP – to have been less of a stubborn, determined pain in the ass to colleagues and bosses alike. Or is this the cross that intrapreneurs and, indeed, their colleagues, have to bear?

My 'north star' ambition remains the same – at its core, to fundamentally challenge the role that business currently plays in society and to seek to harness its transformative power to tackle the global challenges facing humanity. Sure, it's a bit lofty and a tad overly ambitious, but in a world of grotesque inequality and a climate crisis unfolding before our eyes, can we really satisfy ourselves with incremental, piecemeal ambitions for change? Where I've probably shifted, however, is in how this goal can be achieved.

I've moved from running a small social enterprise within a large corporation to seeking to support and encourage other intrapreneurs, who are seeking to do similar things in their own organisations. I also work as an independent consultant and give speeches on an ad hoc basis, but am fortunate to be able to be quite selective about the organisations I do consulting for and the topics I speak about. It is my ambition to explore further the powerful role that print, broadcast and social media might play in helping us re-imagine a new world of business and to even revisit some of the 'crazier' ideas that I've alluded to in this book. Indeed, if there are any CEOs out there open to crowdsourcing their business strategy, then let's go and find a movie producer together. Or if there are any film producers out there who want to buck the business-bashing trend of Hollywood, then let's go and find willing CEOs and help create an insurgency of intrapreneurs. I'd happily work, if not pro bono, then on a 'low bono' basis. Jeff Skoll – you deserve to have first refusal on these ideas.

For the time being, however, I'm focused on promoting this book. As you may recall from the prologue, I decided to write my story for a couple of different reasons. Firstly, I felt I needed to talk openly about mental health in the workplace; it's a significant and growing problem that corporations, large and small, need to take very seriously. We should be more vocal about the challenges employees are facing in jobs that have grown exponentially in size and complexity over the past decade. This has been exacerbated by the constant drumbeat of downsizing in pursuit of economic efficiency, above every other consideration, whether that be people, planet or, indeed, purpose. We're connected 24/7 through our smartphones and there are precious little means of escape when things get tough. No, I don't consider myself an expert on this topic and, thankfully, had a relatively brief flirtation with the mental health community. But, if people like me don't talk about our experiences, then we'll never break the taboo and more people will continue to stay silent, missing out on the help they need and deserve. A serious discussion on this topic across all sectors of society is long overdue.

As I explained in the very beginning, the main reason for writing the book is, however, to seek to inspire others to drive change within their own organisations, to rock the boat, to step away from the herd. This new breed of changemaker, the aspiring social intrapreneur, seeks to fuse business value with social or environmental impact, and is willing to take risks, ridicule and rewards to prove it. No, you won't find that job title on any business card – it's as much a mindset as a skillset.

Intrapreneurs are not content with business as usual and aspire to drive change bottom up and inside out of their own organisations. These are the people who don't change companies when they get frustrated in their jobs or crave more purpose from their careers.

Instead, they stay put and *change the companies* they're in. Might this sound like you? Maybe you're a senior executive struggling to know how to manage these troublesome, budding intrapreneurs within your team. If so, you're exactly the kind of people I'm trying to connect with.

No one ever said that it would be easy. Of course it's risky for your career. Sure, you'll be laughed at. Told you're crazy. Overlooked for promotion. Yes, you might even lose your job. I often think of the reactions that a Picasso or a Jackson Pollock must have had when they shared their first works of art. Or how silly that first person trying to start a Mexican wave must have felt when they stood up screaming with their hands in the air, only to find they were the only one. My point is that you may have to be prepared to appear crazy to others if you're going to be successful in driving positive change in any organisation.

As an aside, I googled 'First Mexican Wave'and was amused to discover that a so-called '*Krazy* George Henderson' is credited with starting the very first Mexican wave at an Oakland v. New York baseball match back in 1981. George may not feel so quite as 'krazy' now, having popularised this fun crowd activity across most sports around the world. I rest my case.

No, intrapreneurship is not for the faint-hearted, but in my experience the rewards far, far outweigh the risks and the downsides. I wouldn't have swapped my career in Accenture and ADP for the world and would do it again in a heartbeat.

The most important thing to do is to take that initial step, or to 'cross the threshold into the field of adventure,' to use Joseph Campbell's terminology from *The Hero's Journey*. No one can do that for you.Only you can decide. And on this note I'll leave you with a parting thought.

As I wrote this epilogue, my intrapreneurial hero, Garmt van Soest, was planning his own funeral. You see, euthanasia is legal in the Netherlands and this brave young man decided to bow out at a time of his own choosing – a decision that, thankfully, very few of us will ever be forced to make. The 23rd October 2017 was his 'date with death,' as he wryly put it. Garmt was about to step across the ultimate threshold – death itself. Not content with having spent the past four years 'Kicking ALS in the Balls', he decided to stick the proverbial boot into the scrotum of the Grim Reaper, too, as a final act of defiance.[3]

I would say this to you: whatever it is that is causing you to hesitate, hold back or procrastinate in crossing that elusive threshold and beginning your own Hero or Heroine's journey, ask yourself this: is it scarier than death itself? Probably not, I suspect. From a personal perspective, I was agonising over the decision to publish this book or not. I'm not short of well-meaning friends who tell me it's madness: 'Do you really want to tell the world you lost the plot?'; 'What if you get sued? You could end up with nothing.' To be perfectly honest, I was starting to get cold feet. Then Garmt told me of the decision that he'd made. He helped me suit up, and it's thanks to him that you're reading this now, which is why I've dedicated this book to him and his memory.

I'd like to wish you all the best of luck in your own intrapreneurial journey – be that in a business, within government or in the charity sector.

There are a growing number of organisations springing up to support the global intrapreneurship movement. Here are just a few you might want to consider:

The League of Intrapreneurs[4]

The Circle of Young Intrapreneurs[5]

Intrapreneur Lab[6]

Impaqt[7]

Business Fights Poverty[8]

For those of you for whom the burnout issue is more front of mind, there are also places you can go for help and advice. Arianna Huffington is championing this cause through books such as *Sleep and*

3. I was pleased to have the opportunity to read this epilogue aloud to Garmt as he sat, eyes closed and smiling in his wheelchair only two weeks before his death.

4. http://www.leagueofintrapreneurs.com

5. http://www.circleofyi.com

6. http://intra-lab.com

7. http://www.impaqt.net/Impaqt/index.php

8. http://businessfightspoverty.org

Thrive. She's created a support platform, which has lots of tips on good practice in the workplace. I'm delighted to see that Accenture is one of their main corporate partners and is putting tens of thousands of employees through the *Thrive* training programmes[9].

As for me? Well, I'm very optimistic about the future and excited about helping to support the global social intrapreneurship movement – both with my own time and also with my share of the proceeds from this book. Changing the world is not an impossible dream – not if we're successful in changing the world of business. Individually and collectively we all have a role to play in making that happen. So what are you waiting for?

Allow me to leave you with one of my favourite quotes for aspiring intrapreneurs, from the 20th-century American psychologist, Rollo May:

'*The opposite of courage in our society is not cowardice, it is conformity.*'

9. https://www.thriveglobal.com

Acknowledgements

Writing a book has strong parallels with intrapreneurship: one assumes it's all about the efforts of one individual, but it's actually a team sport.

Firstly, I would like to acknowledge the financial contributions of all the supporters mentioned in these pages, who played a critical role in bringing the book to life. I'm extremely grateful for your generosity and all the words of encouragement. Special thanks to Zahid Torres-Rahman at Business Fights Poverty for generously stepping up to the sponsor role.

There are many other people to whom I owe a massive debt of gratitude for their support, encouragement and feedback during the lengthy writing process. Louisa Shea, an English Literature PhD and former Harvard Lecturer, was a godsend and invested a huge amount of her time feeding back on early drafts during regular meetings in Geneva. I'm also grateful to Mathew and Xander at Unbound for believing in the concepts behind the book, and to their colleagues Annabel, Lisa, Debbie, Kwaku and Fiona for their help during the production process. Mark Ecob deserves special thanks for the cover design.

Many friends provided useful feedback on early drafts, including Amy Cawthorne, Arianna Brambilla, Brindusa Burrows, Cynthia Hansen, Lincoln McNey, Gene Early, Loobs Cervoni and Chris Magennis. My creative council of David Pearl, Jamie Lister, Mica Ferierra and Chris Magennis helped me review options on the cover design. For legal reviews and support, I'd like to thank Amber Melville-Brown, Peter Finding and Andrew Fremlin-Key at Withers Worldwide and Lorna Skinner at Matrix Chambers.

Lastly, let me say a special thank you to all of my colleagues at Accenture Development Partnerships (ADP) for their hard work and dedication over so many years. Were I to name a few I'd end up missing too many. They are the silent heroes and heroines of this book and I very much hope that their ongoing efforts are given due recognition in the stories I've shared. Without them, there would have been no ADP and as a result, no book. Thank you all.

Patrons

Dan Acher
Philippe Addor
Fran Adenis
David Agoada
Maria Alliaud
Trip Allport
Elisa Alt
Mandar Apte
Ariane
Jennifer Baarn
Michael Balint
George Barr
Patricia Benoit-Guyot
Suzanne Berman
Sarah Bird
Shayna Rector Bleeker
Virginie Bonnell
Sara Bothams
Tim Boyes-Watson
Christopher Breedlove
Dominik Breitinger
Carolien Bruin
Jerónimo Calderón
Meredith Caldwell
Ewan Cameron
Fiona Cervoni
Gordon Cervoni
Elisa Chami-Castaldi
Tim Chong
Nick Clarke
Jeremy Connell
Fiona Cook

Jane Corbett
Joanne Cowie
Rachel Cox
Jo da Silva
Emmanuel de Lutzel
Wouter Deelder
Justin DeKoszmovszky
Mike Dixon
Ruth Dobson
Mhairi Duncan
Paul Ellingstad
Yapincak Erkan
Florencia Estrade
Tony Evans
Lesley Everett
Sheena Ewing
Freddie Fforde
Robert Figgis
Sergio Lopez Figueroa
Catherine Fisher
Samantha Fox
David French
Maria Gaither
George Gicev
Jullie Tran Graham
Ian & Tracey Grant
Terry Gray
David Grayson
Wim De Greef
Glen Gribbon
Asmaa Guedira
Berenice Guerra
Jacques Hämmerli
Vanessa Harding
Bethan Harris
Manuel Hartmann

Tim Heard
Lesley Herrington
Chloe Hill
Julian & Mercedes Hill-Landolt
Martin Wilfred Holland
Tamas Hovanyecz
Insightful Intrapreneur
Johari Ismail
Daniel Jackson
Mark Jacobs
Yunus Jaleel
Jakub Jancovic
Louise Jardine
Jody Jeffcoate
JJ Jones
Al Judge
Emily Kasriel
Hilary Kemp
Thomas Krakau
Sophie Krantz
Neel Lakhani
Karine Geneau de Lamarliere
Mara Lapi
Nic Laz
Eveline Maas
Andy Mac
Sally Maclean
Nicola MacLeod
Sean Magennis
Jan Maisenbacher
Hai Malarkey
Yoko Malbos
Seth Marbin
Anastasia Thatcher Marceau
Archie Mccabe
Carol McDermott

David Mcfie
Scotti McLaren
Nicolai Michelsen
Janice Middleton
Arabella Monro-Somerville
Josef Mueller
Anna Muir
Lucy Murdoch
Lynne Naphtali
Carlo Navato
Lesley Neil
David Nolan
Karoline Nystrøm
Jude O'Reilley
Peter O'Toole
Lisa Obradovich
Russ & Amanda Oliver
Marielle Pacaley
Anil Parekh
Nicky Parkinson
Kathleen Parsons
Marieke Peeters
Samantha Penabad
Geeta Pendse
Harry Pepper
Daniel Pitcher
Duncan Pollard
KD Prince
Jenny Purcell
Cvetanka Radosavljevic
Arjun Raghavan
Maja Ravanska
Dani Redondo
Hannah Reichardt
Colin Reid
Alan Ritchie

Nicola Robb
Vikki Roscoe
Adam Rowlands
Anne Schiettecatte
Juliet Schofield
Nicole Schwab
Ghadeer Abu Shawareb
Catrina Sheridan
John Shirlaw
Tom Shutte
Meghan Siegal
Valeria Ionka Silvestri
Colin Sloman
Jeremy Smith
Ben Solanky
Natalia Stepanova
Viktoria Stepanova
Pieter Talpe
Grace Terroir
Jo Thompson
Heather Tierney
Victoria Titova
Roza B. Trpenoska
Michael Tweed
Suba Umathevan
Roshni Venkatesh
Martin Vogel
Rachel Watts
Annina Wersun
Carla White
Fokko Wientjes
Øystein Wikeby
Donie Wiley
Marlena Wisniak
Susanne Wittig
Mary Woodgate

Yau Yeu
Fiona Zavaroni